A MATTER OF TIME

▲ ▲ ▲ ▲ ▲ ▲ ▲

RISK AND OPPORTUNITY

IN THE

NONSCHOOL HOURS

▼ ▼ ▼ ▼ ▼ ▼ ▼

REPORT OF THE TASK FORCE ON YOUTH DEVELOPMENT
AND COMMUNITY PROGRAMS

CARNEGIE CORPORATION OF NEW YORK
CARNEGIE COUNCIL ON ADOLESCENT DEVELOPMENT
DECEMBER 1992

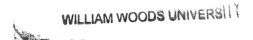

LIBRARY OF CONGRESS CATALOGING-IN-PUBLICATION DATA

Carnegie Council on Adolescent Development. Task Force on Youth
Development and Community Programs.
A matter of time: risk and opportunity in the nonschool hours /
Task Force on Youth Development and Community Programs.
Carnegie Council on Adolescent Development.
p.   cm.
Includes bibliographical references.
ISBN 0-9623154-3-5 (pbk.)
1. Teenagers—United States-Societies and clubs.   2.Youth-United
States-Societies and clubs.   3. Socially handicapped teenagers-
United States.   4. Adolescence.
I. Title.

| HS3260.U5C37 1992 | 92-37832 |
| 369.4 0973—dc20 | CIP |

Designed by Meadows & Wiser, Washington, D.C.
Cover illustration by Melton E. Castro/Meadows & Wiser
Printed by Wolk Press, Inc., Woodlawn, Maryland

CONTENTS

JO UEHARA
Assistant Executive Director for
    Member Association Services
YWCA of the U.S.A.
New York, New York

ROBERTA VAN DER VOORT
Executive Director
United Way of King County
Seattle, Washington

A MATTER OF TIME: RISK AND OPPORTUNITY IN THE NONSCHOOL HOURS

All Americans have a vital stake in the healthy development of today's young adolescents, who will become tomorrow's parents, workers, and citizens. But millions of America's young adolescents are not developing into responsible members of society. Many likely will not lead productive or fulfilling lives. Young adolescents, aged ten to fifteen, do not become mature adults without assistance. They are profoundly influenced by experiences they have at home and in school, but they are also affected by experiences in their neighborhoods and the larger community during the nonschool hours.

The importance of community environments and institutions in contributing to the development of young adolescents is well supported by both research and practice. The opportunity to make that contribution arises largely during the nonschool hours. Yet few American communities work consciously and consistently to seize that opportunity.

The passage through early adolescence—guided by family, encouraged by school, and supported by the community—should result in healthy outcomes. That is the case for many American youth, but not for many others. Instead of safety in their neighborhoods, they face physical danger; instead of economic security, they face uncertainty; instead of intellectual stimulation, they face boredom; in place of respect, they are neglected; lacking clear and consistent adult expectations for them, they feel alienated from mainstream American society.

Why is the period of early adolescence so critically important? With the exception of infancy, no time of life compresses more physical, intellectual, social, emotional, and moral development into so brief a span. The young adolescent is simultaneously coping with the onset of puberty, progressing from the protective neighborhood elementary school to the more distant, more impersonal middle-grade school; growing taller; walking, biking, or using public transportation to travel farther from home without parental supervision; and experiencing a new sense of independence.

Young adolescents are preparing to become adults, and experiences in early adolescence help shape what kind of adults they will be. They are developing skills, habits, and attitudes that will determine whether they succeed or fail in school and establish personal and career goals. It is during this period that young adolescents begin to make their initial decisions about such potentially dangerous behaviors as alcohol and other drug use, sexual activity, and gang involvement. They face risks far more serious than did their predecessors, and they face them earlier in life.

Young people bring many strengths and useful experiences to the tasks of adolescence: seemingly limitless energy, great curiosity about the world, an intense desire to learn skills, and a trusting attitude. But they are not yet able to shape their futures. They cannot negotiate the passage through adolescence alone. Indeed, many of America's twenty million young adolescents are not alone: they enjoy strong family support and needed protection, good health care, and an array of engaging and meaningful experiences during the time they are not in school. In programs right in their own neighborhoods, they learn new skills, meet interesting peers of both their own and the other gender, and encounter adults who can help them thrive. These young people live in communities that provide constructive opportunities that meet their needs during their free time.

But large numbers of other young adolescents face a far different and far more threatening world. Lacking a vision of a productive adulthood and constructive activities to engage them during their nonschool hours, they veer into another course of development. Some injure their health by using tobacco, alcohol, and other drugs. Some engage in premature, unprotected sexual activity, which the presence of AIDS now renders deadly. Some commit acts of crime or live in neighborhoods where fear of violence pervades their daily lives.

Although all adolescents face at least some of these hazards, those who live in urban and rural poverty areas face a higher level of risk.[1] They are likely to have a lower level of personal and social support than their counterparts from more affluent families.[2]

Aside from the damage to individual young lives, American society pays heavily for such outcomes. We pay in diminished economic productivity of a generation. We pay the bills for crime, welfare, and health care. We pay immense social costs by somehow having to absorb millions of alienated people. And we pay the moral costs of knowing that we are producing millions of young adolescents who face predictably bleak and unfulfilling lives.

These outcomes can be reversed, if Americans decide to create communities that support families, educate adolescents for the global economy, promote their health, and provide opportunities for them during the nonschool hours.

THE CRITICAL CONNECTION:
COMMUNITY SUPPORTS

Fundamental changes in American family life and the well-documented shortcomings of American public education have undermined two central sources of healthy growth for young adolescents. American society is now focusing considerable discussion—and some action—on families and schools. This developmental triangle has a third side: It consists of community supports, especially the organizations and programs that serve young adolescents. These youth-serving organizations can be critical to young adolescents learning the skills and developing the confidence they need to enter the adult world.

By any standards, America's young adolescents have a great deal of discretionary time. Much of it is unstructured, unsupervised, and unproductive for the young person. Only 60 percent of adolescents' waking hours are committed to such essentials as school, homework, eating, chores, or paid employment,[3] while fully 40 percent are discretionary.

Many young adolescents spend much of that time alone. The 1988 National Education Longitudinal Study, which surveyed a nationally representative sample of some 25,000 eighth graders, found that approximately 27 percent of the respondents regularly spent two or more hours at home alone after school. Eighth graders from families in the lowest socioeconomic group were more likely to report that they were home alone for more than three hours, while

BY ANY STANDARDS, AMERICA'S YOUNG ADOLESCENTS HAVE A GREAT DEAL OF DISCRETIONARY TIME. MUCH OF IT IS UNSTRUCTURED, UNSUPERVISED, AND UNPRODUCTIVE FOR THE YOUNG PERSON. ONLY 60 PERCENT OF ADOLESCENTS' WAKING HOURS ARE COMMITTED TO SUCH ESSENTIALS AS SCHOOL, HOMEWORK, EATING, CHORES, OR PAID EMPLOYMENT, WHILE FULLY 40 PERCENT ARE DISCRETIONARY.

those in the highest income group were least likely to be unsupervised for that amount of time.[4]

Young adolescents do not want to be left to their own devices. In national surveys and focus groups, America's youth have given voice to a serious longing. They want more regular contact with adults who care about and respect them, more opportunities to contribute to their communities, protection from the hazards of drugs, violence, and gangs, and greater access to constructive and attractive alternatives to the loneliness that so many now experience.

Young adolescents can, in short, be left adrift or they can be involved in community-based programs that are fun and that help them achieve the developmental tasks of youth. Vastly understudied and largely ignored in public policy debates, these programs and organizations deserve society's attention and critical appraisal.

Early in 1990 the Carnegie Council on Adolescent Development convened a twenty-six-member Task Force on Youth Development and Community Programs to conduct just such an examination. The task force undertook two years of study that included an extensive literature review, focus group discussions with young adolescents, interviews with youth development leaders, twelve commissioned papers, site visits to programs and organizations, and a survey of independent youth agencies. The task force concluded that community-based youth development organizations represent a valuable national resource with considerable untapped potential.

COMMUNITY-BASED PROGRAMS FOR YOUTH DEVELOPMENT

More than 17,000 organizations offer community-based youth programs. They include large, well-financed, and well-staffed national groups such as Girl Scouts of the U.S.A. and the YMCA; grassroots independent organizations; religious youth organizations; adult service clubs, sports organizations, senior citizens groups, and museums; and public-sector institutions such as libraries and parks and recreation departments.

Community-based youth programs can provide enriching and rewarding experiences for young adolescents, and many do: their young members socialize with their peers and adults and learn to set and achieve goals, compete fairly, win gracefully, recover from defeat, and resolve disputes peaceably. They acquire life skills: the ability to communicate, make decisions, solve problems, make plans, and set goals for education and careers. They put their school-learned

---

HOW COMMUNITY ORGANIZATIONS CONTRIBUTE TO YOUTH DEVELOPMENT

YOUNG ADOLESCENTS NEED:	COMMUNITY ORGANIZATIONS OFFER:
Opportunities to socialize with peers and adults	Group programs; mentoring and coaching relationships; drop-in activities; structured programs that focus on the development of interpersonal skills; safe places; constructive alternatives to gang involvement
Opportunities to develop skills that are relevant now and in the future	Programs that incorporate the teaching of such critical life skills as goal setting, decision making, communicating, problem solving
Opportunities to contribute to the community	Community service programs; design and implementation of solutions to community problems; participation in decisions of the organization
Opportunities to belong to a valued group	Group programs; formal and informal groups of varying sizes and changing configurations; symbols of membership and belonging
Opportunities to feel competent	Programs that encourage practice of new skills, public performance and recognition, and reflection on personal and group accomplishments

knowledge to use, for example, by working as an intern in a museum. In these activities and others, they prepare themselves for adulthood by interacting with and learning from responsible, caring adults and their peers.

Young adolescents greatly enjoy these experiences. They are especially attracted to those programs that they have a hand in designing and implementing. Furthermore, young adolescents enjoy working in community service programs such as aiding the elderly or tutoring younger children; their visible contributions provide them with a sense of importance, fulfillment, and belonging.

But youth organizations can do much more to meet the needs of the nation's adolescents than they are doing. Current programs are typically fragmented and uncoordinated; programs often address single problems (aimed, for example, at preventing early pregnancy) and may not offer young people a sufficient range of challenging and enriching activities.

Many youth agencies are chronically underfinanced and suffer from the low morale among staff that so often follows when dedicated people must provide limited services. The adults who lead programs have few opportunities for training in working with adolescents.

Most troubling, many existing programs tend to serve young people from more advantaged families.[5] They do not reach millions of young adolescents who live in low-income urban and rural areas. Some programs reach young people for only one or two hours a week, far less time than it takes to give sustained support to those who can most benefit. Fully 29 percent of young adolescents are not reached by these programs at all.[6]

The time has come to change these conditions dramatically. Youth-serving agencies, government, and all sectors concerned about youth must join in an effort to expand opportunities for young adolescents when they are out of school, improve program quality and increase program intensity, and extend these activities particularly to young adolescents who live in low-income, often high-risk, communities.

PROGRAM RECOMMENDATIONS

CREATING NETWORKS OF COMMUNITY SUPPORTS FOR YOUNG ADOLESCENTS

The nonschool hours present a highly promising opportunity for offering young adolescents useful experiences to promote healthy growth and development. Communities must build networks of affordable, accessible, safe, and challenging youth programs that appeal and respond to the diverse interests of young adolescents. These community programs should:

▶ TAILOR THEIR PROGRAM CONTENT AND PROCESSES TO THE NEEDS AND INTERESTS OF YOUNG ADOLESCENTS.

Program designers should actively solicit the views of young adolescents and involve them in program planning and implementation. Young people respond enthusiastically to programs that reflect their needs and desires; they may shun programs that adults plan without their advice. To be truly responsive to the needs and interests of today's young adolescents, many programs will have to modify their content and intensify their levels of involvement with young people.

▶ RECOGNIZE, VALUE, AND RESPOND TO THE DIVERSE BACKGROUNDS AND EXPERIENCE OF YOUNG ADOLESCENTS.

Young adolescents are in a critical period of establishing their identities. Programs must recognize that gender, race, ethnicity, and culture represent essential features of individual development and that, by the time they reach early adolescence, young people have had significantly different experiences based on these factors. This recognition will require programs to deal with specific developmental, organizational, and societal issues that respond to and celebrate such diversity.

▶ EXTEND THEIR REACH TO UNDERSERVED ADOLESCENTS.

Young adolescents who live in low-income neighborhoods are most likely to benefit from supportive youth development services; yet they are the very youth who have least access to such programs and organizations. Youth agencies must work individually and together at local and national levels to extend their reach to young adolescents in low-income areas.

▶ ACTIVELY COMPETE FOR THE TIME AND ATTENTION OF YOUNG ADOLESCENTS.

Social interaction and fun are often cited as reasons why young people are attracted to organized programs outside of school. Young adolescents also consistently identify money and employment as priorities, but few organizations respond to these wants and needs. Recognizing young people's need for safety and status, youth organizations should take a developmental approach to teen employment and offer a fresh alternative to the stultifying, sometimes dangerous, first jobs available to many adolescents. Such an approach, coupled with other skills-oriented prevention and intervention strategies, can attract young people away from involvement in gangs.

▶ STRENGTHEN THE QUALITY AND DIVERSITY OF THEIR ADULT LEADERSHIP.

Greatly expanded training and other forms of staff development are critically needed. Youth-serving agencies report that the nature of young people's response to the adults who work with them is *the* most critical factor in program success. Both paid and volunteer staff members need pre- and in-service training, ongoing supervision and guidance, and public recognition.

▶ **REACH OUT TO FAMILIES, SCHOOLS, AND A WIDE RANGE OF COMMUNITY PARTNERS IN YOUTH DEVELOPMENT.**

Young adolescents benefit most when all major influences work in harmony and provide consistent messages, high expectations, and personal support. Effective community youth programs must establish mutual working partnerships with families, schools, and community institutions such as health and mental health centers.

▶ **ENHANCE THE ROLE OF YOUNG ADOLESCENTS AS RESOURCES IN THEIR COMMUNITY.**

Young adolescents should have the opportunity to participate in all aspects of youth programs: teaching skills to peers, caring for the facility, planning special events, assisting in governance, and representing the organization to the media and policy makers. Young people enjoy and are good at providing community service, such as planting trees, registering adults to vote, working with elders, and staffing soup kitchens. They also gain experience in understanding how to use community resources for their own benefit.

▶ **SERVE AS VIGOROUS ADVOCATES FOR AND WITH YOUTH.**

Children and young adolescents do not vote, cannot be heard in political debate, and command no power commensurate with their needs or their critical importance to the nation. They need strong advocates at all levels of government.

▶ **SPECIFY AND EVALUATE THEIR PROGRAMS' OUTCOMES.**

Successful programs evolve through testing and changing approaches to meet new needs. Every community youth program should incorporate an appropriate level of evaluation into its design, being careful to match organizational needs and the state of the program's evolution with selected assessment measures.

▶ **ESTABLISH STRONG ORGANIZATIONAL STRUCTURES, INCLUDING ENERGETIC AND COMMITTED BOARD LEADERSHIP.**

Effective programs are usually the product of stable, well-governed, and well-managed organizations. Boards of directors should generate and support policies designed to reach out to underserved young adolescents, and they should work with administrative staff to diversify and stabilize their funding base.

GENERATING COMMUNITY RENEWAL THROUGH LOCAL, STATE, AND NATIONAL ACTION

Americans must rebuild a sense of community in their neighborhoods. The nation cannot afford to raise another generation of young adolescents without the supervision, guidance, and preparation for life that caring adults and strong organizations once provided in communities.

The United States has far to go before its national policies on families, children, and youth match those of other industrialized countries, the most effective of which accept broad public responsibility for young people.

▶ **FUNDERS OF ALL TYPES—PRIVATE AND PUBLIC, NATIONAL AND LOCAL—SHOULD WORK IN PARTNERSHIP WITH YOUTH DEVELOPMENT ORGANIZATIONS AND WITH ONE ANOTHER TO IDENTIFY AND ADDRESS THE PRESSING NEEDS OF YOUTH IN COMMUNITIES ACROSS THE COUNTRY.**

Funders should address the four major problems that plague the youth development sector: instability of core support, inadequacy of total financial resources, a crisis orientation toward fixing problems rather than deliberately promoting healthy development, and a single-issue approach to youth problems rather than a comprehensive one. Local United Ways, community foundations, national foundations, businesses, individuals, and government should make it an essential part of their missions to finance youth agencies and to encourage them to adopt the program recommendations in this report.

▶ **LOCAL, STATE, AND FEDERAL POLICIES SHOULD BE COORDINATED, FOCUSED ON INCREASING SUPPORT FOR BASIC YOUTH DEVELOPMENT SERVICES, AND TARGETED TO AREAS OF GREATEST NEED.**

Policies should be built on the best current knowledge and should reflect a view of youth as resources. Local government should provide leadership for, encourage, coordinate, and help finance the improved delivery of comprehensive and integrated youth programs. States can allocate funds from block grants available to localities, enact facilitating legislation, foster genuine working collaboration among state agencies, establish a spirited office of children and youth, and take responsibility for assisting youth in low-income neighborhoods by building alliances with successful community-based programs.

Current federal policy focuses primarily on intervening with young adolescents who are already in trouble, not on helping them keep out of it. Most federal dollars and technical assistance are aimed at crisis intervention, treatment of problems, and control of

COMMUNITY-BASED ORGANIZATIONS: NATIONAL YOUTH ORGANIZATIONS, GRASSROOTS YOUTH AGENCIES, RELIGIOUS INSTITUTIONS, ADULT SERVICE CLUBS, SENIOR CITIZENS GROUPS, SPORTS ORGANIZATIONS, MUSEUMS, LIBRARIES, PARKS AND RECREATION DEPARTMENTS

▶ Expand work with young adolescents, especially those living in low-income urban and isolated rural areas.

▶ Engage in joint planning, share training resources, and collaborate in advocacy with and on behalf of youth.

SCHOOLS

▶ Construct with community agencies alliances that recognize common goals, combine strengths for maximum effectiveness, and respect inherent differences.

PARENTS AND FAMILIES

▶ Help young adolescents make wise choices about the constructive use of their free time.

▶ Direct energies to youth organizations as program leaders and advisers, board members, or fund-raisers.

HEALTH AGENCIES

▶ Increase adolescents' access to health care services, information about disease prevention and health promotion by combining forces with youth organizations and schools.

HIGHER EDUCATION INSTITUTIONS

▶ Help community agencies identify what works in youth programs, improve capacities for evaluation, strengthen professional development, and conduct joint programs that serve youth.

RESEARCHERS AND EVALUATORS

▶ Expand efforts by forming partnerships with community-based youth organizations on program development and evaluation.

FUNDERS

▶ Strengthen and stabilize the funding base for youth development programs by moving from categorical funding to core support of youth agencies, combining public with private funds, and facilitating collaboration among fragmented youth and community organizations and with the schools.

▶ Target new resources to low-income neighborhoods.

▶ Establish as funding priorities the professional development of youth workers, evaluation of programs, replication of programs that work, and vigorous advocacy with and on behalf of youth.

MEDIA

▶ Expand coverage of positive youth activities and success stories by increasing publication and broadcasts of material created by young people, encouraging high-quality programs that feature youth in key roles, and publicizing available youth activities to adolescents and their families.

LOCAL, STATE, AND FEDERAL GOVERNMENTS

▶ Articulate a vision for youth of all communities by coordinating policies for youth at all levels, intensifying support for youth development programs, targeting services to youth in low-income areas, and devoting special priority to locally generated solutions.

YOUNG ADOLESCENTS

▶ Become involved in designing and implementing youth programs.

▶ Serve communities as volunteers.

antisocial and criminal behavior, which leads to incarceration, often without meaningful rehabilitation.

Congress began to consider a more responsive and preventive federal approach in the Young Americans Act of 1989, which offers a first step toward a coherent national youth policy. The act establishes broad public responsibility for the well-being of children and youth and defines a strong federal role in providing leadership, planning, coordination, and funding for supportive services for young Americans. Unfortunately, Congress has not funded the act.

TRANSFORMING RISK INTO OPPORTUNITY

Youth-serving agencies should be in the forefront of action to bring challenging and attractive programs to today's young adolescents, particularly those in low-income neighborhoods. They should be bold in citing the proven value of offering programs that help young adolescents develop into contributing members of their communities.

But they cannot do the job alone. The work of formulating programs and policies that respond to the needs of *all* young adolescents should begin with youth agencies but embrace all concerned groups and citizens. As suggested by the call to action opposite, the Task Force on Youth Development and Community Programs invites all sectors of society to join forces in developing strategies to achieve long-term and constructive social change that can benefit all Americans, especially the nation's young adolescents.

The dedicated effort of all these sectors is needed to achieve a new understanding of and appreciation for young adolescents. Understanding and appreciation must lead to action. Americans can reform vast social systems when they set their minds to the task. A hundred years ago, in the closing decade of the nineteenth century, a surge of reform led to the Progressive Era, a time of sweeping social change that resonated throughout many aspects of American life: the country's laws and other government policies, its education and social welfare systems, and its public and private arenas.

Although different in scope and content, another broad national effort to reform schools and other public services now seems to be gathering momentum. Community-based programs for youth during the nonschool hours are critical to this effort.

We will all benefit from such an effort. For the nation as a whole, the rising new generation will consist of healthy, confident young adolescents who are ready to become fully contributing members of society. For all of America's youth, uncertainty about their futures will be transformed into preparation by a caring community for a promising and fulfilling life. Risk will be transformed into opportunity for young adolescents by turning their nonschool hours into the time of their lives.

YOUNG ADOLESCENTS AND OUR NATION'S FUTURE

Over the past decade, Carnegie Corporation of New York has had the privilege of initiating several activities that have contributed to new understanding of the development of young adolescents aged ten to fifteen.

In 1986 the Corporation established the Carnegie Council on Adolescent Development to place the compelling challenges of the early adolescent years higher on the nation's agenda. One of its first priorities was to explore the condition of education for young adolescents, an effort that produced *Turning Points: Preparing American Youth for the 21st Century*. That report generated wide discussion in the education, health, and youth development communities and resulted in pilot reform programs in dozens of cities and states. The Corporation translated its recommendations into action through a major funding commitment to the Middle Grade School State Policy Initiative, which has supported many of these reform efforts.

The council then turned its attention to the health of young adolescents and commissioned Fred M. Hechinger, former education editor of *The New York Times*, to draw on council work and other sources to write *Fateful Choices: Healthy Youth for the 21st Century*. This book, which warned that poor health among America's adolescents had reached crisis proportions, attracted thoughtful attention across the country. It recommended actions that could shape healthy lifestyles and avoid lifelong casualties.

A Matter of Time: Risk and Opportunity in the Nonschool Hours follows in the tradition of these publications. In this report, the council has put a spotlight on national and local youth organizations, in order to assess their potential to contribute—with schools, families, health organizations, and other community institutions—to the healthy development of young adolescents. A particular focus of our inquiry has been the strengthening and expansion of community-based

youth development programs for young adolescents living in low-income neighborhoods.

This report seeks to answer several important questions: What do young people do during their out-of-school hours? What influences—healthy or otherwise—come to bear on them during those hours? What do young people need and want that they cannot find at school or at home, and what facilities are available to meet those needs and desires? *Turning Points* showed that community-school partnerships could strengthen the educational experience of students during nonschool hours, but more research was needed to clarify the best opportunities; indeed, that initial exploration was one factor that led to this fuller study.

Thus, the council in 1990 created the Task Force on Youth Development and Community Programs to carry out its new initiative and prepare this report. The task force found that a few noted educators and policy analysts had begun to call attention to the importance of out-of-school experience. For example, Vanderbilt University education professor Chester Finn estimates that a young person spends only nine of every hundred hours in the classroom. This 9:91 formula, which is outlined in his recent book, *We Must Take Charge: Our Schools and Our Future*, dramatically emphasizes an important reality: American youth have a great deal of unscheduled, unstructured, and unsupervised time. This reality also presents an opportunity to build adolescents' capacity to make constructive use of this time. Exploring how to maximize this opportunity is the focus of this report.

The reason that this time is important stems from the significance of events that are occurring in the young adolescent's life between the ages of ten and fifteen. Early adolescence is the period of fastest physical growth other than infancy; it brings the onset of puberty; for many it triggers the young person's first ventures away from parents and home and into the larger world. It is a time when the young person is exposed to many new influences: In school, the student enters middle school or junior high, a more challenging and usually more impersonal place than elementary school. After school, young adolescents need for healthy development a variety of stimulating, constructive experiences that can continue to prepare them for passage to competent, mature adulthood.

Families alone cannot meet all needs of the young adolescent. For solid developmental reasons, the young person wants to become more involved outside the home—all the while retaining close ties to home—to engage peers, learn from adults other than parents, master new skills, and try out adult roles. Schools cannot meet all of these needs either. And both families and schools are under increasing pressure, families to produce adequate income while meeting their child's physical and emotional needs, schools to link with child-care providers and social service agencies.

Both families and schools, increasingly, lack the time and resources to attend to the complicated needs of the young adolescent. As a consequence, many adolescents are now growing up lacking some essential ingredients of healthy emotional and physical development.

Early in its study, the task force determined that youth organizations, which rank second only to public schools in the number of young people they reach each year, can have significant effects on the healthy development of young adolescents. Little is known about these organizations—what they do, whom they serve, how effective they are—and even less attention has been paid to future strategies that might enhance their youth development role.

Youth organizations include the large national agencies, such as the YMCA and Girl Scouts of the U.S.A., and independent grassroots organizations that are not affiliated with any national structure. Community-based youth development programs also include activities sponsored by religious institutions libraries, parks and recreation agencies, sports organizations, museums, adult service clubs, and senior citizens groups.

These organizations and programs can provide young adolescents with social support and guidance, life-skills training, positive and constructive alternatives to hazards (such as drug or alcohol use, gang involvement, early sexual activity, and crime), and opportunities for meaningful contributions to the community. They may also provide the young person with an opportunity to earn money, which is often a matter of desperate importance in low-income families.

Because this set of services is remarkably understudied and its potential not yet fulfilled, the Carnegie Council faced an unusual challenge in determining the specific ways to approach our examination. Our first step was to convene a task force of twenty-six seasoned professionals: national policymakers, researchers, youth organization executives, local and national funders, and other civic leaders. This interdisciplinary group was cochaired and superbly led by Dr. James Comer, the noted Yale University child psychiatrist, school reformer, and expert on the needs of children living in poverty areas, and Wilma (Billie) Tisch, who is nationally recognized for her community achievements, particularly in the voluntary sector.

Jane Quinn, staff director for the effort, has been a major contributor in this field. She played a crucial role in this study, working with the leadership team and task force and employing a variety of methods to acquire information about the subject: focus groups with young adolescents; interviews with experts, including the board and staff directors of national youth organizations as well as researchers and local program operators; a survey of independent grassroots youth groups; twelve commissioned papers on topics ranging from cross-national perspectives on youth development to funding of youth work in this country; and an extensive literature review that included both published and unpublished materials from a wide variety of social science fields.

The full task force met six times, and individual members volunteered to conduct organizational interviews and participate in various subcommittees. In addition, all members of the task force reviewed the several drafts of this final report that synthesizes their findings. Altogether, their thoughtful, constructive dedication was essential to producing a report of such quality and foresight. Naturally, the views expressed and recommendations offered are those of the task force and do not necessarily reflect the position of the officers or trustees of Carnegie Corporation of New York.

The purpose of this report, then, like the purpose of the task force itself, is to expand the scope and availability of developmentally appropriate, community-based services for young adolescents, particularly those living in high-risk environments, and to enhance public understanding and support of effective services for America's youth. I am convinced that the potential of such efforts is immense. If they are brought to fulfillment in the years ahead, our young people will suffer many fewer casualties and our nation's future will be greatly enhanced.

David A. Hamburg
President, Carnegie Corporation of New York
Chair, Carnegie Council on Adolescent Development
New York, New York

A GROWING CRISIS IN YOUTH DEVELOPMENT

When David Hamburg called me in February 1990 to ask that I cochair a new task force that would examine the role of America's youth organizations in promoting the healthy development of adolescents, I had no doubt that I needed to respond in the affirmative. My quarter century of work in educational reform, particularly in the public schools of some of our country's most disadvantaged neighborhoods, had taught me that there was indeed a "third leg" to the triangle of human development. If family and school constitute two of these legs, as I believe they do, the third leg is surely those experiences that young people have in their neighborhoods and the larger community. While my school-based work had led me to the notion of turning schools into supportive communities for young people, I recognized also the importance of strengthening the out-of-school environments in which our young people are growing up.

As a child psychiatrist, I received extensive training in principles of child development, and I find that those principles I learned some thirty years ago are still relevant. But the context in which they are applied has changed dramatically, which means that the kind of child development and education needed in our country today is very different from what was called for just three or four decades ago. Growing into productive adulthood has never been a simple process, but it is clearly more complex today than ever before, and the rate of change from 1950 to 1990 has been exponential. What has changed? And what challenges do these changes pose for American society?

In my view, two massive sets of social and economic changes have occurred along parallel tracks, and they intersect most acutely at the point when young people attempt to make the transition from adolescence to adulthood, from dependence to independence—or, better yet, interdependence, for that is what productive

adulthood in our country really means. I see these two tracks as the following: a significant increase in the level and number of skills needed for successful adulthood; and a significant decrease in the ongoing support and guidance offered to young people during their growing-up years. These two trends have created a serious problem in our country—indeed, I believe, a crisis.

The first set of changes, the need for increased knowledge and skills, really began in earnest immediately after World War II as the American economy moved from the late manufacturing age, with a heavy industrial base that could absorb almost all workers, to a postindustrial economy rooted in an information and service base. This new era brought with it a set of greatly accelerated educational requirements. The level of individual development needed to acquire this kind of education became higher than ever before, and adequate family and community functioning to promote that level of development became even more crucial.

But what has occurred on the parallel track has, in fact, moved in the opposite direction for many of our young people. Families and communities have generally become less, rather than more, supportive of children and youth. Some of this can be traced to policy gaps. For example, while other industrialized nations of this world—many of them in Europe—developed coherent, comprehensive family policies in the 1930s and 1940s, America did not. Our country's family policy continues to place most of the responsibility for the raising and rearing of children on the parent or parents with whom they reside. And yet these parents are increasingly unavailable to their children. There are more families with both parents working. There are more single-parent families. And there is more divorce. We have even witnessed, in some of our more disadvantaged areas, the growth of a phenomenon known as the "no-parent family." All of this adds up to a situation in which children are receiving insufficient help with their development; all of this also adds up to a very costly proposition, because these young people may well find themselves unprepared to obtain employment that allows them to take care of themselves and whatever family responsibilities they may subsequently take on.

Just as families have changed, so have communities. Before 1945 America was largely a nation of small towns and rural areas; even the cities tended to be a collection of small towns. Both mobility and communication were limited. Work and play tended to be local phenomena, and there was a great deal of interaction among the authority figures (parents, teachers, principals, ministers, coaches) in children's lives. Under these conditions, children grew up with a sense of place and a sense of belonging. This situation changed dramatically and quickly after World War II, with the advent of mass communication (particularly television) and with the application of increasingly sophisticated science and technology. America became a nation of metropolitan areas with higher mobility and advanced communication. Better transportation also contributed to the movement of both parents and children out of their own neighborhoods for their work and schooling, and this in turn led to a significant decrease in the interaction among the authority figures in the lives of young people. The supportive and protective functions of neighborhoods—two subtle but essential functions—have been all but lost for many of America's youth.

I am more convinced than ever of the importance of reinventing community, both within our schools and within our neighborhoods. This sense of place, of belonging, is a crucial building block for the healthy development of children and adolescents. And it is especially crucial for young people who are growing up in disadvantaged circumstances—the young people who face the most serious obstacles on the pathway to adulthood. America has always produced a few young people who were "at risk" of not achieving productive adulthood—for a host of individual and societal reasons. But the number of young people in this circumstance has reached epidemic proportions. Fully one-fourth of our nation's youth face serious risk of not reaching productive adulthood, and another 25 percent are at moderate risk. Poverty is a major, although not the sole, contributor to these statistics.

While many groups faced discrimination and obstacles to their well-being in past decades, most were able to overcome the negative effects, to improve social conditions, and to obtain needed levels of education. But the recent emergence of an education-based economy has made this task more difficult for many Americans. The consequences of an education-based economy in which many families and schools are not able to provide adequate support for the young people in their charge are unemployment, underemployment, poverty, and dependency among many people who could have participated in the economy forty years ago. Because of their distinctive and more traumatic social histories, several groups—African Americans, Latinos, Native Americans, and now some new Asian immigrants—are today disproportionately affected by the adverse consequences of poverty, community and family stresses, and related anger, isolation, and alienation.

I am certain that our society *could* address these significant problems if it could succeed in developing both an accurate understanding of the causes and the political will to implement the solutions. But there can be no single, simple remedy. Improvement of our formal educational systems is one avenue of solution, and I am heartened by the many worthwhile reform efforts that are under way in locales across the country. But even if we were to greatly improve our country's schools, we must also rebuild the developmental infrastructure for children and adolescents at the neighborhood level. We must make dramatic increases in the scope and availability of developmentally appropriate, community-based services for our young people, particularly those living in high-risk environments. We must attend to all aspects of their development—cognitive, social, physical, emotional, and moral. Adequate development makes adequate education possible, which in turn facilitates participation in the mainstream economy and the ability to fill family, community, and citizenship roles. Therefore, we must give young people as much support as they need, balanced with as much freedom as they can manage. To do anything less is to court disaster, for individuals and for society.

The Task Force on Youth Development and Community Programs has worked for two years to document the current work of America's youth organizations and to chart a course for strengthening their role in promoting positive youth development. While our study has focused to a great extent on institutions, we began our deliberations by analyzing the needs and strengths of the young people themselves, and we attempted throughout our process to keep that perspective at the very center of our analysis. We publish this study in the hope that it will enhance public understanding of this important set of issues and that it will lead to constructive social change.

James Comer
Maurice Falk Professor of Child Psychiatry
Yale Child Study Center, Yale University
New Haven, Connecticut

GIVING ALL YOUTH
A CHANCE

I felt very much as Jim Comer did—although for quite different reasons—when David Hamburg asked me to cochair the Task Force on Youth Development and Community Programs. For the past thirty years, I have been an active participant in the fascinating, rich, and uniquely American voluntary sector. My service over these three decades as a planner, adviser, fund-raiser, board member, officer, and board president of several charitable and cultural institutions has contributed greatly to my own understanding and appreciation of these community resources whose work is central to our quality of life and yet is too frequently hidden from public view. I welcomed the opportunity to provide leadership to an effort designed to look systematically at community programs for young adolescents.

A major focus of our inquiry has been the voluntary sector, because it is this group of organizations—voluntarily sponsored and voluntarily attended—that has historically shouldered the major responsibility for establishing and maintaining community-based youth development programs. When the French social commentator Alexis de Tocqueville visited the United States in the early 1800s, he made the observation that "Americans of all ages, all conditions and all dispositions constantly form associations." This strong and enduring American propensity no doubt reflects our belief that collective action can be directed toward the common good. Even Tocqueville might have been surprised to witness the response of American citizens to the massive social changes during the second half of the nineteenth century—a period marked by deteriorating urban neighborhoods, poor health, child labor, and high rates of crime and delinquency. A major part of this response was directed toward children and youth, with the result that a large number of our country's youth organiza-

tions were born in the early 1900s. What is so striking about this era is the extent to which the public conscience could be aroused by the existence of serious human problems and the extent to which that concern led to constructive social action.

Many contemporary observers see a parallel between the massive economic and social transformations of the late 1800s and those that we are experiencing a hundred years later. Yet to be determined is whether or not the public conscience can be similarly aroused during the last decade of *this* century. Our report seeks to contribute to that debate and to constitute a call to action for all Americans.

While our task force's study has centered on the voluntary sector, this focus has not been an exclusive one. From my own experience within that sector, I recognized the importance of making our examination inclusive of both public and private initiatives (as well as partnerships and collaborations) because American society needs the best efforts of all partners if we are to be successful in addressing the very real problems confronting us today.

Ideal community programming for young people promises a continuum of caring service that includes educational and social enrichment, problem prevention, crisis intervention, remediation, and treatment and rehabilitation. Each community should have a balanced range of such services; in my view, we must invest some considerable proportion of our resources in the enrichment and prevention end of this continuum. We organized the Task Force on Youth Development and Community Programs to focus attention on this set of positive services, even as we were and are fully cognizant also of the critical importance of rehabilitation and treatment approaches.

What is most striking, I think, from our national examination of the institutions at this end of the youth services continuum is the great range and diversity of their work. By any standard, their current reach is immense, and both the breadth and depth of their programming are impressive. There is untold richness in this diversity—a richness that should be respected and harnessed because the needs of young people as we look across the country are also incredibly diverse. As we conducted our two-year examination of the current work and untapped potential of community-based youth development programs, we became increasingly concerned about the young people who are not reached by these efforts. Our sense was that young people who fall between the societal and educational cracks tend to slip also through the net of available extracurricular services. A clear pattern emerged as we looked systematically at the many subsectors within the large universe of organizations and institutions that we had selected for analysis: *without exception, the young people in greatest need had the least access to support and services*. Whether our focus at any particular point in our investigation was publicly funded recreation programs, religious youth groups, sports programs, or private, nonprofit youth organizations, we found that young people in more advantaged circumstances had greater access to current programs and services. The pattern was more persistent and pervasive than any of us on the task force had anticipated.

What can we do to change this reality? What should we do? The heart of this report is a set of recommendations for addressing the inequities that we found. We call on people of good will—and our examination only served to reinforce our own belief in the good will of our fellow citizens in relation to our country's young people—to couple thoughtful consideration of our recommendations with concerted action. We can, and must, build on the extraordinary resources already in place: resources that are flourishing in some few instances, but that are usually underfunded, undervalued, and largely unknown; resources that are almost always run by underpaid staff and dedicated individuals and groups of volunteers. We can, and must, do a better job than we are now doing. We must do everything that is within our power to do, so that all of today's adolescents enjoy equal opportunity to become the workers, parents, and leaders of tomorrow.

Wilma Tisch
Chairman of the Board
WNYC Foundation
New York, New York

PART I

YOUNG ADOLESCENTS: RISK AND OPPORTUNITY

AN AFRICAN PROVERB HOLDS: "IT TAKES AN ENTIRE VILLAGE TO RAISE A CHILD." THIS TIMELESS, UNIVERSAL PROVERB CAPTURES THE ESSENCE OF HEALTHY DEVELOPMENT OF THE YOUNG PERSON: A CARING, SUPPORTIVE FAMILY SURROUNDED BY A CARING, SUPPORTIVE COMMUNITY. IN SUCH A SETTING, THE INFANT IS LOVINGLY NURTURED INTO CHILDHOOD; THE CHILD IS GUIDED CAREFULLY INTO EARLY ADOLESCENCE; THE YOUNG ADOLESCENT EAGERLY VENTURES OUT FROM HOME INTO A FRIENDLY COMMUNITY TO BEGIN TO LEARN THE WAYS OF ADULTHOOD; AND THE OLDER ADOLESCENT BECOMES INCREASINGLY CONFIDENT IN ASSUMING RESPONSIBILITY AS A CONTRIBUTING ADULT.

But contemporary America is, for many young adolescents aged ten to fifteen years old, a far cry from this scenario. Millions of these young people grow up in communities that offer them little in the way of interesting or stimulating activities. They face stultifying boredom or temptations to engage in drug or alcohol abuse or early sexual activity. Many receive no adult guidance; many face physical danger in their own neighborhoods.

A central purpose of this report is to focus public attention on the conditions under which millions of young adolescents in this country grow up. Specifically, the report focuses on the nonschool hours—that great block of time in which the young person explores the community, puts lessons learned in school and home to practical use, meets peers and adults other than classmates or parents, and begins the transition to young adulthood. This report is based on research evidence that young adolescents' ability to grow into healthy and mature adults is greatly influenced by the experiences they have and the people they meet during their nonschool hours. In its recommendations, this report calls on American communities to do far more than they are now doing to support the healthy development of young adolescents—by providing them with ample, accessible, developmentally appropriate activities during their nonschool hours.

Public agencies and private, nonprofit youth organizations should find, attract, and serve young adolescents who face particularly serious risks during their nonschool hours. These young people, often the most neglected and least served of the nation's youth, live primarily in neighborhoods characterized by one common denominator: poverty.

America's interest in youth waxes and wanes. Periods of intense social reform—lasting one or sometimes several decades—occur after longer periods of indifference and neglect. One such surge came around the turn of the century, when the reformers of the Progressive Era worked to protect and support youth through improved services, laws, and other policies. In recent times, however, America has been in a period of indifference and neglect, especially regarding low-income rural and urban areas, and the evidence is everywhere: public schools in many parts of the country have deteriorated and the quality of public education has fallen, city parks and recreation centers are dilapidated, financial support for facilities and programs for young people is decreasing. It is the view of this report that the time for a new era of reform, requiring leadership and collective effort, has arrived.

FAMILY LIFE IN AMERICA HAS CHANGED

Family life in America has changed, and so have the nation's communities. Fewer and fewer young adolescents are raised in a caring, supportive family surrounded by a caring, supportive community.

The presence in the home during the day of a parent or other care-giving adult is no longer the norm. Most children and young adolescents in America today are raised by a single parent or in a two-parent household where both parents work and are away from home during the workday. Many extended families have become widely dispersed as the new generations spread out across the country in search of jobs and opportunity and older family members move to distant retirement. In many cities next-door neighbors barely know each other, much less provide friendship and assistance on an ongoing basis.

As family and social conditions have changed, so too have the needs of adolescents. They must have experiences that will prepare them to live in a technologically complex and ethnically diverse America. The sources of these experiences include parents and other family members as well as teachers, coaches, and classmates. Experiences outside the home and school also greatly influence the teenager. It is to this crucial but often overlooked area—the community and its supports for youth development—that this report turns its attention. First, however, it is useful to find out who America's young adolescents are and what risks they face.

WHO ARE AMERICA'S YOUNG ADOLESCENTS IN THE 1990S?

Nearly one in twelve Americans is between the ages of ten and fifteen.[1] As of July 1990 there were some twenty million young adolescents, roughly 51 percent male and 49 percent female. Approximately 68 percent were non-Hispanic white, while the other 32 percent were black (15 percent), Hispanic (12 percent), Asian/Pacific Islander (3 percent), and American Indian/Eskimo/Aleut (1 percent).[2]

Approximately 20 percent of these young adolescents live in poverty, up from 14 percent in 1969 and 16 percent in 1978.[3] Nearly 30 percent of all adolescents live in rural areas, and one in four is in poverty. Well over 100,000 of America's young adolescents are recent immigrants, most of them faced with learning a new language, adapting to a new culture, and helping their families to do so as well. Some are also refugees who may have suffered oppression or persecution in the country of their origin.

In diversity and numbers, this group will increase over the foreseeable future. The Census Bureau estimates that, by the year 2000, the early adolescent age group will grow from 20 million to more than 23 million, and its racial and ethnic composition will change to approximately 66 percent non-Hispanic white and 34 percent other racial and ethnic groups.

This demographic picture suggests a good starting point for a look at America's young adolescents in the 1990s. Given the wide range of backgrounds, experiences, skills, strengths, and needs, youth-serving organizations must be extremely flexible, and they must know about and understand the diverse nature of youth today. They must be prepared to catch up with new realities.

TODAY'S YOUNG ADOLESCENTS FACE FORMIDABLE RISKS

Early adolescence has always been a challenging time, but youth today face far greater risks than did their parents or grandparents before them. Many young adolescents first experiment with tobacco, alcohol, illicit drugs, and sexual activity during early adolescence, several years earlier than their predecessors. Many drugs that tempt them are far more hazardous and addictive than those available just a generation ago. The number of young adolescents who use alcohol, either on an experimental or abusive basis, is at least equally significant: 77 percent of eighth graders (most of them aged fourteen and fifteen) report having used alcohol, and 26 percent say they have had five or more drinks on at least one occasion within the past two weeks.[4]

Approximately 30 percent of young adolescents re-

A 1989 Carnegie report on the education of young adolescents outlined goals of healthy adolescent development. The maturing fifteen-year-old, as depicted in *Turning Points*,[5] is sound of body and mind and moving toward a lifetime of meaningful work and responsible citizenship.

The arduous but critically important tasks for ten- to fifteen-year-olds are to:

COGNITIVE DEVELOPMENT

▶ Expand knowledge;
▶ Develop critical thinking and reasoning skills; and
▶ Experience competence through academic achievement.

SOCIAL DEVELOPMENT

▶ Increase communication and negotiation skills;
▶ Increase capacity for meaningful relationships with peers and adults; and
▶ Explore adult rights and responsibilities.

PHYSICAL DEVELOPMENT

▶ Begin to mature physically and to understand changes that come with puberty;
▶ Increase movement skills through physical activity;
▶ Develop habits that promote lifelong physical fitness; and
▶ Learn to take and manage appropriate physical risks.

EMOTIONAL DEVELOPMENT

▶ Develop a sense of personal identity;
▶ Develop a sense of personal autonomy and control; and
▶ Develop coping, decision-making, and stress-management skills.

MORAL DEVELOPMENT

▶ Develop personal values;
▶ Develop a sense of accountability and responsibility in relation to the larger society; and
▶ Apply values and beliefs in meaningful ways.

What might be called a developmental perspective also highlights young adolescents' strengths and capacities. Young adolescents typically have great curiosity, high levels of energy, creative imaginations, intense interest in the world around them, a desire to learn new skills, and idealism.

Furthermore, a developmental perspective embraces the idea of continuous growth. What the fifteen-year-old will become is based on a progression from birth, but the adult's makeup is tied especially closely to his or her early adolescent development. One reason for investing in programs for the young adolescent is that many seeds of success or failure in achieving positive development are sown during this period. Americans have come to see the importance of investment in early childhood programs as a cornerstone for positive child development. The nation should begin to look at early adolescent programs in the same way as establishing a necessary basis for later adolescent and adult development.

---

port having had sexual intercourse by age fifteen (27 percent of girls and 33 percent of boys),[6] with nearly six in ten reporting that they did not use any contraception at first intercourse.[7] Of all sexually active adolescents, fully one-fourth will contract a sexually transmitted disease before graduating from high school.[8] The threat of AIDS adds a new deadly dimension to their risks.

Who are the young adolescents most in danger of succumbing to these risks? The Task Force on Youth Development and Community Programs concluded that the single consistently present factor is low income in the household.[9]

That does not mean, however, that all youth in low-income families will develop problems, or that all low-income households will generate young people who engage in risky behavior. Far from it. Parents in many low-income households, faced with the most trying of circumstances, often overcome the odds and raise their children to be healthy, mature, productive adults. Nor does higher income immunize youth from social problems. For example, alcohol use among adolescents rises directly in relation to parental education.[10] Usually, but not always, parental education is related to family income.

But the task force found that the deck is stacked against young adolescents from low-income families. They are the most likely to attend inadequate schools, the most likely to face physical danger in their daily lives, the most likely to spend large amounts of time without adult supervision, and—most significantly for purposes of this report—the least likely to have access to the supports that youth development organizations can offer to them during the nonschool hours.

Millions of young people leave school unprepared for the workplace. Business leaders warn that youth who apply for jobs lack both work skills and basic education: the ability to solve problems, to learn, and to be trained in the complex tasks required in today's workplace.

The problem will soon escalate. The wave of first-born baby boomers is now approaching fifty years of age, leading to further aging of the population. It will fall to today's young adolescents to help pay for increasing Social Security retirement and health care benefits.

Beyond these dollar issues, however, lie fundamental moral reasons for raising youth development to a higher national priority. It is the clear responsibility of adult Americans to prepare today's youth to be tomorrow's guardians of this nation's democratic traditions. The most basic questions posed in this report have to do with the quality of American society. Should this nation continue virtually to abandon so many of its young people in their critical years of early adolescence? Or should it begin to establish a new social compact among the generations? An important element of that compact could be community support of young adolescents during their nonschool hours.

Out-of-school hours constitute the biggest single block of time in the life of a young adolescent. What do teenagers do when they are not in school? Where do they go? What peers and adults do they encounter? What do they need to enable them to fill their nonschool hours effectively and to their satisfaction?

Because few of these questions have been answered, the task force set out to examine nonschool time in light of community resources and to offer guidelines for sound public and private agency policies.

The most striking findings of the task force's analysis of nonschool hours are:

▶ About 40 percent of adolescents' waking hours are discretionary—not committed to other activities (such as eating, school, homework, chores, or working for pay).[11] (See chart, page 29.)

▶ Many young adolescents spend virtually all of this discretionary time without companionship or supervision from responsible adults. They spend the time alone, with peers, or—in some cases—with adults who may exert negative influences on them or exploit them.

IDENTIFYING AND REACHING ADOLESCENTS IN HIGH-RISK ENVIRONMENTS

In *Adolescents at Risk*[12] Joy Dryfoos concludes that approximately 25 percent of American adolescents aged ten to seventeen are at serious risk of not achieving productive adulthood and that another 25 percent are at moderate risk. Dryfoos identified four behaviors that interfere with adolescents' healthy development—substance use, adolescent pregnancy, juvenile delinquency, and school failure and/or dropping out—and sought to identify their common antecedents. She found substantial evidence that these different high-risk behaviors are associated with the following factors:

▶ Early age of initiation of the behavior;

▶ Poor achievement in school and low expectations for achievement;

▶ Acting out, truancy, antisocial behavior, and conduct disorders;

▶ Low resistance to peer influence;

▶ Lack of parental support; and

▶ Living in an economically deprived neighborhood.

For program planners concerned with extending services to adolescents in high-risk settings, the most direct way of targeting such services is by expanding services in low-income neighborhoods. While it is possible to identify particular young people who have initiated problem behaviors at an early age, or whose parents do not provide adequate support, such strategies tend to stigmatize individual youth and to follow a deficit-oriented model, rather than a youth development approach.

The case for focusing on low-income neighborhoods is strengthened by knowledge that economically deprived areas tend also to

have less adequately funded public services, higher crime rates, more drugs, more physical danger, and fewer positive role models for young people. That these factors constitute a high-risk environment in which to grow up seems indisputable.

Because there is evidence that family income serves as the clearest determinant of access (or lack thereof) to community programs for youth,[13] and because life in a poor neighborhood raises adolescents' risks, the task force has adopted the income criterion as the major focus in determining which young adolescents warrant special concern.

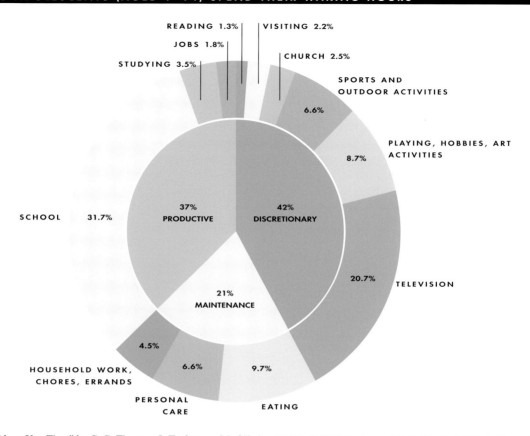

Source: "How Children Use Time" by S. G. Timmer, J. Eccles, and I. O'Brien (1985). In F. T. Juster and F. B. Stafford (Eds.), *Time, Goods and Well-Being.* Ann Arbor: University of Michigan, Institute for Social Research. Adapted by permission of the Institute for Social Research. Note: This chart represents 52 percent of hours during a week. Young adolescents spend 37 percent sleeping and 11 percent in miscellaneous activities.

OUTLINE

11-YEAR-OLD GIRL

Mama says when she was a girl, kids said, "Step on a crack, break your mother's back." I told her our old sidewalk is so cracked the mothers would be laid up day and night. My friends play a different game.

When people get killed on the street, the police draw an outline around him, like they getting ready to play hopscotch. When they take the body away, they leave that outline behind like a ghost. We say, "Step on the body line, be you next time." The macho boys lie down inside the outlines, but even they won't touch them. If you're a boy, it could definitely be you next. Life and death, they kiss too much.

Something good'll happen, like that time when I was a Girl Scout and we got to help at Christmas at the soup kitchen. One night they had a Girl Scout camp-out in a shopping mall, and we did all kinds of stuff. It was awesome. When I flew up from Brownies I gave my uniform to my sister and Mama bought me a brand-new Girl Scout one. I loved Girl Scouts and wearing my uniform to school, but the leader moved away. The new leader's no fun so I quit. She's one of those fake grown-ups who just wants to boss you around, she didn't care what we wanted to do. Now I'm in a church group that's supposed to go camping this summer.

I still fit in my uniform. Maybe they'll get a new Scout leader who really likes to be with kids. There's some computer stuff and crafts things I wanna learn, but I can't teach myself, even though I looked in some books for instructions. Mama might show me how to sew my own clothes on her machine. Not today, though, she says there ain't enough hours in a day for it all.[14]

▶ Positive opportunities available to young adolescents in their free time vary widely, from interesting and challenging activities in some communities to virtually none at all in others.

▶ Negative opportunities, which lead them into risky behavior such as criminal activity and early sexual activity, range from low (although seldom nonexistent) to extremely high in some neighborhoods.

▶ Many communities offer out-of-school activities that are unavailable to those young adolescents who cannot travel to, pay for, or be admitted to them (because of skill requirements or membership restrictions).

▶ Nonschool discretionary time represents an enormous potential for either desirable or undesirable outcomes in the young person's life—a potential that many parents, educators, and policy makers fail to appreciate.

LOTS OF TIME

One reason American youth have so much discretionary time is the comparatively short school day (six to seven hours, not all of which are spent in academic pursuits) and year (180 days). A few communities have adopted year-round schooling, but it usually results in about the same number of hours spent in school: cycles of twelve weeks of school followed by three weeks of vacation, rather than the traditional nine months of school followed by three months of vacation.

GIRL TALK
14-YEAR-OLD GIRL

If I'm not at school, I'm at the mall trying on clothes with my friends. You don't have to buy anything, you know, you can just act like you *might* buy something. I can see how I'd look if I had all the money in the world. My parents say I've got to buy my clothes myself. But how can I do that since I don't have a job? And I can't get a job cause I don't know how.

What can a teenager do? Sometimes I baby-sit, but I wouldn't call that a career and besides, that money's for college. When I grow up, I wanna be somebody, make enough money to buy my own house and have a family. I'm gonna be a lawyer or maybe a scientist since I'm good in biology. But that's when I grow up. Right now I need to learn what I can do to make money, especially since I need more clothes for high school.

There should be an all-girl place with classes on how to get jobs, like how to go on an interview and fill out applications. If the class was all girls, you could just be yourself. We could have sports classes, cooking classes, and sewing classes. Especially sports, so the boys don't yell, "You throw like a girl." Of course I throw like a girl!

We could have a class where we talk girl talk about stuff you worry about. Right now, I'm on the phone with my friends, but they don't have all the answers. What do they know that I don't about boys or how to handle your parents? Someone who knows what it's *really* like could give us tips, like what to do when a boy is after you to go with him and you just wanna say, "Get out of here, you nerd," but in a nice voice, so you don't hurt his feelings.

MY FATHER'S HOME
10-YEAR-OLD BOY

I used to hang out with my friends after school. Most of the time, we just acted stupid on the corner but that got dangerous and our moms said to quit it and come right home. In this city, wear your hat the wrong way and you're dead. Now I go home and watch TV and sleep. I get scared all by myself, even though Mom says there's nothing to be afraid of in the day.

I would make a place for kids called My Father's Home. It would be a love place where there's no killing. They'd have stuff for me to do. Lift weights, eat snacks, play games. I'd make it so all the boys in my neighborhood could go there any time, but no gangbangers or girls'd be allowed. I could ask someone to help me do my homework since I want straight A's this year. Nobody'd tease me 'cause I asked for help.

I'd have beds at My Father's Home, like in a dormitory. Kids could sleep there in the summer when people go crazy on the streets. Last year, Mama and me slept on the floor, praying not to get shot.

You couldn't count all the gangs in this city. If you don't know how to dress, someone'll make a mistake, suspect you belong to one gang or another. Walk on the wrong street or in the wrong neighborhood, someone'll kill you. I only wear black, brown, or gray, colors that mean nothing. At My Father's Home, I'd put on my red starter jacket and my bright green pants. I'd wear my pumps. Then I'd play one-on-one with the guys without feeling scared all the time, like someone might shoot me by mistake.

By way of comparison, adolescents in Japan attend school for nine hours a day, 240 days a year. The average American junior-high school student spends 28.7 hours per week in school and 3.2 hours studying; a Japanese counterpart spends 46.6 hours in school and 16.2 hours in study.[15]

TIME WITH FRIENDS

The important new element in the life of young adolescents, compared with that of younger children, is the opportunity to spend time with friends, and teenagers tend to seize this opportunity vigorously. They form friendships with other young people in the neighborhood. Who will these peers be, and what will the young people do together?[16]

Boys show continued interest in physical activity, such as sports, while girls spend increasing amounts of time socializing with friends, talking on the telephone, hanging out at the mall, or visiting a girlfriend.

TIME WITH PARENTS AND FAMILY

Young adolescents spend little time with parents and other family members, except at meals or watching television. Girls seem to spend more time than boys with family. One study of 1,000 adolescents found that they spend an average of five minutes a day exclusively with their fathers and about twenty minutes a day with their mothers.[17] Today's parents have other commitments that compete for their time, and young teens increasingly seek autonomy to make decisions about how to use their time.

TIME WORKING

Most young adolescents are given some responsibility for household chores. These differ by gender, family income, and racial or ethnic group. Boys work in the yard, and girls baby-sit and shop for groceries. Girls spend more time than boys on assigned chores. In one study, girls reported working about 7.5 hours more per week than boys. Boys tend to enter paid employment earlier than girls and earn higher rates of pay. As many as 20 percent of fourteen- and fifteen-year-olds work for pay outside the home.

Many chores can be constructive, but they tend to reinforce gender stereotypes. Paid employment, if carefully chosen and supervised, can provide useful knowledge, attitudes, and skills; unfortunately, many of the first jobs available to America's young adolescents are routine, boring, and lack positive interaction with adults.[18]

TIME IN YOUTH PROGRAMS

Between 60 and 80 percent of young adolescents participate in at least one activity sponsored by public or nonprofit agencies.[19] Teenagers generally report that they value these opportunities. Yet, overall, they do not spend large amounts of time on such activities.

Some young people participate intensely and continuously in such programs, others virtually not at all, and most do so only occasionally. Factors influencing participation include involvement of friends, access to transportation, availability and image of the activities, interest in the activities offered, and choice.

Much is known about what young people like to do and what attracts them to such activities. But this knowledge has not been widely applied in youth programs.

REESE

12-YEAR-OLD BOY

I'm glad I've got Reese. He says don't bother with "Mister." He goes to the same church as us. He likes kids so he does things for them. My friends from school were on Reese's baseball team last summer, but I didn't join because I didn't think I'd be any good. But they all had fun and were the league champions so I signed up this year.

I like Reese because he takes time to *show* you the right way to do things, instead of just *telling* you. Like when I couldn't hit a fastball and kept striking out, he never yelled when I struck out, he practiced with me more. He pitched fastballs until I could hit them with my eyes closed. The first time I got a hit off one, he cheered like it was the World Series or something. When someone messes up a big play, Reese doesn't give him any grief. He says, "Maybe next time you'll catch it."

Reese is the world's greatest coach. When it was time to pick the All Stars for the church league, he said, "No way—my *team* is All Stars." He doesn't want anyone to feel left out. Mrs. Reese had an All Star picnic at their house and Reese gave us plaques for things we'd done. I got one for a triple play. Mom hung it over the fireplace.

The other thing about Reese is he helps you out if you're having problems. He's more like a friend, even though he's old. When Dad couldn't drive me to the playoffs, Reese did. He has a lot of energy and he always has enough time for you. He loves all kids like they were his own.

American teenagers spend, on average, about twenty-one hours per week watching television. (By contrast, they read for pleasure about 1.8 hours per week and spend 5.6 hours on homework.)[20] One study found that eleven- and twelve-year-old boys watch television an average of twenty-six hours per week.[21] Television viewing peaks at around age twelve and declines through the later teen years. It may represent the only activity some young people share with parents or siblings.

For young people in high-risk neighborhoods, television watching is at least safe and avoids the danger of the streets; but it also represents lost opportunities. Passive television watching offers teenagers no new skills and does not develop their social abilities. Instead, they watch acts of murder and other violence, often coupled with sexual activity, frequently portrayed without any negative consequences.

UNSUPERVISED TIME: OPPORTUNITY LOST OR GAINED?

The 1988 National Education Longitudinal Study indicated that about 27 percent of eighth graders spent two or more hours at home alone after school. Those in the lowest socioeconomic group were most likely to be home alone for more than three hours (17.2 percent), while those in the highest socioeconomic group were least likely to be unsupervised for that amount of time (9.3 percent).[22]

Unsupervised after-school hours represent a period of significant risk; it is a time when adolescents may engage in dangerous and even illegal activities, and is the most common time for adolescent sexual intercourse (usually at the boy's home while his parents are at work).[23] Unsupervised young adolescents stand a greater chance of engaging in substance abuse. In one study, eighth graders who were unsupervised for eleven or more hours a week experienced twice the risk of substance abuse as those who were under some form of adult supervision.[24] Unsupervised teenagers are also more likely to be subject to negative peer pressure.[25]

Many young adolescents have not been taught to take care of themselves, how to handle emergencies, and how to cope with negative pressures from peers or adults. Their neighborhood may be physically unsafe.

Unfortunately, young people from poor families are most likely to live in unsafe neighborhoods and to be unsupervised during the after-school hours. They are least likely to have access to constructive alternatives. They are at extremely high risk; they are the youth whose lives hang in the balance.

Young adolescents surely need some time alone in which to pursue their own interests, to think about

UNFORTUNATELY, YOUNG PEOPLE FROM POOR FAMILIES ARE MOST LIKELY TO LIVE IN UNSAFE NEIGHBORHOODS AND TO BE UNSUPERVISED DURING THE AFTER-SCHOOL HOURS. THEY ARE LEAST LIKELY TO HAVE ACCESS TO CONSTRUCTIVE ALTERNATIVES. THEY ARE AT EXTREMELY HIGH RISK; THEY ARE THE YOUTH WHOSE LIVES HANG IN THE BALANCE.

themselves and their lives, and to cope with the stresses of being young. Growing up is never easy, and young people need time to reflect.

CREATIVE AND CONSTRUCTIVE USES OF NONSCHOOL TIME

Nonschool hours need not be fraught with peril or aimlessness. Young adolescents are eager for opportunities to make creative and constructive use of their free time, and in doing so they reap rich rewards. For example, it is possible to predict with some accuracy success or failure in school by finding out whether the young student spends roughly twenty to thirty-five hours a week engaged in constructive learning activity.[26]

Participation in intensive, well-planned, out-of-school activities can promote development of what one child development researcher calls "the other three R's": resourcefulness, responsibility, and reliability. Nonschool hours are the proving ground on which young people test and master their own interests, thus developing the skills and confidence that promote the other three Rs.[27]

YOUNG ADOLESCENTS AS COMMUNITY RESOURCES

In addition to developing their own skills, young adolescents represent growing resources for their families and community. Many are eager to contribute their time and energies: 58 percent of American adolescents, in a recent sample of fourteen- to seventeen-year-olds, were participating in voluntary community service, and even more expressed a willingness to volunteer. They are, when asked, almost four times as likely to volunteer.[28] Needs in the community—opportunities to contribute by cleaning up a polluted stream, reading to the elderly in a retirement home, tutoring younger children, or teaching them to resist negative peer pressure—currently exceed community service programs organized for young adolescents.

Communities that respond to their teenagers' needs can expect a remarkable gift in return: an outpouring of youthful energy, enthusiasm, and idealism that will benefit both the young people themselves and the community as a whole.[29]

How do communities respond? There is certainly an opportunity for individuals to do so. Even in the poorest of inner-city neighborhoods, the most sprawling and sterile of suburban communities, the most remote of rural areas, caring adults can look out for young people, befriend them, instruct them, encourage them.

The matter should not be left entirely to individual action. Communities act through agencies and

MOM, I'M PREGNANT
15-YEAR-OLD GIRL

After a year of health ed and everything Mom told me, I thought I could write the book about sex and boys. The only thing I didn't learn is how do you tell your mother you're pregnant? And how do I get Joe back? Mom'll be so pissed off, she'll kill me. All she wants is me to get out of high school and go to college. She's been saving money since I was born. That's when Dad left.

I can hear her now. "Why weren't you in school? Why weren't you doing your homework? Don't you have enough chores? I thought you were at the mall. When did you have time?" That one's easy. I had all kinds of time. School's a drag. I do okay, it's not like I'm great or anything. I'm not a brain and I'm not a cheerleader. After school, I used to go to Joe's house cause his parents weren't there. At first, we just watched TV and made out, but that turned into sex before I even thought about saying no. I never knew what Mom meant. You can't go back to holding hands. Now I do. I thought we were having fun, not babies.

Joe used to love me and now he doesn't know my name. I thought if I kept the baby I'd have something to call my own. It's not like I have anyone else except Mom and she's not there half the time. How am I gonna tell her? She was always talking about the Pill. Now instead of buying the Pill, I'll be buying Pampers. I don't even know what a diaper looks like. Sometimes when I think about this baby who's going to be all mine, it's excellent. The next day, it's a nightmare. I'm gonna be old and I'm not even sixteen. How will I finish school? At least the baby'll love me even though Joe doesn't. I can learn what cherish means. She's all mine, to have and to hold. Mine forever.

organizations: private, nonsectarian, nonprofit; churches and other religious institutions; civic clubs; and public agencies such as libraries, museums, and parks and recreation departments.

Both accepted theory and empirical evidence strongly support the idea that community-based programs are essential to the healthy development of young adolescents.[30] Individuals develop as the result of experiences with a variety of persons and systems.[31] Young adolescents bring to these experiences both assets (e.g., talents, parental standards, positive school climate, involvement in community organizations) and deficits (e.g., unsupervised time, fear and stress, experience with physical abuse, negative peer pressure).

Young adolescents with such assets are least likely to engage in high-risk behavior (alcohol, drug, or tobacco use; sexual activity; misbehavior in school; and antisocial conduct). One researcher found that sixth- through eighth-grade students with no key assets (family support, positive school climate, involvement in structured youth activities, and involvement in church or synagogue) show an average of four risk indicators (such as substance abuse), while those with one asset show three risk indicators, those with two show two, and those with three assets show only 1.4 risk indicators.[32] Furthermore, every system that surrounds the young adolescent—family, school, peer group, and community—contains both protective and risk factors.[33]

Community-based youth development programs apply such research through interventions designed to help youth build personal resilience. A resilient individual has these attributes:

▶ Social competence;

▶ Problem-solving skills;

▶ Autonomy (sense of self-identity and an ability to act independently and to exert control over his or her environment); and

▶ Sense of purpose and of a future.[34]

Shifting the balance from vulnerability to resilience requires action on three levels: helping individual youth build these four characteristics; ensuring that there is at least one caring, consistent adult in each young person's life; and developing a sense of security in the lives of all young people and their families. Community support means building a range of formal and informal structures that surround, encourage, and protect young individuals and their families.

These structures offer adolescents and their families opportunities to participate in organized groups; ways of contributing to the well-being of others; and access to and use of facilities and events including museums, libraries, parks, civic events, and celebrations.[35]

BOTH ACCEPTED THEORY AND EMPIRICAL EVIDENCE STRONGLY SUPPORT THE IDEA THAT COMMUNITY-BASED PROGRAMS ARE ESSENTIAL TO THE HEALTHY DEVELOPMENT OF YOUNG ADOLESCENTS. INDIVIDUALS DEVELOP AS THE RESULT OF EXPERIENCES WITH A VARIETY OF PERSONS AND SYSTEMS.

Home and neighborhood provide key influences on the young adolescent and also influence how well the young person is likely to do in school and later in life. A noted educational researcher has examined the relationship between out-of-school activities and students' performance in school and later in life. The results: young people who devote more time to reading, discussing, problem solving, and decision making do better in school and beyond.

Through extensive case studies of Asian, African American, Hispanic, and white families, Reginald M. Clark found one predictor of success in school was whether a young person spent twenty to thirty-five hours a week (of the sixty to seventy waking hours available) engaged in "constructive learning activity."[36] Such activity would, in a given week, consist of four or five hours of discussion with knowledgeable adults or peers, four or five hours of leisure reading, one or two hours of writing (grocery lists, a diary, letters, etc.), five or six hours of homework, several hours devoted to hobbies, two or three hours of chores, and four or five hours of games (especially games such as Monopoly, Scrabble, or Dominoes that require the player to read, spell, write, compute, solve problems, and make decisions). Constructive learning activity also includes theater, movies, and sports.

"The reason that youngsters who do these things outside school are more likely to be achievers is because they receive appropriately rich opportunities to extend their learning within a well-rounded array" of activities, says Clark. In contrast, the activity diet of underachieving young people is "top-heavy" with recreation that is largely passive and often not challenging or instructive.

Clark juxtaposes these two scenarios in the following way:

High-yield leisure: These activities — "leisure" in the sense that they are fun — include reading a book or talking with a parent about political campaigns, about why it is important to get an education, or about ways to handle a sticky job situation. Participating in organized youth programs, summer camps, or museum visits are other examples.

Recreation: Examples include television, games, music, playing outside, hanging out, partying, skipping rope, nature hikes, or family vacations.

According to Clark, "Achieving youths tend to pursue an activity pattern that is wholesome, nurturing, and balanced in the sense that these youngsters spend approximately twenty to thirty-five hours a week or more doing various high-yield leisure and deliberate learning activities. The rest of their out-of-school time is spent doing health maintenance and recreational activities." Clark's research emphasizes the need for a balanced activity diet that is currently unavailable to many of America's young adolescents.

For adolescents, community supports link family and school with a wider world of issues, events, and people. Community supports offer opportunities to learn practical and social skills and to apply and consolidate academic skills and interests. They provide forums for discussion of adult roles such as caring for others. They offer chances to test a variety of potential work roles, to seek and supply support across generations, and to develop a sense of competence and responsibility.

Finally, some of the most compelling evidence for strengthening community youth programs comes from the field of formal education. For many individuals — including adolescents — learning is enhanced when education is offered in real-life settings outside the classroom.[37]

In summary, current social science theory strongly suggests the great potential value of community-based youth development programs. This theory builds on educational and human development research that indicates (1) the needs of adolescents for supportive environments that provide engagement in a variety of active, socializing experiences; and (2) the potential of community programs to employ methods that are especially appropriate for young adolescents' development and that appear to have a good likelihood of success with that group.

How well do youth and community organizations live up to that potential? An examination of their practices and of research on their actual effectiveness provides important answers.

HOW COMMUNITY ORGANIZATIONS
FOSTER YOUTH DEVELOPMENT

Community organizations and programs for young adolescents have long seen their primary goal as promoting positive youth development. Although organizational definitions vary, positive youth development is best described as the process through which adolescents actively seek, and are assisted, to meet their basic needs and build their individual assets or competencies.[38] Parents, teachers, school administrators, peers, siblings, religious leaders, coaches, librarians, and youth group leaders can all serve as agents in this process.

Youth organizations typically place adolescents in small groups led by a paid or unpaid adult leader or by an older teen who also serves as a role model and mentor. Individual programs emphasize cooperative learning, peer leadership, and education through hands-on experience. Youth participate voluntarily, which makes their involvement fundamentally and qualitatively different from attending school.

Although they sometimes conduct their programs on school grounds, community-based organizations complement rather than compete with schools. Where schools focus primarily on imparting knowledge and often sort young people according to academic achievement, community organizations focus on social, physical, emotional, and moral development without openly labeling the gifted and the average. As community organizations begin to emphasize their role in the "informal education" of young people, and schools increasingly adopt reforms consistent with youth organizations' tradition and practice, the two developmental organizations may reach a common ground that meets the overall needs of youth.

A CLEAR PLAYING FIELD
13-YEAR-OLD BOY

I'd rather play soccer than play Nintendo, but I wish we had a field without glass, no drunks who throw bottles or pee all over the place. Every day before practice, Coach makes the guys who come late do glass patrol. They've gotta look for broken bottles and clean up the field. He started that after the game when a kid on another team got a piece of glass in his knee and had to get a zillion stitches.

I play soccer all the time. I don't care if any of my friends play or not, if it rains, if it's February or August. I'm kicking that ball and practicing every day of the week, except when Mom calls me in for dinner. She doesn't understand how great I am, but Dad calls me Little Pele. Last week, I made the winning goal.

Soccer teaches you to play on a team so you help each other win. It's not like tennis or gymnastics, where one guy gets all the glory. In soccer, even if you wanna be a superstar, someone has to back you up.

EMPIRICAL EVIDENCE SUPPORTS
STRENGTHENED YOUTH PROGRAMS

In looking for empirical evidence of the effects of community programs on healthy youth development, the task force examined research literature that had not been synthesized before or was unpublished and not accessible through traditional databases. This literature included surveys of youth and their parents, surveys of past participants in youth organization programs, national longitudinal studies of youth, and actual program evaluations conducted by national youth organizations. Five themes emerged from this material:

▶ Young people, their parents, and other adults want such programs;

▶ Young people value and want more opportunities to help them build personal and social skills;

▶ Young people and adult alumni value their own participation in nonschool youth programs;

▶ Participation in community-based youth development programs is especially appreciated by minority youth and young people growing up in single-parent families; and

▶ Participation in community-based youth development programs can promote positive behavior and reduce high-risk behavior.

These themes are found in a host of opinion surveys and program evaluation studies. Surveys of community leaders, parents, youth, and former program participants tell part of the story:

▶ In a 1988 survey of the National Association of Elementary School Principals, 84 percent of responding elementary and middle school principals said that children in their communities need increased access to organized before- and after-school programs, and 37 percent believed that children may perform better in school if they are not left unsupervised for long periods during nonschool hours.[39]

▶ A 1986 survey of Minneapolis parents and children revealed that young people wish to participate in sports and outdoor activities, acquire personal and social skills, and learn about possible career choices.[40]

▶ A 1987 survey of alumni of 4-H and other youth groups found that, on average, alumni believed that participation in the program contributed to their personal development by giving them pride in accomplishment, self-confidence, the ability to work with others, the ability to set goals and to communicate, employment and leadership skills, and encouragement of community involvement.[41]

Recent evaluations of community youth programs confirm this story:

▶ Four annual evaluations of the Association of Junior Leagues' Teen Outreach Program, a school-based, life-skills management and community service program for middle and high school students, found that participants were less likely than peers who did not participate in the program to become pregnant, drop out, or be suspended from school.[42]

▶ A multiyear evaluation of a targeted intervention developed by Girls Incorporated, called Preventing Adolescent Pregnancy, indicated that participation in all program components was associated with lower overall rates of pregnancy, and that participation in individual components led to specific pregnancy-related effects (e.g., young adolescents who took assertiveness training to learn to refuse early intercourse were only half as likely as nonparticipants to become sexually active).[43]

▶ An evaluation of WAVE, Inc.'s drop-out prevention program found that those who participate showed improved school attendance, lower drop-out rates, and improved scores on job readiness, mathematics, reading, and self-esteem.[44]

▶ An evaluation of Boys and Girls Clubs of America's SMART Moves (substance-abuse prevention) initiative showed substantial differences between housing projects that had clubs and those that did not. Residential areas with clubs experienced an overall reduction in alcohol and other drug use, drug trafficking, and other drug-related crime.[45]

Taken together, current social science theory and field evaluations provide a solid rationale for strengthening and expanding the role of community-based programs in promoting healthy adolescent development. More must be learned about what types of programs are most likely to be effective with individual adolescents and with particular groups of them. But enough is known to launch the process of reform in programs for America's young adolescents.

CONSTRUCTIVE OPPORTUNITIES FOR YOUTH DEVELOPMENT ORGANIZATIONS

What is the picture of community-based organizations serving youth in the United States today? How many are there, and where did they come from? What youth populations do they attract, and what services do they offer? How effective are they in meeting the needs of the youth they serve?

These questions about community-based youth-development organizations have not previously been systematically answered. A gaping hole exists in knowledge of, and attention to, these organizations and programs that provide constructive opportunities for young people beyond what is currently available in their neighborhoods. In Part II, this report analyzes, for the first time, the characteristics and operations of groups that provide community-based youth activities during the nonschool hours.

COMING TO AMERICA
13-YEAR-OLD GIRL

My best friends still live in the city, so to them I'm history. We don't even talk on the phone anymore because it costs too much. When you live in the suburbs, if you can't drive or your friends don't have a car, you can only go as far as your feet take you. Papa says be quiet when I say there's nothing to do here. He says, "What about your studies and that bad grade in math?"

Because I'm a TV lover, I could stay home all day and watch the stories. Mama only lets me watch one a day, then I've gotta go outside. I'm making one good friend with this girl so we go to each other's house a lot. She's real popular. I like to dance and play with her other friends. We teach each other new dances and I'm so good they call me Mrs. Patrick Swayze. They're always so psyched when they get the steps right. I think maybe I'll be a dance teacher. When I help other people, I feel happy that I really did something.

Sometimes, though, we just watch TV and eat and try to think of something to do. I wish there was a place like a community center where I could meet other Salvadoran girls who are new in the States and we could have English classes, maybe with a Salvadoran lady who's bilingual. She would help me speak better English. If she was young, like a college student, she could help girls learn what it is like to live here. We could talk and get help from each other and improve our lives. I would help the new girls because some people don't have anybody to help them with their problems. Maybe I would teach them to dance like Americans.

PART II

UNTAPPED POTENTIAL: COMMUNITY PROGRAMS FOR YOUTH

WHEN THE TASK FORCE ASKED YOUNG ADOLESCENTS WHAT THEY WANTED MOST DURING THEIR NONSCHOOL HOURS, THEY REPLIED: SAFE PARKS AND RECREATION CENTERS; EXCITING SCIENCE MUSEUMS; LIBRARIES WITH ALL THE LATEST BOOKS, VIDEOS, AND RECORDS; CHANCES TO GO CAMPING AND PARTICIPATE IN SPORTS; LONG TALKS WITH TRUSTING AND TRUSTWORTHY ADULTS WHO KNOW A LOT ABOUT THE WORLD AND WHO LIKE YOUNG PEOPLE; AND OPPORTUNITIES TO LEARN NEW SKILLS.[1]

Youth-serving organizations are the primary vehicle offering these kinds of services and relationships to young people. America's youth organizations are second only to public schools in the number of young people they reach. A vast network of agencies—public and private, secular and religious, national and local—serves millions of youth. Collectively, fifteen organizations alone, including the Girl Scouts, Boy Scouts, Boys and Girls Clubs, Camp Fire Boys and Girls, 4-H, Girls Incorporated, and the YMCA and YWCA, reach approximately thirty million young people each year.[2]

Despite the broad scope and reach of the youth-serving sector, its substantial base of financial support, and its enormous potential to promote positive youth development, it is largely ignored in public policy debate. Especially lacking is an analysis of how existing youth development organizations and programs can better respond to the needs of today's young adolescents, particularly those from low-income backgrounds. The Task Force on Youth Development and Community

Programs sought to fill this knowledge gap through a multipart study that included commissioned papers written by youth development specialists, interviews with many of the organizations themselves, focus group discussions with young adolescents, site visits to programs and organizations, and a review of the professional literature, including national surveys and program evaluation reports.

This report contains the first large-scale national study of their services and program structures that has ever been undertaken.[3] Part II describes the current status of major providers of youth development programs (such as national youth organizations) and smaller organizations with potential for expansion (such as intergenerational programs). It focuses on the expansion of programs whose primary purpose is to enhance positive development or prevent youth problems from starting. Programs that focus principally on remediation and treatment, such as juvenile justice, foster care, or protective services, are not included.

The task force examined five kinds of organizations that deliver community-based youth development programs and services:

▶ Private, nonprofit, national youth organizations (including those that are primarily or exclusively youth-serving in their focus as well as multiservice organizations that offer substantial service to youth);

▶ Grassroots youth development organizations not affiliated with any national structures;

▶ Religious youth organizations;

▶ Adult service clubs, sports organizations, senior citizens groups, and museums that run youth programs; and

▶ Selected public-sector institutions, including libraries and parks and recreation departments, that offer youth services.

The picture that emerges from the task force study is both heartening and troubling. It is heartening to learn that so many Americans give so much of themselves and their resources in the interests of youth. It is troubling to find that so many young adolescents, especially those who need it most, are excluded from the potential benefit of this effort.

PRIVATE, NONPROFIT NATIONAL YOUTH ORGANIZATIONS

Some 400 national organizations either serve youth exclusively or offer substantial services to them.[4] The twenty largest such organizations are described in this section—of which thirteen are primarily or exclusively youth-serving, and seven are multiservice.[5]

These organizations are committed to youth development, emphasize prosocial values, rely on small-group techniques and involved adult leaders, and use hands-on education, cooperative learning, and age-appropriate programming strategies.

Many of these national organizations have increasingly come to define their work as "informal education" and "youth development" rather than recreation, which for several groups reflects a return to an earlier focus. Also, many agencies are placing greater emphasis on building specific skills and competencies rather than self-esteem and self-confidence.

Although private national organizations share many common aspects, each has unique components within the structure of its program. For instance:

▶ Some organizations are facility-based, others are group- or troop-based, and still others rely on a one-to-one match between a young person and an adult volunteer mentor.

▶ Troop- or group-based agencies tend to meet once a week, for an hour or two, while facility-based agencies generally offer services for twenty to thirty hours per week (although the extent to which individual members make use of the entire array of services varies).

▶ Some programs are led by volunteers, others (usually the facility-based organizations) rely primarily on paid staff.

▶ Program content and approaches vary. Some organizations offer a comprehensive "core" program, while others focus on one or two aspects of overall youth development, such as academic enrichment or leadership skills. Even when several organizations offer specific programs in the same content area, their approaches may be quite dissimilar.

▶ The demographics of service populations can differ in composition in terms of socioeconomic status, race and ethnic background, age, and gender and in total number of youths served.

▶ Some organizations are well funded (e.g., Boy Scouts of America and Girl Scouts of the U.S.A.), while others struggle. Some national groups rely heavily on affiliate dues and on revenues from the sale of equipment, products, and supplies, while others receive the bulk of their support from government or from charitable contributions.

▶ Every organization defines its membership differently—in general, the national organizations try to maximize their membership numbers, occasionally by including leaders and others.

▶ Most organizations try to encourage active youth participation in program planning at the local level, but they seldom permit young people to take part in genuine decision making. Only a few national organizations appoint youth members to boards or committees.

Tables 1, 2, and 3 present information on the service demographics[6] and finances of the twenty organizations studied.

CURRENT TRENDS AMONG NATIONAL YOUTH ORGANIZATIONS

Many of today's largest national youth organizations were founded early in this century in response to the massive social dislocations brought on by the Industrial Revolution and World War I. Although rooted in history and tradition, these groups have continually modified their programs to meet the contemporary needs of America's youth. Most groups evolved in response to social changes, including those in the funding environment. Some changes improved youth services, others did not. Finally, some national youth and multiservice organizations have adapted to shifts in demographics, but many have not.

TREND: EXPANDING SERVICE TO YOUNGER CHILDREN

In recent years, several national agencies have established new programs for younger children, such as the Tiger Cub Scouts for first-grade boys, the Daisy Girl

Scouts for five-year-old girls, and the Camp Fire Sparks for boys and girls of that same age. In addition, 4-H recently launched a new program for elementary-level children ages five through eight. These efforts respond to the developmental needs of young children and to the changing child-care needs of families; they are also strategic, in that they push membership statistics and revenue bases to a higher level. They may also involve troubling trade-offs, however, because some agencies appear to have undertaken these efforts at the expense of programs for adolescents, who are viewed as more challenging and expensive to serve.

Almost every national agency is now experimenting with ways to extend programs to underserved youth. Here are some examples:

▶ Big Brothers/Big Sisters of America is offering training and technical assistance to some school-based

TABLE 1: CHARACTERISTICS OF YOUTH SERVED BY SELECTED NATIONAL ORGANIZATIONS

ORGANIZATION	TOTAL YOUTH SERVED	PERCENTAGE ADOLESCENTS[a]	PERCENTAGE FEMALE	PERCENTAGE MINORITY[b]
American Camping Assn.	5,300,000 including adults	NA	NA	NA
American Red Cross	1,025,756	NA	NA	NA
ASPIRA	17,000 ages 3–20	NA	NA	100 Hispanic
Big Brothers/Big Sisters of America	90,073 (77% matched with adults)	67.2 ages 10–15	49.6	31.3
Boy Scouts of America	4,292,992 ages 6–20	25 ages 11–13	3	18
Boys and Girls Clubs	1,700,000 ages 6–18	44 ages 11–16	30	51
Camp Fire Boys and Girls	600,000 ages 5–18	50 ages 10–15	62	26
Child Welfare League	2,000,000 ages 18–under	NA	NA	49
4-H Clubs	5,657,657 ages 9–19	68 ages 9–14	52	23.5
Girl Scouts of the U.S.A.	2,560,718 ages 5–18	6 ages 11–14	100	14.1
Girls Incorporated	250,000 ages 6–18	63 ages 9–18	71	51
Junior Achievement	1,300,000 ages 9–18	68 ages 9–14	NA	37
National Association for the Advancement of Colored People	40,000 ages 20–under		NA	Primarily black
National Coalition of Hispanic Health and Human Services Organizations (COSSMHO)	20,000	NA	NA	Primarily Hispanic
National Network of Runaway and Youth Services	404,279	38 ages 14–under	53	36
National Urban League	150,000 ages 12–14	NA	NA	85 black
Salvation Army	349,541 ages 3–19	NA	NA	NA
WAVE, Inc.	10,068 ages 14–21	NA	49	NA
YMCA of the USA	5,800,000 ages 6–17	NA	46	NA
YWCA of the U.S.A.	700,000 ages 18–under	26 ages 12–17	74	29

Source: Information presented in this table was obtained from each group's most recent annual report and organizational interviews conducted by the task force. These numbers reflect the fact that methods of counting or estimating youth served vary from agency to agency. As indicated (NA), many organizations do not have information in some of these categories.

[a] These figures reflect the fact that methods of age grouping vary from agency to agency.
[b] These figures reflect the fact that some of the studied organizations serve primarily one racial or ethnic group. Others serve a more diverse population. Five do not have data available on this aspect of their service demographics.

TABLE 2: FINANCIAL STATUS OF SELECTED NATIONAL YOUTH DEVELOPMENT ORGANIZATIONS

ORGANIZATION	ANNUAL EXPENSES	SURPLUS/DEFICIT	TOTAL ASSETS
American Camping Association	$ 2,958,574	$ 83,398	$ 1,549,418
ASPIRA	1,187,408	103,308	677,132
Big Brothers/Big Sisters of America	3,995,088	(205,929)	1,946,030
Boy Scouts of America	75,491,000	9,723,000	255,639,000
Boys and Girls Clubs of America	16,097,026	(532,407)	31,819,100
Camp Fire Boys and Girls	4,116,579	(298,150)	3,111,430
Child Welfare League of America	6,269,838	154,156	10,635,220
Girl Scouts of the U.S.A.	32,631,000	3,529,000	90,492,000
Girls Incorporated	3,670,248	(22,998)	5,953,420
Junior Achievement	8,440,405	805,834	10,365,625
WAVE, Inc.	5,880,455	48,873	1,623,075
National Network of Runaway and Youth Services	783,748	(1,501)	124,172

Source: Most recent annual report available from each organization.

Note: Because of generally accepted principles of not-for-profit accounting, surplus and deficit figures may include both unrestricted and restricted funds as well as land, property, and equipment funds.

TABLE 3: FINANCIAL STATUS OF SELECTED NATIONAL MULTISERVICE ORGANIZATIONS WITH YOUTH DEVELOPMENT PROGRAMS

ORGANIZATION	ANNUAL EXPENSES	SURPLUS/DEFICIT[a]	TOTAL ASSETS
American Red Cross[b]	$ 1,402,108,000	$ 7,911,000	$ 1,802,939
National Coalition of Hispanic Health and Human Services Organizations (COSSMHO)	2,512,157	235,423	1,534,233
NAACP	7,697,320	(633,928)	7,306,528
National Urban League	26,208,003	593,449	13,211,175
Salvation Army	7,012,958	2,286,283	24,105,147
YMCA of the USA	35,355,634	(477,609)	84,039,724
YWCA of the U.S.A.	12,108,987	(3,265,779)	41,989,411

Source: Most recent annual report available from each organization.

[a] Because of generally accepted principles of not-for-profit accounting, surplus and deficit figures may include both unrestricted and restricted funds as well as land, property, and equipment funds.

[b] Represents combined national and local financial figures.

and school-linked mentoring programs, in addition to providing such services to its own affiliates;

▶ Boy Scouts of America's new in-school Learning for Life program seeks to extend scouting values and life skills to young people in underserved urban and rural areas;

▶ Boys and Girls Clubs has launched an aggressive expansion campaign in public housing projects;

▶ Camp Fire has supplemented its basic club and camping programs with school-age child-care services and topic-specific courses that promote self-reliance and life skills;

▶ 4-H recently launched a major national Youth-at-Risk Initiative in an effort to reach a wider spectrum of young people and to meet the contemporary needs of today's young people in both rural and urban environments;

▶ Girl Scouts has established a National Center for Innovation that is experimenting with facility-based programming (e.g., in community centers in public housing developments) in low-income neighborhoods;

▶ Girls Incorporated has developed partnerships with other national organizations, including the YWCA and the Salvation Army, to reach more girls and young women;

▶ Junior Achievement is allocating several million dollars to new school-based programs for elementary-aged students and adolescents in low-income areas; and

▶ WAVE, Inc., has initiated WAVE in Schools as a drop-out prevention effort that supplements its WAVE in Communities program for young people who have already discontinued their formal education.

A trend toward expansion of services for young people living in high-risk environments is discernible, but change is occurring at a glacial rate.

TREND: CUTTING BACK IN RESPONSE TO
SHRINKING FUNDING

During the early 1980s reductions in federal expenditures for social programs put financial pressure on most groups in the human services sector. Between fiscal year 1982 and fiscal year 1989, private giving offset only 46 percent of the cumulative reductions in federal spending in areas of interest to nonprofit organizations.[7] National youth organizations and their affiliates never relied on federal funds for the bulk of their support, but the cutbacks took their toll throughout the youth services sector. In addition to offering program funding, federal dollars at one time provided youth agencies with other types of support—for example, staff salaries through the Comprehensive Employment and Training Act.

In recent years, national and local youth agencies have actively sought to achieve financial stability by

A TREND TOWARD EXPANSION OF SERVICES FOR YOUNG PEOPLE LIVING IN HIGH-RISK ENVIRONMENTS IS DISCERNIBLE, BUT CHANGE IS OCCURRING AT A GLACIAL RATE.

diversifying funding sources, competing harder for national foundation grants, increasing efforts to solicit contributions from individuals and corporations, retrenching staff and cutting back on services to affiliates, and seeking support from both traditional and nontraditional federal sources.

Youth organizations must compete aggressively for grant dollars:[8]

▶ Affiliates of the largest national youth-serving organizations receive a greater share of their support from local United Ways than do smaller independent agencies, but the former's share is decreasing;

▶ National youth-serving organizations receive the lion's share of foundation dollars directed toward preventive youth services, although the total proportion of foundation grants allocated for this purpose is quite small (approximately 2 percent);

▶ Smaller, independent agencies are considerably more dependent on government funds than are large national organizations;[9]

▶ Unrestricted support is increasingly difficult to obtain, and funders are reluctant to pay for indirect or administrative costs;

▶ Funders prefer to make categorical grants for specific projects or purposes, rather than for overall support of the organization; and

▶ Changes in federal tax policy have reduced the charitable contributions on which these organizations depend.

Overall, the funding base of many youth-serving organizations is extremely precarious.

TREND: CHANGING ORGANIZATIONAL STRUCTURE TO REDUCE COSTS

National youth organizations have traditionally followed either a top-down program development policy or a confederation model that grants local affiliates autonomy in determining program content and approaches. With money in shorter supply and supporters questioning what they are getting for dues paid to the headquarters, national youth organizations are centralizing much of their program development work.

Several implications of this trend emerge: clearly the organizations are under rising financial pressure and are attempting to streamline their structures to spread dollars further. Because program development is costly, it makes good sense for national operations to absorb at least some of these costs and free their affiliates to allocate resources to actual program delivery. At the same time, however, these organizations recognize the need for some flexibility in program content to allow affiliates to respond to local youth needs.

TREND: REACTING TO LEGAL ACTIONS AND CONCERNS

A young adolescent is injured while participating in a program sponsored by a national youth organization; alleging negligence in oversight of the young person, the parents sue the national organization and the local board of directors.

This kind of legal action, among others, has led many national youth organizations to adopt policies regarding exposure to risk. Many local boards of directors have also believed that they must incur the cost of directors' and officers' liability insurance to protect themselves against suits and to be able to attract qualified new board members. Furthermore, skyrocketing costs of general liability insurance have caused several organizations to modify their current programs to reduce potential risk.

Lawsuits against youth organizations have risen in number and in size of potential award. Youth-serving groups face suits from these quarters:

▶ For-profit firms challenge their tax-exempt status on grounds of unfair competition (such as health and fitness clubs contending that the local YMCA and YWCA offer the same services at a competitive advantage because of preferential tax status);

▶ Parents or members of the population served seek to change policies that restrict membership by gender, religion, or sexual orientation; and

▶ Parents or young people sue for damages from sexual abuse by the organizations' staff or volunteers.

Lawsuits are expensive to defend, and the threat of them drives up costs of insurance and of screening and training staff.

TREND: RESPONDING TO GENDER ISSUES

During the past two decades almost every major single-gender national youth organization has been forced to address the question, at the national policy level, of whether to provide services to both boys and girls. They are responding to lawsuits demanding access to programs, rising demand from families with school-age children who want youth services, philosophical considerations, and their own desire to increase membership.

Although most traditionally male organizations have become coeducational, their female counterparts have mostly recommitted themselves to single-gender programming. Organizations have changed policy on gender in a variety of ways. Boy Scouts of America, for example, has opened two programs (Explorer Scouts and Learning for Life) to girls; Big Brothers and Big Sisters merged two separate organizations into a single national group; the YMCA and Boys Clubs changed their missions and became fully coeducational; and Camp Fire adopted a deliberately nonsexist program philosophy in 1977 when it decided to start serving both genders.

During the late 1970s and early 1980s, a number of national organizations broadened their missions to include family- or adult-centered programs. This shift was intended to respond to community needs and stabilize funding in such organizations as the YMCA and YWCA. Within the past two years, however, the YMCA, YWCA, and the American Red Cross have countered the trend, reaffirming in public declarations their earlier commitment to youth programs on the national level.

FUTURE CHALLENGES FACING NATIONAL YOUTH ORGANIZATIONS

Approximately half of the twenty organizations studied have a long-standing commitment to serve young people from low-income and minority backgrounds: ASPIRA, Big Brothers/Big Sisters of America, Boys and Girls Clubs of America, Child Welfare League of America, National Coalition of Hispanic Health and Human Services Organizations (COSSMHO), Girls Incorporated, National Network of Runaway and Youth Services, National Urban League, Salvation Army, and WAVE, Inc. Several of these groups, however, serve a relatively small number of youth, have small budgets, or are multiservice agencies that focus only part of their resources on young people. The challenges for these groups include finding ways to extend their current services to more young people, expand their financial resources, and form partnerships with other organizations. In particular, these agencies may have valuable lessons to teach other organizations about outreach techniques and program adaptation.

The young people served by this country's largest, most heavily funded youth groups are disproportionately white and from middle- to upper-income families, partly because that is the groups' tradition but increasingly because they charge fees for services that poorer youth cannot afford. The challenges facing these groups include adapting their programs to the needs of a more diverse group of participants, retraining current staff, recruiting multicultural staff, developing new outreach strategies, and overcoming image barriers in some communities and among some previously excluded groups.

Different challenges face the large multiservice agencies. These agencies must find creative ways to translate and support their national recommitment to youth work at the local level. Crafting national policy is an important first step, but it must be supported by developing youth programs, recruiting culturally diverse staff, training local affiliate staff and board members, and (for most) generating financial resources to underwrite the costs of these efforts.

GRASSROOTS YOUTH DEVELOPMENT ORGANIZATIONS

About 17,000 youth development organizations now operate within the United States. Several thousand are independent. The remainder are affiliated with national youth organizations such as the YWCA of the U.S.A. or Boys and Girls Clubs of America. If little has been written about national youth organizations, even less is known about their grassroots counterparts. The task force undertook an exploratory survey of grassroots organizations for this report.[10]

Most of the 252 responding grassroots groups were established during the 1960s and 1970s to work with youth perceived to be facing risks in a particular community. At least two-thirds were set up without previous models; the founders relied on their own ingenuity to develop organizational structures and programs. Many continue to go their own way in relative isolation, following their own lead as they see fit.

Moreover, until Independent Sector, the national association of nonprofit organizations in Washington, D.C., established a taxonomy of nonprofit organizations within the National Center for Charitable Statistics database in 1990, no systematic way existed to identify these organizations, much less document or analyze their contributions to youth development. Current data about them remain rudimentary, but even with this limited information, the basic picture that emerges is a testament to the importance of their work.

Only 25 percent of all grassroots youth development organizations operate with annual budgets of more than $25,000. This fact suggests that the majority of these groups are small, are being run by local volunteers, and may be relatively modest in the scope of their services and operations.

Of the larger organizations (those with annual budgets of more than $25,000), better than two-thirds of respondents report that they provide life-skills training and substance-abuse education, as well as general counseling for families, groups, and individuals and specialized counseling for sexual and child abuse. Moreover, 40 to 50 percent also offer crisis intervention, community service, academic tutoring, communications skills, peer counseling, sex education, job readiness and career awareness, health education, physical fitness and sports, other education programs, and a place for youth to have fun and hang out.

CURRENT TRENDS AMONG GRASSROOTS YOUTH DEVELOPMENT ORGANIZATIONS

Based on this exploratory survey, grassroots youth development organizations appear to represent a vig-

"The main ingredient of our success is that we've stayed close to the community, even as we've grown older and larger," notes Chris Baca, executive director of Albuquerque's Youth Development, Inc. (YDI). Founded in 1968 and incorporated in 1971, YDI has evolved from a single program site to thirteen neighborhood locations and from an initial annual budget of $150,000 to one of $3.6 million in 1991. The organization's current services, which range from after-school recreation to residential treatment, can truly be described as comprehensive, reaching nearly 18,000 young people with some twenty programs last year.

According to Baca, the founders of YDI had a clear vision of "tapping the roots of family tradition" by supporting families and building on their strengths and by responding to the needs of local neighborhoods with caring and compassion.

Specific programs for adolescents include summer youth employment, substance-abuse prevention and treatment, AIDS education, sports and recreation, drop-out prevention, a youth theater troupe, other arts programs (including music, dance, and rap), outreach counseling, GED preparation, scholarship assistance, and several juvenile justice efforts.

Nontraditional staffing patterns contribute to the effectiveness and innovative quality of these programs. Ruben Chavez, director of the Gang Prevention and Intervention Program, now in his mid-thirties, was a gang member when growing up in Los Angeles. "The kids believe me and they trust me," says Chavez. "I can be a bridge between gang members and the community, and between rival gangs, because I've been there." Chavez says his work is directed toward preventing initial gang involvement among younger teens and providing constructive, nonviolent activities for current gang members. In a structured seven-week program gang members become involved in community service, learn nonviolent conflict-resolution skills, visit adult corrections facilities, obtain employment and legal assistance, and receive counseling with family members.

Baca observes that "the constant struggle for funding, the grants that fall through, and the bureaucracies that fail to validate your efforts are all low points. If it weren't for the kids and the top-notch people who work here, I'd have given up long ago."

---

orous network of services for America's young people. Many of the larger groups are well established within their communities, offer a wide range of services to the low-income families they serve, and receive broad public and private support. The task force survey showed that:

▶ At least two-thirds of young people served by the responding organizations are from low-income families and are defined by agency directors as facing serious risks, and about the same proportion has had some involvement with the juvenile justice system;

▶ About two-thirds of these organizations serve mostly or all white youth, while 15 percent serve mostly or all black youth, 10 percent mostly Hispanic youth, 4 percent mostly Asian youth, and 2 percent Native American youth;

▶ Boys and girls are served in about equal numbers;

▶ In contrast to some large national organizations, such as the YMCA of the U.S.A. and Girl Scouts of the U.S.A., these groups serve mainly adolescents: youth ten to eighteen years old make up almost two-thirds of their total service population (young adolescents, 35 percent, and older teenagers, 28 percent);

▶ Almost half of the responding organizations report that "enhancing youth development" is their most important function (as opposed to preventing problem behaviors, short-term intervention, or long-term treatment).

FUTURE CHALLENGES FACING GRASSROOTS ORGANIZATIONS

Federal, state, and local governments sustain two out of five of the grassroots groups that responded to the task force survey, with support ranging from 70 to 100 percent of their operating revenues. Such high levels of government support leave the recipients vulnerable to shifting political winds. Responding groups reported the following sources as providing these percentages of their annual budgets: 50 percent from government grants, 7.5 percent from fund-raising events, 14.7 percent from fees for service, 2.3 percent from membership dues, 8 percent from federated campaigns, 16.3 percent from other charitable income, and 1.2 percent from other sources.[11]

Judges, lawyers, and concerned citizens started

many of these agencies with juvenile justice funds to assist youth in trouble with the law, and these agencies still rely on such funds. These origins explain why the agencies serve young people at high risk, and also why they rely so heavily on government funds.

Most nonprofit organizations know that it is imprudent to rely on any one source for more than 50 percent of annual income and that they must diversify their funding bases. Many grassroots organizations experience difficulty in becoming accredited agencies of the local United Way or other federated campaigns, which tend to fund older, more established, and nationally affiliated agencies.[12]

Beyond that, these organizations encounter lack of public understanding of their work. They must cope with the increasingly complex and serious problems that young people face, which require a greater variety of approaches than before. Many agencies are ill-equipped to cope with the changing needs and rising demands of today's young adolescents. For example, survey respondents consistently named housing as a major unmet need of youth in their communities; yet few of the groups can meet this high-cost need.

Organizational isolation is another challenge. Many groups lack the capacity to follow what is going on in the wider world of youth development. Yet knowledge of effective practice in youth development work is advancing and could be made more readily available to these organizations. They could learn about new ideas and practices, share technologies, and save money in one of the most expensive areas for such agencies: program development. These agencies need information especially in three areas: pending legislation and government programs, fund-raising techniques, and program development and evaluation.

RELIGIOUS YOUTH ORGANIZATIONS

Religious activities[13] are popular with youth: from 30 to 50 percent of America's young people report that they participate in some kind of religious youth group.[14] One out of every three organizations now listed in the *Directory of American Youth Organizations*[15] is church-affiliated—and many local organizations and denominational programs are not included in that directory. Religious youth organizations have many common features:

▶ Most foster moral and faith development as a primary goal; many also promote the healthy development of the whole person, paying attention to social and emotional aspects of development.

▶ Program structures generally include a mix of small groups of same-age peers coordinated and led by committed adult leaders; formal instruction (such as classes to prepare youth for full membership in church

or synagogue); worship services, often planned and conducted by youth themselves; special events (such as camps and retreats); youth leadership councils; community service projects; and community centers (such as the network of Jewish Community Centers). In addition, many congregations sponsor Boy Scout, Girl Scout, or Camp Fire groups, and may add their denominational component to the basic program of these organizations.

▶ Programs attempt to instill both social and spiritual awareness. Youth are assisted in developing their personal identities, including faith and cultural identity. Most programs seek to enhance young people's capacity to put their beliefs and values into practice by providing opportunities for community service.

▶ Approximately 80 percent of adults in youth ministry programs are volunteers, 15 percent are full-time employees with other responsibilities within the church or synagogue, and the remaining 5 percent are part-time employees.

For many adolescents, their religious organization and its leaders are often as trusted as family. This sense of familiarity, combined with the commitment adult church leaders have to nurture young church members, lends strength to church-based youth programs.

Other strengths include an emphasis on youth empowerment and leadership; cohesive national structures; reliance on relationship-intensive processes and on nondidactic, hands-on educational approaches; traditional and continuing emphasis on youth as resources to the church or synagogue community; "other-directedness," resulting in opportunities to engage in community service and community action; and an ethics orientation that encourages young people to reflect on and question the materialistic values of the larger culture.

CURRENT TRENDS AMONG RELIGIOUS YOUTH ORGANIZATIONS

Participation trends differ by denomination. For the past thirty years, participation in Protestant youth programs has declined, in part because of diminished financial support for youth work, while the Catholic Church has enjoyed a resurgence because of increased program funding and more energetic national leadership, including publication of national program guidelines in 1976. During this same period, the evangelical youth ministry has grown moderately, while Jewish youth work has remained relatively stable.

Although religious youth work traditionally emphasized older adolescents—particularly high school-aged students—for the past decade, such organizations as the Search Institute, the Center for Early Adolescence, and Group Publishing have played a major role in expanding outreach to young adolescents and in developing programs, resource materials, and staff training approaches that respond to their developmental needs. Religious youth leaders currently report noticeably higher involvement among ten- to fifteen-year-olds than among older teenagers, estimating that between 50 and 75 percent of youth involved in their denominations' youth programs are under fifteen.[16] The age of approximately thirteen is critical for many young adolescents in deciding whether to continue to participate. Formal programs for teenagers, such as Hebrew school and confirmation classes, are stressed during early adolescence. Once they complete these rites of passage, many young people face either nothing to "graduate into" or programs that do not meet their changing needs.[17]

While churches made considerable progress in recent years in their ability to address the needs of young adolescents, they were not so sanguine about the efforts of religious youth organizations to respond to the youth development and primary prevention needs of young people. Youth ministry specialists generally agree that the country's major denominations,

BLACK CHURCHES SUPPORT YOUTH DEVELOPMENT THROUGH PROJECT SPIRIT

Since 1978 the Congress of National Black Churches (CNBC) has worked to build on and strengthen the black church's ministry by serving as an organizational umbrella for the eight major black American religious denominations: African Methodist Episcopal, African Methodist Zion, Christian Methodist Episcopal, Church of God in Christ, National Baptist Convention of America, Inc., National Baptist Convention, USA, Inc., National Missionary Baptist Convention, and Progressive National Baptist Convention, Inc. Headquartered in Washington, D.C., CNBC represents approximately 19 million African Americans in more than 65,000 local churches.

CNBC seeks to harness the historical willingness of black churches to respond to not only the spiritual, but also the economic and social, needs of the black community. The organization launched its first major national demonstration effort— Project SPIRIT—in 1986, with funding from Carnegie Corporation of New York and the Lilly Endowment. Project SPIRIT, which stands for Strength, Perseverance, Imagination, Responsibility, Integrity, and Talent, aims to instill those very qualities in African American youth. The typical young person enrolled is an underachiever—bored with the traditional school setting, earning low grades, and already experiencing discipline problems. The project focuses on three target populations: young people, parents, and black pastors.

The youth component revolves around daily after-school programs conducted in church facilities by elder volunteers. Program activities include:
▶ Snacks, prayer, and time for meditation;
▶ Tutoring in reading, writing, and mathematics;
▶ Activities that teach practical life skills through games, skits, songs, and role-playing;
▶ Activities aimed at developing black cultural and ethnic pride; and
▶ A weekly rites-of-passage curriculum that culminates in an end-of-the-year ceremony.

Parents participate in weekly education sessions based on *Systematic Training for Effective Parenting* but adapted to be more culturally relevant to black parents. This Afro-centric approach to parent education aims not only to give information on child development and effective parenting techniques but also to help parents become strong advocates for their children both at school and in the community.

The Pastoral Counseling Training Component of Project SPIRIT provides pastors and clergy of participating churches with a fifteen-session workshop designed to help them become more effective in the care, education, and guidance of African American youth. Because this type of training is missing from most seminaries and in-service education programs for black ministers, it is a critical component of Project SPIRIT.

Over the lifetime of the demonstration, Project SPIRIT has served more than 2,000 youth and their parents in Atlanta, Oakland, and Indianapolis. Since the demonstration, the project has been replicated in Kokomo, Savannah, Washington, D.C., and several communities in northern California.

According to Vanella Crawford, director of Project SPIRIT, "the program's fundamental goal is to encourage African American children to explore and affirm their blackness and self-identity." Other goals are to provide constructive after-school activities for young people growing up in low-income communities, to expand their network of relationships with caring adults, to support academic achievement, and to teach relevant and practical life skills.

for the most part, are not currently reaching young people living in at-risk environments; that many religious organizations are beginning to seek ways to do so; and that if youth in high-risk environments are being served by religious youth programs, these efforts are largely local and small or involve treatment and remediation initiatives (offered by such groups as Catholic Charities and Lutheran Social Services). Two notable exceptions are Youth for Christ, a nondenominational religious organization that has targeted many of its services to teenagers living in high-risk environments, and the Congress of National Black Churches, which has launched several innovative programs designed to provide educational and social enrichment to African American youth.

The failure of many religious youth organizations to reach young people who face the most daunting developmental obstacles is particularly compelling in light of research indicating that religious participation and values often serve as protective factors against high-risk behaviors. The strength of religious beliefs and practices is inversely related to drug and alcohol use, sexual activity, and delinquency among adolescents.[18]

FUTURE CHALLENGES FACING RELIGIOUS YOUTH ORGANIZATIONS

For all their strengths, religious youth groups sometimes fall short of achieving their potential because of discrepancies between the stated value of youth work and the resources allocated for its implementation. Adults are often inadequately prepared to lead their classes—most receive little or no training, supervision, or assistance. Religious organizations are often only minimally accountable, in terms of numbers served and outcomes achieved. Finally, these organizations tend to serve only the children of church members.

Religious organizations have both the facilities and the volunteers needed to provide more extensive youth programs. Their challenge is to harness those resources to:

▶ Reach unserved young adolescents, particularly specific underserved groups, such as low-income urban adolescents, adolescents of color, and adolescents living in high-risk environments;

▶ Develop the comprehensive and flexible programming needed to meet a full spectrum of adolescent needs;

▶ Strengthen adult leadership—beginning at the seminary level for clergy—and adapt that training for volunteers and youth educators;

▶ Improve networks, especially human networks, so that the resources available to religious youth workers can be broadened and the professional isolation that many practitioners experience can be minimized;

▶ Find ways to reduce institutional isolation and promote multi-institutional cooperation and collaboration; and

▶ Clarify the goals and objectives of religious youth work and measure progress against them.

PRIVATE COMMUNITY GROUPS: ADULT SERVICE CLUBS, SPORTS ORGANIZATIONS, SENIOR CITIZENS GROUPS, AND MUSEUMS

Private community groups sponsor a broad spectrum of youth programs and bring commitment and energy to their work. Their programs reach many young people, although usually not the ones who need service the most, but their potential remains largely untapped.

ADULT SERVICE CLUBS

Adult service clubs are composed of adult volunteers who want to improve communities through the delivery or support of voluntary efforts—including programs for youth.[19] Although many of these organizations have international components or affiliates, the clubs are uniquely American. All have headquarters in the United States. These organizations include cause-oriented groups, groups rooted in a historic benevolent tradition, fraternal organizations, and ethnic minority sororities and fraternities.

Adult service group membership rolls range from the 8,000 members of the Links, Inc., to the 1.5 million Elks; annual operating budgets from the Links' $300,000 to Lutheran Brotherhood's $42 million; and activities for youth in at-risk environments from nonexistent to significant. (See table 4.)

CURRENT TRENDS AMONG ADULT SERVICE CLUBS

Studies of adult service groups are rare, and no studies of their youth programs exist. What is known is that:

▶ With the exception of the youth organizations directly affiliated with clubs such as the Interact Clubs of Rotary International, the Squires Program of the Knights of Columbus, and the Key and Builders Clubs of Kiwanis International, few adult service groups sponsor youth activities that are truly national in scope; and

▶ Much of adult service clubs' youth-related work involves sponsoring local youth groups such as the Boy Scouts, Girl Scouts, Camp Fire, and 4-H, sports teams, college scholarships, recognition awards, and short-term projects such as one-day career fairs and other educational events.

Furthermore, few adult service club programs are targeted toward young adolescents. Exceptions are the Kiwanis International's Builders Clubs, which provide community service opportunities for young adolescents at the middle-grade level, and the Association of Junior Leagues' Middle School Improvement Program. Several organizations do, however, sponsor specific programs for adolescents, some with positive evaluation results. For example, the Association of Junior Leagues' Teen Outreach Program, cited earlier, has undergone systematic outcome evaluations and has proven effective in preventing adolescent pregnancy and in promoting positive attitudes and behaviors toward community service.[20]

Several minority organizations appear to place high priority on services for adolescents living in low-income and other high-risk neighborhoods. For instance:
▶ Alpha Kappa Alpha sorority offers education and health programs for African American youth, including the AKAdemics Plus drop-out prevention program; and
▶ Since 1929, the Alpha Phi Alpha fraternity has sponsored a program, Go to High School, Go to College, that counsels African American youth on postsecondary education and careers, provides information on college entrance requirements and financial aid, and contains a scholarship program.

FUTURE CHALLENGES FACING ADULT SERVICE CLUBS

Adult service clubs have the human and financial resources and communications vehicles, the ability to train volunteers, and the commitment to community betterment needed to provide strong youth programs. In many American communities, these groups currently play a strong supportive role as funders, as supplemental program providers, and as providers of scholarships, speakers for specific topics, and the like. But, compared with contemporary youth needs, the touch of most of this work is light.

Furthermore, the largest organizations, both in membership size and financial resources, continue to direct most of their youth-related efforts to youth in low-risk environments. They may not be aware of the needs of young people living in high-risk environments, or their members may be concerned about the difficulty and possible physical danger in working in distressed neighborhoods. Even those programs that specifically target youth in at-risk neighborhoods have reached only a small number of young people.

TABLE 4: CHARACTERISTICS OF SELECTED NATIONAL ADULT SERVICE ORGANIZATIONS WITH YOUTH DEVELOPMENT PROGRAMS, 1991

ORGANIZATION	NUMBER OF MEMBERS	NUMBER OF CHAPTERS	NATIONAL BUDGET	PROGRAMS FOR LOW-INCOME YOUTH	ADVOCACY FOR YOUTH
AAUW[a]	140,000	1,900	$ 4,500,000	No	Yes
Alpha Kappa Alpha	110,000	750	8,000,000	Yes	Yes
Alpha Phi Alpha	125,000	700[c]	1,800,000	Yes	No
Assn. of Junior Leagues	184,000	277[c]	6,100,000	Yes	Yes
BPW/USA[b]	120,000	3,000	2,500,000	No	No
Delta Sigma Theta	175,000	760	2,000,000	Yes	Yes
Elks	1,500,000	2,300	1,500,000	No	No
Kiwanis	315,000	8,500[c]	10,500,000	Yes	No
Knights of Columbus	1,473,128	9,192[c]	NA	No	No
Links, Inc.	8,000	240[c]	300,000	Yes	No
Lions	1,365,000	39,250	NA	No	No
Lutheran Brotherhood	1,000,000	811	42,000,000	Yes	No
National Council of Jewish Women	100,000	200	3,800,000	Yes	Yes
National Council of Negro Women	40,000	250	1,500,000	Yes	Yes
Rotary International	1,077,211	24,413[c]	30,000,000	No	No
U.S. Jaycees	240,000	4,500	3,100,000	No	No

Source: *Adult Service Clubs and Their Programs for Youth* by A. K. Fitzgerald and A. Collins, 1991. Unpublished manuscript prepared for the Carnegie Council on Adolescent Development, Washington, D.C.

[a]American Association of University Women   [b]Business and Professional Women/USA   [c]National and International

Youth development work can be a two-way street. "Our organization is better, it's stronger, for having established this effort," says Marion Sutherland, president of the Links Foundation, Inc., after five years of implementing Project LEAD: High Expectations. "Project LEAD [Links Erase Alcohol and Drug Abuse] has moved our members from checkbook charity to hands-on participation. In communities across the country, Links chapters have become deeply involved with young people—not because they were made to, not because they were paid to, but because they wanted to."

The Links Foundation is the charitable arm of the Links, Inc., a national women's organization dedicated to improving the quality of life for African Americans. Founded in 1946, Links has 241 chapters throughout the United States and in Nassau, the Bahamas, and Frankfurt, Germany.

Project LEAD: High Expectations was developed as a national demonstration program in 1987 with financial support from the federal Office for Substance Abuse Prevention (OSAP). The program is designed to help African American youth refrain from using alcohol and other drugs or engaging in other high-risk behaviors. It also seeks to enhance young people's self-esteem and pride in their cultural heritage, to teach about career options, and to help youth establish high education and career aspirations.

According to Vivian L. Smith, OSAP's acting director, "One of our goals in funding this project was to identify successful program elements that could be adapted in communities nationwide. We have not been disappointed. This project has already demonstrated remarkable success with young people in nearly 150 communities across the nation—from public housing developments to community centers to public schools." To date, more than 5,000 trained adult volunteers have delivered the program to nearly 10,000 young people.

Local Links chapters sponsor Project LEAD: High Expectations in their own neighborhoods or cities. Local chapters build a project team with other groups such as the YWCA, churches, or the Boys and Girls Club. Projects frequently obtain support from fraternal and civic organizations, corporations, churches, and the media.

Young people participate in Project LEAD: High Expectations sessions two to four hours per week for a period of three to nine months, depending on the frequency and length of sessions.

National Project Director Flavia Walton says the most important benefit of participating in Project LEAD: High Expectations is the opportunity to interact with African American adults: "Project LEAD volunteers and resource persons are individuals from all walks of life who are engaged in a wide variety of occupations. Contact with these adults reinforces the concept that participants can set high expectations for themselves and achieve their goals."

The reasons may be that the programs are new or are sponsored by small organizations with modest budgets.

If they are to reach their full potential, adult service clubs must accept the challenges of overcoming the lack of awareness of youth needs, organizational isolation, social distance, lack of documentation and evaluation of current efforts, and reliance on short-term projects. Well-designed national efforts, such as the Links Foundation's Project LEAD: High Expectations and the Association of Junior Leagues' Teen Outreach Program, stand as a strong testament to the potential of adult service clubs in harnessing their national and local power in the direction of more intensive, meaningful, and effective youth programming.

SPORTS ORGANIZATIONS

An estimated 35 million children and adolescents aged six to eighteen participate in youth sports programs[21] each year.[22] About 6 million are enrolled in school-sponsored programs, and some are involved in club sports programs. But most participate through agency-sponsored and community recreation programs run by municipal parks and recreation departments, and it is these programs that are of interest here. (Club sports generally operate on a for-profit and fee-for-service basis; intramural and interscholastic programs are sponsored by schools and thus fall outside the context of this report.)

Agency-sponsored local sports programs receive much of their support from adult service clubs such as Lions Clubs and Kiwanis Clubs. One community

TABLE 5: CHARACTERISTICS OF SELECTED NATIONAL YOUTH SPORTS PROGRAMS

ORGANIZATION	AGE RANGE	COMPETITION AT NATIONAL LEVEL	EMPHASIZE FUN, SOCIAL AND SKILL DEVELOPMENT	PROVISION FOR LOW INCOME	FEE FOR PLAY
Amateur Athletic Union	NA	Yes	Yes	Yes	Yes
American Youth Soccer Organization	5–19	Yes	Yes	Yes	No
Dixie Youth Baseball	8–17	No	Yes	Yes	Yes
Hershey Track and Field	NA	Yes	Yes	No	No
Little League Baseball	6–18	Yes	Yes	No	Yes
National Jr. Tennis League	8–18	Yes	Yes	Yes	Yes
National Youth Sports Program	10–16	No	Yes	Yes	No
Police Athletic League	NA	Yes	Yes	Yes	NA
Pony Baseball	5–18	Yes	Yes	No	Yes
Pop Warner Football	6–16	Yes	Yes	No	Yes
Soccer Association for Youth	6–18	Yes	Yes	No	Yes
U.S. Ice Hockey Association	5–18	Yes	Yes	No	Yes
U.S. Volleyball Association	6–adult	Yes	Yes	No	Yes
U.S. Wrestling Association	8–adult	Yes	No	No	Yes
U.S. Youth Soccer Association	4–19	Yes	Yes	Yes	Yes
Young American Bowling Alliance	8–21	Yes	Yes	No	Yes

Source: *Overview of Youth Sports Programs in the United States* by V. Seefeldt, M. Ewing, and S. Walk, 1992. Unpublished manuscript prepared for the Carnegie Council on Adolescent Development, Washington, D.C.

agency generally sponsors a particular sport—to the exclusion of both other agencies and other sports. As a result, programs for different sports often share no common structure or philosophy about working with adolescents. Local agencies generally affiliate with national sports-specific organizations, which exposes participants to district, regional, or national competition. Agency-sponsored athletic programs are, therefore, greatly influenced by rules mandated in all competitions beyond the intracity level. Little League Baseball, Pop Warner Football, U.S. Ice Hockey Association, and the American Youth Soccer Organization are examples of these types of national programs. Also included in the definition of agency-sponsored programs are those offered by such groups as Boys and Girls Clubs, Girls Incorporated, Boy Scouts of America (Varsity Scouts), YMCA, and YWCA.

Sports programs sponsored by the affiliates of national youth organizations differ from those conducted by sports agencies in that their programs are more likely to provide opportunities to participate in:
▶ A variety of sports;
▶ Activities developed by the national organization, such as Boys and Girls Clubs' Olympic Sports and Super-Fit All Stars programs, and Girls Incorporated's Sporting Chance program; and
▶ Competitions organized through national organizations such as Boys and Girls Clubs and YWCA.

Local chapters of these organizations may also coordinate leagues and affiliate with sports-specific national governing bodies.

CURRENT TRENDS AMONG SPORTS ORGANIZATIONS

TREND: EXCLUDING YOUTH IN HIGH-RISK ENVIRONMENTS

Table 5 describes characteristics of selected national sports programs.[23] Although these programs report no restrictions based on race, creed, or socioeconomic status, most do not include special provisions for youth in low-income or otherwise high-risk environments. Few of these groups compile data on the race and socioeconomic status of their participants and only seven of the sixteen offer special provisions for low-income youth. Also worthy of note is the extent of gender differences in participation rates. Although all of the programs listed serve both boys and girls, either on a single-gender or coeducational basis, boys are 1.5 times more likely to participate than girls.

TREND: PARTICIPATION DECLINES DURING EARLY ADOLESCENCE

A 1989 nationwide study of about 8,000 young people, aged ten to eighteen, showed that 55 percent had participated in agency-sponsored sports—mostly on one or more sports teams.[24] Also:

▶ The highest rates of participation occurred at age ten and then showed a steady decline from ages ten to eighteen;

▶ Both boys and girls participated in agency-sponsored sports programs to have fun, learn skills, become fit, and enjoy competition; although few racial differences in reasons for participation appeared, younger children were more interested in becoming part of a team than in competing, while older children were more interested in competing; and

▶ Youth dropped out of programs because they were no longer having fun or had lost interest, but would consider staying or returning if improvements were made in coaching, scheduling, organization, and programs.

TREND: IGNORING TRAINING AND QUALIFICATION OF COACHES

The coach in an agency-sponsored and recreational sports program in the United States is most likely to be one of the players' parents. Without these 2.5 million volunteer coaches, many programs could not exist. Because volunteers generally have no special preparation other than previous athletic experience, they are often not competent to teach their sport, coach youth with a wide range of physical abilities, or deal skillfully with young adolescents, who respond more positively to encouragement than to criticism.

Competent coaches know the techniques, scientific bases, and psychological aspects of coaching; how to train and condition athletes; and the growth, healthy emotional development, and learning of young athletes. Competency guidelines for coaches were proposed in 1986 by the Youth Sports Coalition of the National Association for Sport and Physical Education.[25] Thirty-three national sports governing agencies and institutes endorsed the guidelines, but to date no national sports governing agency has required its coaches to meet them.

TREND: FAILING TO INTEGRATE YOUTH DEVELOPMENT CONCEPTS

Many agency-sponsored sports programs fail to integrate current knowledge of youth development into their programs. Youth sports programs should enhance physical, social, emotional, cognitive, and moral development in youth by teaching physical skills and promoting teamwork, cooperation, fair play, and healthy competition. Moreover, youth can gain self-confidence, self-esteem, fitness, a sense of belonging, and the satisfaction of achieving goals by participating in sports.

Sports can also be used to promote academic achievement; the Police Athletic League, for example, is working to help the three million young people in its programs build their academic skills and understand the importance of staying in school. Some 500 local PAL chapters direct their efforts toward neighborhood youth who have few other recreational opportunities and who face boredom, apathy, loneliness, and the temptations that lead to delinquency and crime.

These benefits are achieved only, however, if the structure of the program, and the interaction it engenders, foster a healthy learning and growth environment. Sports programs can also have a detrimental effect if, for example, they reward only winning—to the exclusion of sportsmanship, cooperation, fair play, and dealing with defeat.

FUTURE CHALLENGES FACING SPORTS ORGANIZATIONS

The overriding challenge for agency-sponsored sports programs is to achieve their potential in youth development. Considerable change will be necessary:

▶ Age-appropriate guidelines should provide for varying levels of competition, systematic preparation and evaluation of coaches, a focus on instruction, and a philosophy that encourages coaches and youths to assess performance relative to personal improvements rather than competitive outcomes. These guidelines are particularly important for young adolescents (especially girls and late-maturing boys), many of whom may not have acquired basic movement and sports skills during their elementary education.

▶ Outreach to low-income and minority youth should be expanded. Many children and adolescents are now excluded from agency-sponsored programs for economic reasons. Some young people cannot participate in these programs because they cannot afford to pay program and equipment fees; others cannot travel safely to the neighborhoods (often in suburbs) where the programs are located.

▶ Greater equity in participation by girls as well as boys should be encouraged. Boys become involved in sports at younger ages and drop out less often than girls because their skill levels are generally higher, and there is more parental and peer support for sports activities. In addition, the lack of women in adult leadership of youth sports programs has resulted in an insufficient number of female role models for girls.

▶ Youth sports programs should be evaluated, particularly as they contribute to overall youth development.

SENIOR CITIZENS GROUPS

Community elders can offer a wide variety of useful and challenging experiences to young adolescents; and young adolescents can, in turn, make valuable contributions when they work with older adults.[26]

The assumptions behind involving elders in youth development include these:

▶ Elderly people who are lonely, have lost some interest in life, and suffer a diminished sense of self-worth benefit from contacts with youth;

▶ Many young adolescents who are turned off, angry, disadvantaged, or failing in school need the kind of one-to-one attention that older people can provide;

▶ Age integration can help alleviate intergenerational tensions that may become more critical as the U.S. population ages; and

▶ Programs that involve elderly people with young adolescents build a sense of community between the groups and help prepare the young people for adult life.

A quiet revolution was launched with creation of the Older American Volunteer Programs a generation ago, but the revolution remains incomplete today. Proposals for an "elder service" or a "senior corps" surface from time to time but have not been enacted, and a considerable gap remains between the promise of elder service with youth and what is found in practice.

The Foster Grandparent program, sponsored by the federal agency ACTION, grew from 782 volunteers in 1966 to 27,200 by mid-1991, from thirty-three projects to 263, and from $5 million in federal appropriations to just under $60 million. Other federal programs include the Retired Senior Volunteer Program (RSVP), whose volunteers help staff soup kitchens, for example, or serve as museum docents, visit the homebound elderly, bring companionship to AIDS patients, and read to the blind.

Some 400,000 older adults are enrolled in RSVP and 27,000 in Foster Grandparents, receiving a small stipend for their work, which sometimes involves children and youth growing up in poverty. These programs have survived for more than a generation and several changes of administration in Washington: RSVP is twenty-two years old and Foster Grandparents is twenty-seven.

Furthermore, evaluation shows strong evidence that these programs benefit both the elderly and youth: an examination of selected Foster Grandparent programs in the country found that 75 percent of the elders considered the undertaking one of the most important events in their lives over the preceding five years. Other studies showed that young people in the program experienced an improvement in the quality of their daily lives, including an enhanced sense of competence.[27]

Both Foster Grandparents and RSVP are excellent examples of public-private partnerships, as both use their federal funds to leverage substantial state, local, and private funds to underwrite about a third of Foster Grandparents' support and half of RSVP's.

CURRENT TRENDS AMONG SENIOR CITIZENS GROUPS AND OTHER INTERGENERATIONAL PROGRAMS

TREND: NATIONAL DEMONSTRATION PROJECTS

Current demonstration projects around the country illustrate the wide variety of programs in which elders serve youth:

▶ Big Brothers/Big Sisters of America, which relied on older volunteers in past decades, found in a 1988 survey that fewer than 1,400 of its approximately 60,000 volunteers were over age fifty-five, and almost half the local agencies had no older adult volunteers. With funding support from the Charles Stewart Mott Foundation, BB/BSA has undertaken a demonstration project to engage older men and women in helping children from at-risk environments to have enriching experiences in their lives. An evaluation of this highly collaborative effort will be reported in 1993.

▶ A demonstration project to reduce delinquency and strengthen families by providing them with older mentors from church organizations is under way in Hartford, New York City, and Washington, D.C. The National Crime Prevention Council operates and will document the project, which is funded by the Florence V. Burden Foundation. Called Mission Possible, the project draws on churches and divinity schools to train elderly church members as mentors to parents and families by serving as liaison to school and social service agencies, teaching child-raising skills, and involving families in the church.

▶ The most ambitious of the demonstration projects involving elders and young people from at-risk environments is Linking Lifetimes, which was developed by the Temple University Center for Intergenerational Learning and is funded by private foundations. The project links older adults with young people and draws on the youth service, education, and criminal justice systems. Mentors fifty-five or older receive training in helping youth develop social competency and life-coping skills and are paid either a modest stipend or reimbursable expenses. Elder mentors are recruited from a variety of sources (e.g., Foster Grandparent, RSVP, from within public housing developments and churches). Of the original eleven sites around the country, nine sites have continued. Seven are focused on adolescents in schools and community organizations and two work with adjudicated youth in institutional settings. By the end of 1991, Linking Lifetimes had engaged 172 elder mentors and 307 youth.

TREND: STARTING INTERGENERATIONAL YOUTH SERVICE

Young adolescents can also provide valuable services to older adults. These programs offer additional avenues for elder-youth contact that can help young people develop in a healthy manner. Some examples are:
▶ The New York City Department of Aging in 1987 launched an Intergenerational Work/Study Program for high school students in danger of dropping out or being unable to obtain a job or continue their education. Some 400 students are assigned to more than ninety sites to work in senior centers, nursing homes, or home care agencies. They work ten to fifteen hours a week, spending at least 25 percent of their time with older adults, and receive both a stipend and academic credit.
▶ The City Volunteer Corps, another New York City endeavor, signs up youth for one year of full-time paid work. Among other tasks, the young people visit homebound elders, do heavy cleaning to enable elders to remain in their homes, visit hospice outpatients at home, and provide escort service and apartment painting for elders.

FUTURE CHALLENGES FACING SENIOR CITIZENS GROUPS AND OTHER INTERGENERATIONAL PROGRAMS

The central challenge for elder service is to close the gap between theory and the much more modest reality that occurs in practice. Federal programs, namely those sponsored by ACTION under Older American Volunteer Programs, are far more established than their private-sector counterparts, but neither program operates at full potential.

Elder service programs, particularly those serving youth in low-income neighborhoods, have a typically short lifespan; efforts quickly expire when the money

COMMUNITY ELDERS CAN OFFER A WIDE VARIETY OF USEFUL AND CHALLENGING EXPERIENCES TO YOUNG ADOLESCENTS; AND YOUNG ADOLESCENTS CAN, IN TURN, MAKE VALUABLE CONTRIBUTIONS WHEN THEY WORK WITH OLDER ADULTS.

runs out or the entrepreneur burns out or moves on. Programs also tend to be small. Even Linking Lifetimes, a premier endeavor in the field, struggles to maintain fewer than 200 mentors across its nine current sites, while Mission Possible has managed to train and involve a total of only about fifty mentors at its five sites. Other problems include a shortage of evaluation research on what works and little technical assistance or advocacy.

Additionally, young people and the elderly are often segregated by age, with the elderly living in retirement communities or apartments and spending their time at close-by senior centers. Age segregation is a barrier to organizational cooperation: aging and youth organizations are unaccustomed to working together and tend to focus on age-specific missions. Recruitment and training for elder volunteers may have to be different from those designed for volunteers of other ages. Program managers are wary of spending scarce dollars on intergenerational efforts that might not work.

Senior citizens groups and others who wish to expand intergenerational programs must continue to build the knowledge base of theory, program implementation experience, and evaluation; expand roles for older adults in existing youth programs; forge effective working partnerships between senior citizens groups and youth-serving agencies; direct some of their collaborative efforts toward expansion of federally supported programs, particularly those that benefit low-income young people; systematically address the training and safety needs of seniors in intergenerational programs; and expand and stabilize the funding base for such efforts.

MUSEUMS

Museums open the worlds of art, history, science, and other subjects to adults and young people alike. Most museums receive both public and private support. Some are governed by private, nonprofit organizations; others are sponsored by municipal and state governments, as well as the federal government; and still others are run by schools, colleges, and universities. For all their differences, most museums assert that informal educa-

BROOKLYN CHILDREN'S MUSEUM PROVIDES SAFE HARBOR AND A CAREER LADDER FOR NEIGHBORHOOD YOUTH

The Brooklyn Children's Museum, one of the first recipients of a Youth ALIVE! Leadership Grant, shows how a museum can successfully attract young adolescents from low-income neighborhoods and offer them useful experiences in healthy development. Founded in 1899, the Brooklyn Children's Museum is believed to be the first museum designed expressly for youth and was one of the first to admit unaccompanied children. It serves about 175,000 young people and their families annually in Crown Heights, New York City's largest minority community, whose 100,000 residents are primarily African American, West Indian, Hispanic, and Hasidim.

Based on ideas drawn from young people themselves, the Museum Team program gives them a chance to become mature and confident adults. Youths aged seven to fifteen who visit the museum on their own can enroll in Kids Crew, which operates afternoons, weekends, holidays, and during school vacations. More than 1,500 young people are members, including about 100 who visit one to four times a week. The next step up is Junior Curators, for ages ten to seventeen, who are trained to assist staff in almost all areas of the museum: twenty Junior Curators at a time participate.

Teen Interns, for ages fourteen to eighteen, enter their first jobs that offer pay and meaningful employment and carry a degree of genuine responsibility. They work part time in the exhibition, education, collection, or administration departments, where they can learn and apply basic and higher-order thinking and problem-solving skills. Fifteen Teen Interns work at the museum, and thirty have "graduated" from the program.

The museum invites families of youth involved in Museum Team to programs conducted during evenings, weekends, and holidays. Each year, the museum presents more than a hundred public performances, events, or workshops that encourage audience participation in music, dance, theater, puppetry, creative writing, and photography. For many adults and their children who attend, it is their first opportunity to participate in the performing arts.

"It's frustrating for staff to work in an underserved community," notes Director of Youth Programs Troy Browne. "The kids have pressing social and emotional needs that sometimes feel overwhelming. So we've concentrated a lot of energy on developing our staff—on enabling them to address kids' real concerns, to mentor them, to facilitate adult-youth partnerships. There's no question that ours is a needs-driven program."

tion is their primary goal.[28] Thus, they are potentially important contributors to youth development.

CURRENT TRENDS AMONG SCIENCE AND YOUTH MUSEUMS

Science and youth museums have recently embarked on a common mission—to expand programming for young adolescents, particularly those from disadvantaged backgrounds. One major national effort is YouthALIVE!, a new initiative funded by the DeWitt Wallace–Reader's Digest Fund and coordinated by the Association of Science-Technology Centers (ASTC) in cooperation with the Association of Youth Museums (AYM). The four-year, $7.1 million initiative is designed to build the capacity of some eighty science centers and children's museums to provide adolescents with hands-on learning experiences and the opportunity to do volunteer work and paid part-time work.[29] The program seeks to expand services to youth who have the fewest opportunities for education and social support. Specifically, the program targets young people who have low family income, have limited English proficiency, are located in an economically depressed community (which may be a rural area with few resources), attend a low-achieving school, or have an unstable family structure.

A needs assessment survey, commissioned by the fund in 1990, found that better than 30 percent of responding museums operate programs for adolescents, aged ten to seventeen.[30] Programs range from a handful of volunteers or small science clubs to extensive paid "explainer" (docent) programs, day camps, overnight summer camps, scientific field research, workshops, classes, after-school programs, and youth advisory committees. Approximately 20 percent of the museums have volunteers or paid explainers from minority groups. Nearly 250,000 youths are being reached through the programs of these museums. The survey found that:

▶ Youth-centered programs in museums that address the developmental needs of adolescents are interesting and challenging, ask students to make meaningful contributions, offer involvement by caring adults, assume that mentoring is part of the program aims, and, in some instances, open doors to careers; and

▶ Programs for underserved youth require subsidy through grant funding. Most public programs are funded by fees charged to program participants, a practice that works against the involvement of disadvantaged youth.[31]

One of the first Leadership Grants went to the Children's Museum of Indianapolis. Since its founding in 1926, the museum has offered innovative programming for young people. In the 1980s the museum focused on young adolescents when it launched the Youth Partner-

ship Program. This program involves young adolescents in interpreting exhibits to visitors and helping to plan exhibits, and it involves youth in a wide range of decision-making settings: board meetings, staff meetings, the exhibit design process, and special events planning.

FUTURE CHALLENGES FACING SCIENCE AND YOUTH MUSEUMS

YouthALIVE! builds on these museums' existing strengths and attempts to address some virtually universal challenges facing museums across the country, such as:

▶ The brief duration of many of the existing workshops, camp-ins, and special events;

▶ A limited ability to reach larger youth audiences for the intensive internship and explainer (or docent) programs;

▶ A tendency to target programs to fourteen- to sixteen-year-olds, rather than ten- to thirteen-year-olds or seventeen-year-olds;

▶ The small percentage of staff time and resources devoted to services for adolescents;

▶ The failure to include youth in program planning and organizational decision making; and

▶ The need to develop programming that is sensitive to the kinds of youth who participate in their programs, by race, gender, or physical disability, for instance, and the need to develop mechanisms for determining the effects of youth participation in museum programs.[32]

PUBLIC-SECTOR INSTITUTIONS: PUBLIC LIBRARIES AND PARKS AND RECREATION DEPARTMENTS

The task force found that most public-sector agencies are not focused on youth development but rather emphasize treatment or remediation, and are therefore outside the scope of this report. Two exceptions stand out: public libraries and parks and recreation departments.

PUBLIC LIBRARIES

At least one out of every two individuals who enters a public library is under the age of eighteen,[33] and libraries generally offer a broad range of services for these children and youth. Besides lending books, libraries provide college and career information, reader advisory services for independent and school needs, personal computers, loans of videocassettes for older adolescents, summer reading programs, story hours, and reading booklists for youth up to age fifteen.

Yet, in 1987, only 11 percent of the nation's 14,000 to 15,000 public libraries employed a young adult librarian,[34] and in 1989 less than half of the public libraries

An unheralded piece of federal legislation, the Library Services and Construction Act, has provided financial support over the past two years for a well-designed effort to encourage nine library systems in the San Francisco area to branch out beyond walls of brick and tradition and expand their services for adolescents.

Each participating library system in the Bay Area Youth-at-Risk Project received funding to underwrite community surveys and focus group studies that involved young people (aged twelve to eighteen) and service providers from area youth agencies. Plans that resulted from the needs assessment process include:

▶ The San Lorenzo Branch Library of the Alameda County System sponsored youth forums on topics that teens identified as major needs (jobs and job skills, multicultural relations, health and sexuality). The library also established a teen advisory council to suggest ideas about acquisition of library materials, help plan the youth forums, and assist in publicizing the library's services through area high schools.

▶ The Berkeley Public Library found that employment was a major unmet need for African American and Hispanic teens and that, as in other jurisdictions, teens were unaware of resources offered by the library. The library hired teens to conduct an outreach campaign among their peers to raise awareness of library and community services.

▶ The Oakland Public Library learned that dropping out of school and below-grade literacy levels were among the most serious problems faced by area teens. The library created after-school tutoring/homework centers at the Martin Luther King Jr. Branch. The center serves twelve- to fifteen-year-old students who attend six middle, junior, and high schools in the vicinity. The library recruits tutors from all walks of life, including junior- and senior-high school students, college students, senior citizens, and other adults from the neighborhood.

▶ The libraries in San Francisco, Contra Costa County, Hayward, Livermore, and Richmond also developed responsive plans that incorporate elements similar to those outlined above.

Two strong emphases throughout all of these efforts are active youth participation in both planning and implementation, and increasing the library's role as part of a network of community services for youth. Project Director Stan Weisner comments: "We really believe the slogan for our project—Information Is Empowering—and we hope that by being proactive, libraries can help to empower young people and those who work with them on a daily basis."[40]

employed a children's librarian.[35] The importance of these statistics is illustrated by another 1987 finding: libraries with young adult librarians are used by youth more frequently.[36]

In addition to the lack of specialized librarians, only 19 percent of the nation's libraries require that young adult librarians and other librarians who primarily serve young adults participate in appropriate ongoing, in-service training.[37]

Libraries also face other current concerns that relate to operations in general and young people in particular, especially accountability. Libraries often cannot document the full extent of their work or evaluate outcomes or services they provide.

CURRENT TRENDS AMONG LIBRARIES
TREND: TREATING LIBRARIES AS MAKESHIFT CHILD-CARE CENTERS

Young people have begun to use libraries as shelter. In many localities, young people are using the public library in the absence of supervised day care during nonschool hours, and children and other young people are remaining in libraries at closing time.[38] These children and youth can create problems for library staff when they are sick, unhappy, too energetic, or starved for adult attention. Although increasing use by young people is a goal for most public libraries, decreasing their misuse is an emergent issue.

TREND: ADDRESSING UNMET NEEDS OF YOUTH

If libraries are to serve youth better, they must develop thoughtful and responsive policies and programs to address the unmet needs of young adolescents. Programs could include library-based clubs, self-care and self-reliance courses, drop-in activities, paid employment, and volunteer opportunities such as working with younger children. In addition, libraries should help focus community attention on the welfare of children and serve as active sources of information on existing community programs for children, youth, and families.[39]

The biggest challenge facing libraries today is funding. In the past few years, library budgets have been slashed, and a number of systems have closed their smaller libraries or satellite branches. Some libraries have responded by curtailing hours and days of operations and by decreasing specialized staff. Others have established nonprofit arms to supplement their public support.

Funding shortages generate other challenges, such as increasing the number of young adult specialists on library staffs, broadening the racial and ethnic diversity of staffs, expanding in-service training on adolescent issues, strengthening services for young adolescents, stepping up outreach efforts to underserved teens, and improving accountability.

PARKS AND RECREATION DEPARTMENTS

Parks and recreation programs, like some of the national youth organizations, were first organized in the late 1800s to provide places for city children left unsupervised for long hours while their parents worked in the factories.[41] Organized recreation programs were then developed to provide children and youth with safe places to play and to offer an alternative to involvement in delinquent behaviors. As those services evolved, many recreation departments greatly expanded their purview, seeking to provide a full range of athletic and social opportunities for all citizens—young and old, wealthy and lower income.

Community recreation services are usually the domain of municipal or county governments and are generally offered by a combined recreation and park department. The agencies usually operate under the direction of a citizen board or commission and are managed by a professional staff, with the assistance of part-time staff and volunteers. In order of payment level, general fund appropriations, user fees and charges, facility rental proceeds, and government grants provide the revenues.

Recreation agencies operate community centers, parks, pools and other aquatic facilities, athletic fields, golf courses, playgrounds, play fields, winter sports facilities, outdoor nature centers, stadiums, camps, beaches, and zoos. They take a leadership role in sports and games, arts and crafts, dance, drama, music, social recreation, outdoor recreation, special events, and other activities. Children and youth are the major users, with youth participation dropping off at around age thirteen.

IF LIBRARIES ARE TO SERVE YOUTH BETTER, THEY MUST DEVELOP THOUGHTFUL AND RESPONSIVE POLICIES AND PROGRAMS TO ADDRESS THE UNMET NEEDS OF YOUNG ADOLESCENTS. PROGRAMS COULD INCLUDE LIBRARY-BASED CLUBS, SELF-CARE AND SELF-RELIANCE COURSES, DROP-IN ACTIVITIES, PAID EMPLOYMENT, AND VOLUNTEER OPPORTUNITIES SUCH AS WORKING WITH YOUNGER CHILDREN.

CURRENT TRENDS AMONG PARKS AND RECREATION DEPARTMENTS

For fifteen years, funding for recreation services has steadily declined. Recreation agencies are reducing staff, decreasing hours of operation of facilities, and eliminating programs that are not self-supporting or funded by outside sources.[42] Publicly supported recreation programs are evolving into a two-tier system, with more and better services available in suburban areas than in less affluent rural and urban areas.[43] The current fiscal cutbacks are serving to increase the disparity between upper- and lower-income areas, meaning that youth most dependent on public recreation services are increasingly less likely to have access to such services.

This trend is particularly unfortunate because community leaders agree on the value of recreation for youth. Furthermore, the 1991 Office of Technology Assessment Report on Adolescent Health called for the expansion of community recreation services, noting that youth participation in organized recreation programs can:
▶ Help ensure appropriate use of discretionary time;
▶ Offer the potential for adult guidance;
▶ Reduce personal distress;
▶ Provide youth with opportunities to learn life skills and social competence;
▶ Provide opportunities for work; and
▶ Possibly reduce substance abuse, especially among disadvantaged youth.[44]

Good program models for low-income neighborhoods abound. Several recreation departments have experimented successfully with innovative afterschool care programs, midnight basketball leagues, summertime urban camping initiatives (some in public housing projects), and a variety of outreach efforts that include mobile vans and collaborations with school systems.

FUTURE CHALLENGES FACING PARKS AND RECREATION DEPARTMENTS

Municipal parks and recreation departments must find ways and means to respond to the needs of young adolescents and of young people living in high-risk neighborhoods. These departments must cope with budget cutbacks and with aging and vandalized facilities and secure alternative funding sources. They must advocate increased resources and greater equity of service, paying particular attention to gender and income. They must recruit, retain, and train qualified staff—particularly staff who are skilled in working with youth. Finally, they must increase co-

operation and collaboration with schools and other community agencies and improve documentation and evaluation of services.

ASSESSING THE UNIVERSE OF YOUTH DEVELOPMENT ORGANIZATIONS

From a national perspective, the universe of youth development organizations in America is vast and diverse, yet it is largely unexplored in the research literature. Its work appears to be central to the healthy development of young people, yet is largely ignored in public policy debate. Especially lacking is an analysis of how existing youth development organizations and programs can make their services more responsive to the needs of today's young adolescents, particularly those from low-income backgrounds.

PARTICIPATION RATES SHOW VAST INEQUITIES

In addition to its study of the five kinds of youth-serving organizations, the task force used two other methods to assess the universe of youth development organizations. First, it analyzed available data to determine levels of participation of young adolescents in youth development programs. Second, it reviewed the professional literature on local youth development activities as a means of testing the validity of its findings at the national level.

Little is known about the participation of young adolescents in youth programs; the subject of youth activities during out-of-school hours has barely been studied. What little information exists, however, reinforces task force findings of vast inequities in availability of programs to youth. The best single source of national information about the participation of young adolescents in community programs is the 1988 National Education Longitudinal Study (NELS 88). This survey of a nationally representative sample of 25,000 eighth graders found 71 percent of respondents to be involved in some type of organized activity outside of school. The four activities that these young people participated in most frequently were nonschool sports, religious youth groups, summer programs, and hobby clubs; however, taken together, the programs of national youth organizations account for the greatest amount of participation (with 49.5 percent of the sample reporting some such involvement).[45] Although the proportion of boys and girls who engaged in at least one activity was about the same, the survey revealed that boys were twice as likely as girls to be involved in scouting and nonschool team sports, and girls were more likely to participate in religious youth groups and summer programs. Table 6 summarizes the NELS data on participation in out-of-school activities.

Although the NELS study did not uncover significant participation differences according to race and ethnicity, it did identify a wide disparity in participation between upper- and lower-income groups. Only 17 percent of eighth graders from families in the highest socioeconomic quartile did not participate in organized out-of-school activities, while fully 40 percent of low-income youth reported no such involvement.[46] Because parents and children in low-income neighborhoods express a desire for increased services, the likely explanation for differences in program participation levels is access (including cost) and availability.

Confirmation of this explanation can be found in other studies. For example, a recent national child-care survey reported sharp differences by socioeconomic levels in school-age children's enrollment in structured after-school activities. Parents from higher-income groups relied on lessons, clubs, sports, and similar enrichment activities to supplement other child-care arrangements to a much greater extent than did lower-income parents.[47]

EVIDENCE AT THE LOCAL LEVEL CONFIRMS TROUBLING CONCERNS

Only a handful of studies have examined youth development programs at the local level, where services to youth are actually delivered. The task force reviewed this published material to test the validity of its findings at the national level. The task force sought evidence on the quality, quantity, and effectiveness of delivery of programs that stimulate healthy development of young adolescents.

The evidence not only confirms the task force's

TAKIN' IT TO THE STREETS: TEENS ARE FULL PARTNERS IN PHOENIX RECREATION PROGRAMS

What would it take to coax more than 200 teenagers to come to a meeting at 8:30 on a Saturday morning? City officials in Phoenix, Arizona, found out. They offered young people, aged thirteen to nineteen, an opportunity to advise the city's leaders, including its mayor, on youth issues as part of a day-long Teens in Living Color Conference sponsored by the Phoenix Parks, Recreation, and Library Department. They also offered food (lots of it—breakfast, lunch, and dinner), music, workshops, a fashion show, and several breaks to allow participants time to socialize with one another.

The conference was part of the City Streets Program that was initiated in 1985 by citizens of West and Southwest Phoenix who were concerned that "local teens had too much idle time and not enough constructive things to do," according to Raul Daniels, City Streets' teen coordinator. The program's characteristics include:
▶ Active youth participation in planning and implementation;

▶ Varied locations;
▶ Interesting, challenging, fun activities;
▶ Extended hours;
▶ Ongoing assessment, including feedback from teens; and
▶ Collaboration between the parks department and other community agencies.

City Streets, now citywide, sponsors rap sessions on teen issues, teen councils, career fairs, health fairs, drug education, dance troupes, modeling, cooking, Nintendo tournaments, D.J. lessons, talent shows, fashion shows, teen festivals, and custom car and truck shows—in addition to ongoing sports and recreation programs. These events are held at parks and recreation centers and at other popular teen hangouts such as shopping malls, civic centers, and area high schools. Many of the recreation department's own centers are open seven days a week, often until 10:00 P.M., and special summer programs for older teens (aged fifteen and up)—called Midnight

Madness—run from 10:00 P.M. until 1:00 A.M. at some locations.

A fifteen-member Teen Advisory Board participates in program planning and in facility reviews and advises the adult board and director of the Phoenix parks department. The chair of the Teen Advisory Board serves ex officio on the adult board.

A new experiment works in partnership with the Arizona Cactus Pine Girl Scout Council. A mobile teen center visits ten Phoenix neighborhoods that have been identified as having high rates of gang violence, substance abuse, and truancy. The mobile program currently offers recreation and limited computer skills programs and will eventually offer job training and assessment and bilingual health education.

According to Eddie Villa, City Streets coordinator, active teen involvement is the key to the success of City Streets: "We listen to kids and take their ideas seriously. Teens are full partners in everything we do."

TABLE 6: PERCENTAGE OF EIGHTH GRADERS PARTICIPATING IN OUT-OF-SCHOOL ACTIVITIES, BY SELECTED BACKGROUND CHARACTERISTICS

BACKGROUND CHARACTERISTICS	ANY OUTSIDE-SCHOOL ACTIVITY	SCOUTS	BOYS OR GIRLS CLUB	'Y' OR OTHER YOUTH GROUP
TOTAL	71.3	14.2	10.7	15.3
SEX				
Male	70.7	18.9	11.2	14.3
Female	71.8	9.8	10.2	16.2
RACE / ETHNICITY				
Asian and Pacific Islander	67.9	13.1	9.1	12.7
Hispanic	60.3	10.9	13.2	13.9
Black	65.6	20.0	23.7	23.0
White	74.4	13.7	8.1	14.3
American Indian/Native Alaskan	60.9	17.3	18.0	15.7
SES QUARTILE				
Lowest Quartile	60.0	12.9	14.5	14.0
25–49%	68.5	13.6	11.1	15.5
50–74%	74.2	14.4	9.5	14.8
Highest Quartile	82.6	16.0	8.0	16.7
LOCATION				
Urban	69.1	15.2	14.6	17.9
Suburban	71.5	14.0	9.1	14.2
Rural	72.8	13.9	9.9	14.8

Source: *National Education Longitudinal Study of 1988: A Profile of the American Eighth Grader* (p. 55) by U. S. Department of Education, Office of Educational Research and Improvement, National Center for Education Statistics, 1991. Washington, D.C.: U.S. Government Printing Office.

findings at the national level but also brings into sharp relief the consequences of the lack of youth policy in this nation. The task force found at the local level a virtual microcosm of the picture at the national level: fragmented program delivery, inequity in access to services, and wide disparity in services between upper- and lower-income communities.

FRAGMENTATION INSTEAD OF COORDINATION

In many communities, no one organization or person is responsible for planning and coordinating youth services. Even when an individual or agency has responsibility for planning and coordination, resources may not be sufficient for the job. Even if reasonable planning exists, often individual agencies have no incentive to participate in coordination efforts—there may in fact be subtle but significant disincentives,

given the intensely competitive environment that surrounds the funding of many youth services. Finally, the complexity and multifaceted nature of the funding streams that support youth programs may encourage a categorical, rather than needs-oriented, approach to youth problems, which in turn leads to fragmented services that react to problems rather than focus on youth development.[48]

INEQUITY IN ACCESS TO SERVICES

American communities differ dramatically according to their demographics, economic bases, and physical layouts. It is not surprising, then, that there is little or no consistency in their support of young adolescents. And because wealth is distributed unevenly, it is not surprising to find tremendous disparities among communities in resources and in their ability to offer ade-

4-H	RELIGIOUS YOUTH GROUPS	HOBBY CLUBS	NEIGHBORHOOD CLUBS	SUMMER PROGRAMS	NONSCHOOL TEAM SPORTS
9.3	33.8	15.5	12.7	19.2	37.3
8.5	29.5	17.1	13.6	16.3	45.1
10.0	37.9	13.9	11.7	22.0	29.9
4.7	27.4	16.7	11.8	24.2	32.0
6.1	24.6	15.5	13.3	19.5	31.3
13.8	30.0	22.4	23.4	29.6	33.9
9.1	36.6	14.1	10.7	17.1	39.1
10.0	27.5	20.6	17.6	22.0	34.1
11.1	22.7	16.3	14.1	16.5	29.5
10.0	30.1	15.0	13.3	16.6	35.6
9.4	35.9	15.1	11.6	18.7	38.4
6.7	45.6	15.5	11.7	24.7	45.2
5.9	29.6	17.7	16.7	23.7	35.6
7.1	33.3	14.9	11.3	18.5	40.0
14.9	37.9	14.7	11.2	16.7	35.1

quate, responsive, and comprehensive youth services.

These wide differences among communities suggest that communities have a lot to learn from each other about how to meet the needs of youth with the resources at hand. Furthermore, few mechanisms now exist to help communities learn from experience elsewhere in the country, and federal and state government policies on youth development must attempt to take into account the uniqueness of every community in the nation.

UPPER-INCOME VERSUS LOWER-INCOME COMMUNITIES

That per-pupil expenditures for schools in upper-income areas exceed those for lower-income areas is well documented; similar disparities in the provision of community-based youth services are just beginning to be rec-ognized and documented. Low-income communities—particularly urban communities with high-density youth populations and isolated rural areas—are the least likely to offer consistent support and an adequate array of services.[49]

The absence of coordination of and support for youth development services, at both the national and local levels, lies at the heart of these current dilemmas. No one worries about these problems, so no one is responsible for addressing them. Each organization—from the smallest local program to the largest national organization—is virtually on its own as it seeks to assess current efforts and plan future initiatives. In addition, the highly local nature of these services all but ensures that young people in economically disadvantaged neighborhoods will have the least access to needed programs.[50]

In synthesizing the results of its study of the universe of America's youth organizations, the task force identified ten clear themes:

▶ Many strengths characterize the existing array of community-based youth development programs. These strengths include tradition, durability, commitment, credibility, diversity, widespread support, and an extensive current reach;

▶ Many youth programs nonetheless are not responding as fully as they might to the needs and wants of young adolescents and are thus failing to attract young people after the age of twelve or thirteen—even to such potentially attractive offerings as sports;

▶ In particular, youth programs are failing to reach out to young people in low-income environments, to solicit their views, listen to them, and act on their suggestions for appealing, accessible activities;

▶ Programs do not adequately address the needs of young adolescents, especially those in low-income neighborhoods, for earned income and initial paid employment experience;

▶ In general, programs do not adequately acknowledge the role of youth gangs in addressing young adolescents' needs (for safety, status, meaningful roles, a sense of belonging, a sense of competence), and they do not actively compete with gangs for youth membership;

▶ Intensity levels of many programs are far below what it takes to be effective in helping young adolescents mature in a healthy manner;

▶ Financial support for youth programs is grossly inadequate to current needs and is, in the eyes of many fund-raising experts, likely to become even worse. As libraries, parks and recreation departments, and other public-sector institutions increasingly compete for private dollars, and as both public and private agencies cope with deepening government cutbacks, support for youth-oriented programs will doubtless become more difficult to generate;

▶ Recruiting, training, and retaining mature, dedicated, top-quality adult leaders—both paid and pro bono—is a constant challenge to these organizations;

▶ Many organizations that offer programs for youth know little about the characteristics of the youth they currently serve, and therefore find it difficult to plan effective outreach strategies, and fewer still conduct regular and systematic evaluations of their programs; and

▶ In most communities, and on the national level, delivery of youth programs suffers from a lack of communication among agencies as well as inadequate coordination and integration of services.

For more than a century, this nation has built and sup-

MANY STRENGTHS CHARACTERIZE THE EXISTING ARRAY OF COMMUNITY-BASED YOUTH DEVELOPMENT PROGRAMS.... MANY YOUTH PROGRAMS NONETHELESS ARE NOT RESPONDING AS FULLY AS THEY MIGHT TO THE NEEDS AND WANTS OF YOUNG ADOLESCENTS AND ARE THUS FAILING TO ATTRACT YOUNG PEOPLE AFTER THE AGE OF TWELVE OR THIRTEEN....

Although communities can clearly provide an array of resources that contribute to the healthy development of young people, little is known about the nature or availability of these resources, patterns of use, or the role these resources play in young people's lives.

Researchers from the Chapin Hall Center for Children at the University of Chicago studied community resources for sixth, seventh, and eighth graders (eleven- to fourteen-year-olds) in two very different neighborhoods in the Chicago area.[51] Julia Littell and Joan Wynn examined a low-income, 97 percent black community ("Innerville") on the west side of Chicago and an affluent, 96.5 percent white suburban municipality ("Greenwood") of metropolitan Chicago, both pseudonyms.

In 1980, 43 percent of Innerville residents, but only 4 percent of Greenwood residents, lived below the poverty line; the median family income today is $9,000 in Innerville and was $29,400 in Greenwood in 1980. Innerville is almost half the geographic size of Greenwood but contains more than 2.5 times as many people and about three times as many eleven- to fourteen-year-olds (5,400 in Innerville, 1,800 in Greenwood).

Organized activities available to Innerville young people most commonly were sports, particularly basketball, followed by church choirs, Sunday school programs, prevention-oriented programs (sex education, drop-out prevention, and gang prevention), and tutoring and literacy programs. Private, nonprofit groups sponsored the majority of the programs. For every 1,000 young adolescents (eleven to fourteen years old), approximately twenty-three organized activities were available per week. On average, nine community facilities were available per week for every 1,000 young adolescents.

The scene in Greenwood was different. Sports were, again, the most common activity for young people, but they included a wide range of options: tennis, swimming, gymnastics, karate, and soccer. In addition, activities included many arts (dance, crafts, and choirs and bands), youth groups, hobby clubs, scouts, and a wide array of elective classes. Public and private nonprofit organizations were equally active in offering opportunities to youth. For every 1,000 young adolescents, seventy-one activities were available in a typical week—more than three times the number available to Innerville youth. On average, forty-two community facilities were available per week for every 1,000 young adolescents.

Overall, in organized after-school programs, Greenwood aimed at enrichment while Innerville aimed at personal support and tutoring. Greenwood offered thirteen types of classes, ranging from baby-sitting to dog obedience training to typing; Innerville offered five (in employment training, drop-out prevention, and pregnancy prevention) that had no parallel in Greenwood. Thus, a young person in Greenwood stood a much higher chance of finding a program or class to suit a particular personal interest.

Greenwood's out-of-school activities involved more organizations of greater diversity than those in Innerville, and they provided more resources per child. Public organizations in Greenwood generated a greater proportion of activities and facilities than those in Innerville; public schools offered almost seven times as many extracurricular activities for middle school young people per week, and public park districts provided eight times (adjusted for population differences) the number of activities during an average week. Churches played a larger role in Innerville.

Equity is an important issue. Given that all young people have similar developmental needs, it would seem only fair that all would enjoy access to similar types of activities, facilities, and events. Organized activities may have additional functions, serving as safe havens for young people living in dangerous or stressful conditions, and helping compensate for their lack of other opportunities; for these young people, community resources may be especially important, the researchers speculated.

ported thousands of agencies that serve the interests of young people. The work of these agencies has doubtless been of incalculable benefit to millions of young people over the years. But the successes of the past offer only limited help in charting the course for the future now needed in this country. Part II has raised and left unanswered troubling questions about the willingness and ability of many youth-serving organizations to reach young adolescents most in need of service. Part III takes this line of reasoning to the next level: the design of programs and policies that will promote the healthy development of today's young adolescents.

RECOMMENDATIONS AND CALL TO ACTION

E NCOURAGING EVIDENCE IS ACCU-
MULATING THAT AMERICAN POLITICAL ATTITUDES TOWARD CHILDREN AND YOUTH
ARE SHIFTING. NATIONAL POLLS INDICATE THAT THE PUBLIC GENERALLY SUP-
PORTS REFORM IN EDUCATION AND OTHER ASPECTS OF YOUTH DEVELOPMENT,
AND IN FACT WOULD ACCEPT TAX INCREASES IF THE FUNDS WERE USED FOR
THESE PURPOSES. SEVERAL OF THE NATION'S LARGEST GRANT-MAKING FOUN-
DATIONS HAVE IDENTIFIED YOUTH DEVELOPMENT AS A TOP PRIORITY. IN ITS
APTLY NAMED REPORT, *BEYOND RHETORIC,* THE NATIONAL COMMISSION ON
CHILDREN CALLED FOR PLACEMENT OF YOUTH ISSUES SQUARELY ON THE NA-
TIONAL AGENDA.[1] AMONG CALLS FOR REFORM, NONE EXCEEDS THAT OF THE
BUSINESS COMMUNITY IN WARNING THAT THE ECONOMIC AND SOCIAL WELL-
BEING OF THE NATION DEPENDS ON HEALTHY YOUTH DEVELOPMENT.[2]

Part III of this report consists of the recommendations for reform of the nation's approach to youth
identified by the Task Force on Youth Development
and Community Programs. The recommendations are
intended to help guide a wide variety of decision makers: those responsible for governance of youth-serving agencies and for creation and implementation of
programs for youth; those in charge of funding agencies and those in government who are responsible for
youth programs; and the many others at the national,

state, and local levels whose help is needed to make
reform a reality.

The task force turns the spotlight on that mar-
velous asset of youth—time, specifically the nonschool hours. The task force, consisting of individuals
whose life work is with youth, believes that this asset
represents a sterling opportunity for significant advance in American social and public policies. The results of successful reform will benefit the nation for
generations to come.

STRENGTHENING COMMUNITY PROGRAMS FOR YOUNG ADOLESCENTS

IN A YOUTH-CENTERED AMERICA, EVERY COMMUNITY WOULD HAVE A NETWORK OF AFFORDABLE, ACCESSIBLE, SAFE, AND CHALLENGING OPPORTUNITIES THAT APPEAL TO THE DIVERSE INTERESTS OF YOUNG ADOLESCENTS. YOUTH DEVELOPMENT SERVICES WOULD PROVIDE MEANINGFUL OPPORTUNITIES FOR YOUNG PEOPLE TO PURSUE INDIVIDUAL INTERESTS AS WELL AS TO CONTRIBUTE TO THEIR COMMUNITIES. THEY WOULD GRANT YOUTH APPROPRIATE DEGREES OF AUTONOMY. THEY WOULD BE ORGANIZED THROUGH RESPONSIVE PROGRAM, ORGANIZATIONAL, AND COMMUNITY STRUCTURES. THEY WOULD BE ROOTED IN A SOLID FOUNDATION OF RESEARCH- AND PRACTICE-BASED KNOWLEDGE OF THE NEEDS OF CHILDREN AND ADOLESCENTS AND SUPPORTED BY A DEPENDABLE AND DIVERSE FINANCIAL BASE. FINALLY, THEY WOULD BE GROUNDED ON SUGGESTIONS FROM YOUTH THEMSELVES.

The reality, however, is that adolescents are rarely asked what they want or need, when and where programs should be offered, or what characteristics they would like to see in the adults who lead youth activities. As a result, many youth programs are ill-suited to their ultimate users. Improving the quality of programs and services and increasing adolescents' participation, therefore, require input from the young people who will be served.

Teenagers know what they like and what they want. They are generally more than happy to talk about the needs of young people in their community. For example, the task force asked focus groups of young adolescents how they would describe an ideal youth center. They consistently stated that the center would:

▶ Have a staff that listened to and respected them;

▶ Provide a safe, protected environment where they could be themselves; and

▶ Offer interesting programs—including organized sports and classes on a variety of subjects.[3]

People, places, and programs—these are the key ingredients of success, according to young people in the focus groups and in other youth surveys. These themes are consistent with current research knowledge as well as with the experience of seasoned practitioners within the youth development field.[4] Integrating its

NEEDS	PRACTICES
INFORMATION	Some youth organizations skirt controversial issues, often the very issues that teens identify as important. A striking example of such an issue is human sexuality. Many American youth organizations avoid or water down discussions of human sexuality in their programs and materials, despite the fact that teens consistently voice their need for help in understanding and exploring this topic.
LIFE SKILLS	Some programs are too didactic in their methodology; skills are developed through experience, not lectures. Some programs are of insufficient frequency and duration; skills develop through practice.
CRITICAL HABITS OF MIND	Some programs are so focused on only one aspect of development (e.g., recreation) that they miss opportunities to promote the acquisition of thinking skills and to foster academic achievement.
DEPENDABLE RELATIONSHIPS	Many programs experience high staff turnover because of low salaries and inattention to staff development. Similarly, insufficient funding within the sector leads to organizational instability, which contributes to lack of dependability in staff and volunteer relationships with youth.
RELIABLE BASES FOR DECISION MAKING	Although social indicators clearly point out that young adolescents *are* making life-altering decisions about substance abuse, sexual activity, gang involvement, and a host of other behaviors, some youth organizations cave in to political pressures that they not deal with "controversial" issues or that they not recognize adolescents' autonomy in making behavioral choices. For example, the "Just Say No" programs that seek to prevent substance use and adolescent sexual activity generally provide no practice in active decision making.
USEFULNESS	American adolescents have few opportunities to be and feel useful, in their families, in their schools, in their communities. Although many youth organizations do provide young people with community service opportunities, these opportunities are not available to enough youth. In addition, youth agencies provide insufficient opportunities for young people to participate in organizational decision making, to determine the goals and methods of programs, and to make meaningful contributions throughout the organization.
BELONGING	Many youth organizations place too much emphasis on symbols of membership that are good for the organization (such as uniforms, which provide revenue and visibility) and not enough emphasis on relevant symbols and real ownership. Young people say they want to belong to a valued group of peers, in partnership with respectful, caring, committed adults. They want to determine for themselves what, if any, symbols of membership are appropriate in that context. Youth gangs address many developmental needs in this arena.
AUTONOMY	The agendas of many youth organizations are decided by adults, often at a national level, and the choices offered to young people are limited to those that adults determine. The voluntary nature of youth agencies suggests that young people should have a great deal of autonomy in structuring and selecting activities in which they will participate.

discussions with young people and program operators with its review of relevant research and practice literature, the task force concluded that there are ten principles of best practice in community-based youth development programs.

Responsive proactive community programs for young adolescents should:

▶ Tailor their content and processes to the needs and interests of young adolescents;

▶ Recognize, value, and respond to the diverse backgrounds and experiences that exist among young adolescents;

▶ Work collectively as well as individually to extend their reach to underserved adolescents;

▶ Actively compete for young adolescents' time and attention;

▶ Strengthen the quality and diversity of their adult leadership;

▶ Reach out to families, schools, and other community partners in youth development;

▶ Enhance the role of young people as resources to their community;

▶ Serve as vigorous advocates for and with youth;

▶ Specify and evaluate their intended outcomes; and

▶ Establish solid organizational structures, including energetic and committed board leadership.

In this section, the task force elaborates on and illustrates these ten principles of best practice.

PROGRAMS MUST ATTRACT YOUNG ADOLESCENTS, BE USEFUL TO THEM, AND HOLD THEIR ATTENTION. TO SUCCEED, COMMUNITY PROGRAMS SHOULD TAILOR THEIR CONTENT AND PROCESSES TO THE NEEDS AND INTERESTS OF YOUNG ADOLESCENTS.

CONTENT

Program developers in all kinds of community settings should talk with and listen to young people as they design activities and interventions. They should offer program content that is relevant to the current interests and future needs of youth, recognizing that such relevance is affected by many individual and group factors, and that these needs and interests change.

Community programs for youth should not be afraid to deal with issues that some adults perceive as controversial, if young people say they need help dealing with these topics. Members of the focus groups interviewed for this project echoed concerns heard in other youth surveys about social issues that might not have been of such immediate worry to previous generations of eleven- or fifteen-year-olds: developing job skills,

earning money, learning about birth control, handling sexual relationships and issues of sexual orientation, and coping with violence.

The kind of program content that teenagers say they want parallels almost precisely what experts say they need. Not surprisingly, experts recommend building programs around the developmental tasks of adolescence, calling for content that addresses at least one of the following needs of youth: health and physical well-being, personal and social competence, cognitive or creative competence, vocational awareness and readiness, and leadership and citizenship.[5] Such content might include:

▶ Health and physical well-being: health education, including substance abuse, sexuality, and AIDS education; health promotion; health services; sports; physical fitness; and other recreation.

▶ Personal and social competence: life-skills training; independent living skills; individual and group counseling; peer education and counseling; mentoring; interpersonal relationship skills, including conflict resolution; and child and sexual abuse prevention.

▶ Cognitive or creative competence: academic tutoring; homework clinics; English as a second language; communications skills; computer skills; visual and performing arts; and culture and heritage.

▶ Vocational awareness and readiness: career awareness; job readiness; job-skills training; internships; summer jobs; and in-house paid employment.

▶ Leadership and citizenship: community service; community action; leadership-skills training; youth advisory boards; and civics education and political involvement.

PROCESS

Although community programs should address the serious concerns of today's young people, they should also respond to adolescents' desire for "fun" and "friends," providing many opportunities for young people to socialize, hang out, and choose from an assortment of interesting and challenging activities.

Community programs for youth should actively engage young people by providing opportunities to practice new skills, make new friends, have new experiences, and explore new options. Such active processes include experiential (hands-on) education, cooperative learning, and peer leadership. Young people should be offered many opportunities to develop new skills through practice and reflection, and their accomplishments should be recognized frequently. Programs should foster supportive relationships with peers and adults and provide opportunities to teach same-age or younger peers.

Many community programs should increase the level of their involvement and make their services more in-

For more than three decades, the Washington, D.C., Youth Orchestra Program has provided year-round arts activities to young people, aged five to nineteen. Open to all youth in the metropolitan area, the program currently has more than 900 active members who voluntarily spend several hours each week—as many as fourteen hours a week during the summer—in music instruction and performance.

The program's clear youth development philosophy has evolved over time and has been strongly shaped by Lyn McLain, founder and current director. McLain views music as a vehicle for teaching important life skills and attitudes, such as persistence, hard work, patience, teamwork, and self-reliance. "Many of these benefits can only be realized to the fullest when students mature and enter the adult world," he notes. "These sentiments have been conveyed to me by many program graduates over the years."

Erika Schulte, assistant to the director for music, echoes these ideas: "Kids learn how to concentrate and to delay gratification. These are lost abilities in our high-tech world. Young people also gain a sense of membership and of belonging to something larger than themselves. Even when students have to leave the program—perhaps because their

families move to another part of the country—they will say, 'I wish I could stay here just to be with the people.' That sense of belonging and of teamwork is very strong." Staff seem to feel a similar sense of belonging and commitment. Schulte has been with the program for nine years.

"THE KIDS NEED TO BE EXPOSED TO PEOPLE WITH REAL SKILLS AND REAL JOBS IN THE ARTS."

For McLain, high-quality instructors are the most important ingredient in implementing his vision of a comprehensive youth development arts program. He works hard to minimize the paperwork required for other staff in an effort to free them to teach. And he works hard to recruit adults who love music, who want to work with young people, and who earn their living as musicians. "The kids need to be exposed to people with real skills and real jobs in the arts. That skill level is critical. Why don't we bring out the strongest troops for the most important work?"

The orchestra operates primarily during nonschool hours. It was organized as part of the District of Columbia's public schools but is now a nonprofit organization that contracts annually with the public

schools. It receives less than one third of its annual budget (now about $500,000) from that source. Foundation grants, individual contributions, and ticket sales provide the remaining two-thirds. Fund-raising is an ongoing challenge, according to both McLain and Schulte.

Who are the young people who join the program? Many have had no previous experience playing any musical instrument, and they join at the introductory level. The current D.C. Youth Orchestra has members from ages eleven to nineteen. The program offers variety in other ways as well. Its members come from the District of Columbia and from suburban Maryland and Virginia; from public and private schools; from low-income, middle-income, and high-income families; and from all of the major racial and ethnic groups represented in the Washington metropolitan area. Schulte goes on to note additional variety in the fact that some program participants are not high achievers in school. "But we stick with our kids, even when they are in trouble. For us, 'trouble' usually means problems at school. Few are in trouble with the law. And our kids don't take drugs. They don't need drugs to fill the emptiness. These kids are not empty. They are challenged every day."

tensive in both frequency and duration. Evidence is growing that, to be effective, community-based interventions—particularly those designed to serve young people from less advantaged backgrounds—must be intensive and sustained.[6] Not every program or service must be comprehensive and intensive, but young people should have access to services that meet these criteria. The frequency and duration of any particular program's activities should be adequate relative to its own goals and objectives and to the needs of the young

people it serves. If a program is building-based, the facility that houses the program should be open long hours, at times that are convenient for young people. Effective community programs should actively seek ways to intensify their contact with young people—for example, by providing camping or retreat experiences, particularly when youth have more discretionary time (weekends and summer).

Finally, a comfortable atmosphere and safe and predictable environment can help young adolescents feel welcome and encourage them to participate. Community programs should have high expectations and clear rules and may provide symbols of belonging (such as T-shirts and membership cards) as well as recognition of progress (for example, recognition ceremonies, public performances, and certificates of accomplishment).[7]

> YOUNG ADOLESCENTS ARE SEEKING THEIR IDENTITY AND NEED ACCEPTANCE AND ENCOURAGEMENT ON THE BASIS OF WHO THEY ARE— THEIR GENDER, RACE, ETHNICITY, AND CULTURE. COMMUNITY PROGRAMS SHOULD RECOGNIZE, VALUE, AND RESPOND TO THE DIVERSE BACKGROUNDS AND EXPERIENCE THAT EXIST AMONG YOUNG ADOLESCENTS.

Community programs should be sensitive to the differences among young adolescents, particularly differences based on gender[8] or on race, ethnicity, or culture.[9] Because the formation of a personal identity is central to the "work" of adolescence, these critical issues in personal identity must be considered by program developers.

GENDER

Concerns related to gender have dominated the thinking of some youth development organizations and have been far less consciously addressed in others. New attention to gender-equity issues has sometimes been thrust on organizations through litigation or political action. Current practice finds youth development organizations serving girls and boys in a variety of settings—coeducational, separately for girls and for boys, and a mixture of these options—and taking a variety of perspectives on gender and its importance to program development. No research basis exists for concluding that it is preferable to offer youth development programs on a single-gender (or conversely, on a coeducational) basis. However, there is a strong body of research that can inform decisions about how programs of either configuration can be responsive to the needs of young adolescents of both genders.

A key consideration in programs for youth is the fact that, by the time they reach early adolescence, boys and girls have had differing experiences based on their gender. These experiences arise from at least four basic factors. Young adolescents have spent middle childhood in single-sex groups during discretionary time where topics of conversation are different. The information about gender roles that they receive from their families and the broader culture varies considerably,

depending on whether they are boys or girls. Gender stereotyping continues in the popular culture, in many adults' attitudes, and in toys and other children's products. And youth development opportunities for young adolescents have a long history of being sex-typed, such as teaching girls to cook and boys to play sports.

Program planners should actively consider and plan around the physical and psychological effects of puberty. During early adolescence, young people of the same chronological age may have reached quite different stages of pubertal development. They may be of dramatically different sizes and shapes. Programs that take young adolescents' similarities and differences into account are more likely to be attractive to them and can also serve to raise young people's understanding of the other gender. Adolescents themselves are aware of and sensitive to such gender issues. The focus groups conducted by the task force revealed that girls frequently expressed a preference for some separate-gender programs, particularly in sports, sexuality education, and interpersonal relationships. Many of the boys also wanted separate sports programs if girls did not have adequate skills to compete. These views are not necessarily discriminatory; rather, they can reflect the reality that many girls do not have the same physical strength as boys and have not had the same opportunities as boys to develop basic sports skills early in childhood.

Several program content areas lend themselves to differential programming, based on gender. These areas include math, science, and technology; altruism expressed through community service; sports; human sexuality; the arts; and violence and conflict resolution. While both boys and girls should have access to programs in all of these subject areas, their varying experiences during childhood and the current challenges they face as adolescents suggest that the specifics of any given program should be adapted to their needs, interests, and skill levels.

For example, youth organizations are well known for their role in providing opportunities for community service and for fostering habits of voluntarism; early adolescence is an ideal time to offer young people meaningful opportunities to contribute to the community. Boys are less likely to report valuing altruistic activities and goals,[10] and fewer boys than girls spend time in social and community service.[11] Girls have more experience in helping others yet often lack opportunities to move from community service into community action and problem solving. Given these considerations, youth organizations may find that community service is an excellent setting in which to overcome gender barriers by encouraging boys to engage in meaningful service activities and by providing both genders with opportunities to move from

community service to community advocacy and action.

One overarching strategy in regard to gender is to recognize that all young people must be prepared for the adult roles of paid worker, family member, and community citizen. Yet this is not easily accomplished because preparing young adolescents to be members of an equitable society requires attention to today's continuing inequities. Youth organizations are well positioned to provide both boys and girls with experiences that encourage the development of interests and skills that have been associated in the past with the other gender (e.g., community service and arts for boys, sports and science for girls).

RACE, ETHNICITY, AND CULTURE

America's young adolescents today represent a rich array of racial, ethnic, and cultural backgrounds,[12] and this diversity will increase in the coming decades. Community programs must be prepared to understand and respond to this diversity.

Much of the established knowledge base concerning youth development in this country represents, in fact, the experience of white youth. As a result of this implicit bias, the perspectives and experiences of youth of color have, by and large, been rendered invisible or conceptualized as deficient. Some programs adopt a "color-blind" approach, assuming that the similarities among adolescents are so great that it is acceptable and perhaps practical to ignore the differences. Yet this conclusion trivializes the fact that race, ethnicity, and culture are powerful forces in American society—forces that strongly affect all youth.

At least three kinds of issues confront developers of youth programs as they work to recognize, value, and respond to the diverse backgrounds of today's adolescents: developmental, societal, and organizational.

DEVELOPMENTAL ISSUES

Race, ethnicity, and culture take on particular salience during adolescence, as young people struggle to learn about themselves and their place in the world. While the work of defining one's personal identity is an ongoing process that begins at birth and continues into adulthood, early adolescence represents a particularly critical period in the resolution of this task. This means that early adolescence (aged ten to fifteen) covers a significant portion of the identity-forming years.

Youth of color confront a special challenge: to achieve a positive orientation toward both cultures, white American and their own. Affirmation of ethnicity—through observation of ceremonies, retention of native language, and reinforcement of specific attitudes, beliefs, and practices—confers beneficial outcomes on young people. For example, African American parents

HOW DO BOYS AND GIRLS DIFFER FROM EACH OTHER DURING ADOLESCENCE?

A host of studies have pointed to the importance of gender as an issue in such behaviors as violence, eating disorders, sexual behavior, substance abuse, and child and sexual abuse. For example:

▶ Among young people aged twelve to seventeen, boys are about twice as likely as girls to die, with the death rate substantially higher among African American males than among their white counterparts.[13]

▶ More boys than girls engage in physical fights,[14] are involved in serious criminal offenses, and are arrested for crimes.[15]

▶ Boys aged twelve to seventeen are three to six times more likely to die from suicide than are girls, although girls are more likely than boys to contemplate and attempt suicide.[16]

▶ More girls than boys are at risk for nutritionally based diseases, including obesity, anorexia nervosa, and bulimia.[17]

▶ By early adolescence, depression is more common among girls than boys.[18]

▶ More girls than boys report being victims of physical abuse, and many more girls than boys report being victims of sexual abuse.[19]

▶ Boys and girls are about equally likely to report using harmful substances, with more boys than girls among heavy users of alcohol and illicit drugs.[20]

▶ The average age at first sexual intercourse is lower for boys than for girls, even though girls mature sexually about two years ahead of boys on average.[21]

who strive to instill ethnic pride and to teach skills for coping with and overcoming social barriers to minority achievement appear to produce children who succeed in school.[22] Some youth development organizations are experimenting with rites of passage for adolescents that emphasize the traditional values and ceremonies of particular ethnic groups. These programs seek to foster the development of healthy individual identity by consciously introducing young people to positive group history and norms. Deliberately Afro-centric programs inculcate traditional African values of kinship, community, collective responsibility, spirituality, and appreciation of nature.[23] Similarly, programs for recent immigrants help young people maintain their ties to their countries and cultures of origin, while also assisting them in adapting to the language and mores of their new country.

SOCIETAL ISSUES

Many minority youth live in economically poor families and neighborhoods. Subtle discrimination and overt racism are facts of life for these young people and their families. Program operators must recognize that many face the substantial risks associated with low-income status, social stratification, and limited resources. They must therefore avoid replicating these structural inequalities, however inadvertent, and develop concrete strategies to assist young people in overcoming negative effects. Specific strategies they can employ include initiating satellite programming in settings where youth reside, ensuring safety in program settings, providing youth with a variety of credible adult role models, implementing targeted job-skills programs, and providing paid employment for youth.

Youth development programs can also counteract prejudice, racism, and discrimination. They can teach by example—by becoming themselves models of fairness and nondiscrimination. They can also diminish racism's harmful consequences. Explicit programs in racism and oppression awareness can assist youth in developing effective communication skills in a multicultural context. Such programs can benefit not only minority teens but also those from majority groups by helping both groups realize the nature and extent of racism.

ORGANIZATIONAL ISSUES

Youth programs and organizations face important issues in their attempts to take a multicultural approach to their work. These issues are often construed to mean program content, when in fact they also include such considerations as staffing, governing boards and advisory councils, outreach activities, program philosophy, and program goals.

The recognition that services must be made cultur-

YOUTH PROGRAMS AND ORGANIZATIONS FACE IMPORTANT ISSUES IN THEIR ATTEMPTS TO TAKE A MULTICULTURAL APPROACH TO THEIR WORK. THESE ISSUES ARE OFTEN CONSTRUED TO MEAN PROGRAM CONTENT, WHEN IN FACT THEY ALSO INCLUDE SUCH CONSIDERATIONS AS STAFFING, GOVERNING BOARDS AND ADVISORY COUNCILS, OUTREACH ACTIVITIES, PROGRAM PHILOSOPHY, AND PROGRAM GOALS.

ally relevant has gained impetus during the past twenty-five years. Early attempts of health, mental health, education, and some youth development programs focused on adding information components and special ethnic or cultural awareness events to existing organizational structures and content; while these efforts at cultural addition served to increase awareness, they tended to reinforce the white, European cultural system on which many services are based. A second generation of multicultural models emphasized special classes and programs for members of minority groups, such as English as a second language, remedial education, and acculturation training.[24] Although some benefits accrued from this substitution approach, it too was limited in its scope (viewing people of color as disadvantaged and deficient in certain skills) and outcomes (having no discernible effects on majority individuals or organizations themselves).

A fully multicultural approach views ethnicity and culture as core features of identity and behavior, and it emphasizes pluralism in all aspects of organizational life.[25] This approach stresses that the white, European-based culture is one of many as it attempts to draw on the strengths of other cultural systems for its goals as well as its operations. In this model, all youth are made to feel welcome and empowered; staff members reflect the ethnocultural characteristics of programs' participants; all staff are trained to be culturally competent; program participants and their families are equitably represented on boards, advisory councils, and other governing structures; and program content is culturally appropriate and relevant to the needs of participants.

Youth development programs should recognize that the specific content of adolescent tasks and competencies varies by culture. For example, although the attainment of individual autonomy constitutes a universal task of adolescence, the specific meaning of autonomy is constructed differently across cultural groups.[26] Similarly, conceptions of proper social relationships vary. Dating and socializing with friends outside of the home may be considered appropriate adolescent behaviors among Americans, but are viewed as inappropriate among many recently arrived Southeast Asian families.[27] Youth programs that ignore such realities risk being unsuccessful with some populations.

Youth organizations also have a crucial—perhaps even unique—role to play in helping young people learn about, understand, and appreciate people with backgrounds different from their own. Such work, although not easy, is consistent with the missions of many youth organizations, is sorely needed in American society, and can flow directly from their regular ways of interacting with young people. Even youth organizations that are located in homogeneous communities, with no significant number of potential minority participants, can design programs that convey the value of diversity and that create opportunities for multicultural awareness and appreciation.

Youth organizations should purposefully create environments that not only meet psychosocial needs and develop competencies but also celebrate and build on aspects of participants' racial and ethnic backgrounds in the process. Young adolescents are poised to take risks, to widen their circle of relationships and affiliations, and to explore actively their worlds and themselves. Youth development programs can take advantage of these predispositions by opening new vistas for youth and by fostering the development of skills and competencies that complement and supplement those provided by schools and families.

FINDING AND ATTRACTING YOUTH MOST IN NEED OF SERVICES WILL REQUIRE THE CONCERTED, COORDINATED EFFORT OF ALL AGENCIES. COMMUNITY PROGRAMS SHOULD WORK COLLECTIVELY AS WELL AS INDIVIDUALLY TO EXTEND THEIR REACH TO UNDERSERVED ADOLESCENTS.

Increasing the access of young people living in low-income areas to supportive community programs will require individual and collective action at both the local and national levels. Community programs for youth should view themselves as actors in a network of services, and these networks should engage in systematic planning and coordinated decision making. Youth and community needs, rather than organizational concerns, should remain at the center of these efforts from their inception. An expanded and realigned set of services should build on the strengths of current programs and organizations, but all actors in the network should anticipate that ongoing adaptation and change will be required.

On the local level, youth programs should participate in comprehensive community-wide planning processes designed to identify gaps in current services and to develop plans for filling these gaps. These processes should involve both older, established and newer, emerging organizations as well as funders of youth programs. Community foundations and local United Ways have particularly salient roles to play in convening such networks and in facilitating their planning and decision-making processes. Public funders and policymakers can also contribute valuable ideas and resources.

Local planning should include attention to issues of

access for all young adolescents, especially those living in high-risk environments. Access concerns include transportation, fees, and publicity as well as more subtle aspects of staffing (are there people like me at the program?) and environment (are people like me welcome there?).

On the national level, interagency networks, such as the National Collaboration for Youth, should turn their attention to joint planning designed to extend their collective reach to underserved adolescents. From a national perspective, young people from low-income neighborhoods seem to be least well served by community programs. The National Collaboration for Youth (NCY) should conduct a systematic assessment and planning effort targeted toward low-income populations. NCY should expand its membership from fifteen national agencies by actively recruiting other national organizations, especially minority organizations such as the National Urban League, ASPIRA, and National Coalition of Hispanic Health and Human Services Organizations (COSSMHO), and other organizations that currently reach low-income youth, such as the Police Athletic League. Working together, these national organizations should use census figures, the National Education Longitudinal Study, and other social indicator data to assess the needs of low-income youth; match these needs to their current services and resources, with a focus on identifying gaps in service; and develop joint plans, which might include working partnerships between two or more NCY agencies as well as individual organizational plans that are part of a larger national plan.

> YOUTH PROGRAMS SHOULD ACTIVELY COMPETE FOR YOUNG PEOPLE'S TIME AND ATTENTION BY DEVELOPING STRATEGIES THAT ADDRESS THE CONTEMPORARY REALITIES FACING TODAY'S ADOLESCENTS.

Although young adolescents consistently name economic and employment issues as a priority for them, few organizations respond overtly to these concerns. Untapped opportunities abound for community youth programs to take a developmental approach to teen employment needs—an approach that offers a fresh alternative to the stultifying, sometimes dangerous, first jobs available to many of America's adolescents. Some youth organizations offer young people a "career path" that includes voluntary service within the organization or club to learn and practice basic skills, with movement to junior counselor or leadership roles (usually with a stipend of some sort), and then progressing toward paid employment on a part-time basis. This step-wise approach has the added

advantage of introducing young people to possible careers in the youth-work field.

In addition to offering paid employment when possible, youth organizations should capitalize on the interest of young people in the world of work by providing career awareness, preemployment training, job-skills training, and internship programs on an ongoing basis. These programs can connect young people with an array of community resources, opening doors not only to future employment but also to possible mentors and role models.

Paid employment in the mainstream economy represents one real attraction for many young people; youth gangs constitute another. American society has witnessed several waves of youth gangs throughout its history, and much is known about their formation, organization, and functioning.[28] Recent research on gang involvement indicates that early adolescence represents the critical decision period for initial gang activity.[29] Youth gangs address many of young adolescents' developmental needs, including safety, status, meaningful roles, income, and a sense of competence and belonging. One researcher has correlated the rise of youth gangs in Los Angeles over the past fifteen years with the dismantling of social programs available to youth. He notes, for example, that the city of Los Angeles sponsored 130 inner-city Teen Posts in the late 1970s and that only five such centers remain in the 1990s.[30]

Youth development programs can—and in some cases do—actively compete with gangs for the time, attention, energy, and commitment of young people. But to do so, these prosocial programs must offer meaningful alternatives to gang involvement.

Both prevention and intervention strategies are required. Prevention programs should reach out to young teens before initial gang involvement occurs, while intervention efforts should focus on providing constructive, skill-oriented activities for current gang members (for example, nonviolent conflict resolution skills, basic academic skills, job training, and employment assistance).

> ADULTS CANNOT LEAD AND INFLUENCE YOUNG ADOLESCENTS IN A HEALTHY WAY UNLESS THEY ARE QUALIFIED AND TRAINED. COMMUNITY PROGRAMS SHOULD STRENGTHEN THE QUALITY AND DIVERSITY OF THEIR ADULT LEADERSHIP.

Across all of the vast universe of community programs studied by the task force, the quality of adult leadership was consistently named as both vitally important and inadequately addressed. Youth-serving agencies, religious youth groups, sports programs, parks and recreation services, and libraries all report that the adults who work with young people in their systems, whether serving on a paid or voluntary basis, are *the* most critical factor in whether a program succeeds, but do not receive adequate training, ongoing support and supervision, or public recognition.

Training and supervision problems are reported to be the result largely of resource constraints, although they may also be tied to the widely held views that work with youth is neither highly valued nor particularly difficult.

The importance of adult leadership in program delivery is well documented in the research literature,[31] and the qualities that contribute to program success in these empirical studies are strikingly similar to the qualities that adolescents say they value in leaders of community programs.[32] These qualities include competence in group processes; ability to act as a guide and facilitator, as opposed to seeking a dominant authority role; respect for adolescents; and ability to empower them to make good decisions and to encourage freedom of choice and individual self-determination. Adolescents want leaders who are kind, nurturing, consistent, trustworthy, and genuinely interested in young people. They want leaders who know how to create a welcoming and supportive atmosphere in the organization or program, and who do not single out, exclude, or embarrass individual young people. Youth of color want assurances that leaders will not discriminate against them, and many immigrant and refugee youth want bilingual leaders who can speak with them in their own language as well as help them learn English.

Improving the quality of adult leadership involves matters of pre- and in-service training, recruitment and retention, and paid and unpaid (or volunteer) staff at all levels. An immediate first step is for community programs to expand greatly the availability of appropriate training and other forms of staff development for all adults who work directly with young people on either a paid or volunteer basis. Program administrators should begin by assessing the effectiveness of existing training models to identify what works for whom and why. They should then promote a range of successful models that include one-on-one coaching, mentoring, and supervision in addition to experience-based workshops and courses.

Youth organizations themselves should advocate the importance of adequate support for professional development, including in-service training, with national and local funding sources in both the public and private sectors. On both the local and national levels, youth organizations should develop collaborative approaches to in-service training that encourage agencies to tap one

IMPROVING THE QUALITY OF ADULT LEADERSHIP INVOLVES MATTERS OF PRE- AND IN-SERVICE TRAINING, RECRUITMENT AND RETENTION, AND PAID AND UNPAID (OR VOLUNTEER) STAFF AT ALL LEVELS. AN IMMEDIATE FIRST STEP IS FOR COMMUNITY PROGRAMS TO EXPAND GREATLY THE AVAILABILITY OF APPROPRIATE TRAINING AND OTHER FORMS OF STAFF DEVELOPMENT FOR ALL ADULTS WHO WORK DIRECTLY WITH YOUNG PEOPLE....

another's strengths and cooperate to tackle weaknesses. Valuing diversity is a critical issue because many organizations are actively trying to reach unserved groups. Existing staff may need opportunities to acquire information and skills that are relevant to this focus.

Youth organizations should work in partnership with professional schools that currently conduct pre-service education of youth workers (social work, education, recreation, human development, and theology) to increase their academic emphasis on the philosophy and knowledge base of youth development. These partnerships should also emphasize supervised field-work in youth organization settings and linkages to postgraduate employment. Pre-service education of youth workers should also take place at the community college level, and youth organizations should actively seek to influence the curriculum of these programs and to place their graduates in youth development settings.

Recruitment of youth workers should allow for multiple entry points into the field. Adolescents should have access to information about youth work as a possible and valued career choice, and indigenous community residents should be encouraged to work with young people in their own neighborhoods. Community programs for youth should work to develop standards for entry into and progression within the youth development field; develop public information networks in the local and national media that portray youth development work as important and valuable; and advocate with governments at the local, state, and federal levels to provide scholarships and fellowships to encourage individuals to enter and/or stay in youth development work. Salary levels must be high enough to attract people into the field. Specific outreach efforts should be aimed at youth and adults residing in low-income communities.

Community programs for youth should also work to retain current staff by providing recognition, ongoing support, adequate compensation, and opportunities to grow professionally, take on new responsibilities, and move up in the organization.

Finally, national organizations (either directly youth-serving or supportive intermediary groups) should increase communication and networking within the field of youth development, by such means as a professional membership association,[33] a widely distributed journal,[34] and a youth development information center that would actively disseminate research and program knowledge to paid and unpaid staff of youth development organizations.

YOUNG ADOLESCENTS NEED CONSISTENT, HEALTHY SUPPORT IN EVERY ASPECT OF THEIR LIVES: AT HOME, IN SCHOOL, AND DURING NONSCHOOL HOURS. FOR THEIR PART, COMMUNITY PROGRAMS SHOULD REACH OUT TO FAMILIES, SCHOOLS, AND OTHER COMMUNITY PARTNERS IN YOUTH DEVELOPMENT.

Positive development is enhanced when the major influences in adolescents' lives work in harmony with one another, providing consistent messages, expectations, and support.[35] Effective community programs for youth see themselves as partners with families, schools, and other community institutions in the youth development process. They work hard to maintain solid working relationships with their partners, and to clarify how their role complements, supplements, and differs from that of others.

PARTNERSHIPS WITH FAMILIES

There are at least five constructive ways to involve parents and other family members in the work of youth organizations:
▶ Keep families informed of organizational activities and give them opportunities to consult in the planning process;
▶ Invite family members to contribute their time and energies to the agency's efforts through such roles as board members and program volunteers;
▶ Design activities that encourage young people to consult with and learn from the experience of family members;
▶ Support families in their teen-rearing responsibilities; and
▶ Provide direct services to families.

At a minimum, youth organizations should keep parents and other family members informed of their activities, through written materials as well as through personal contact. Because young people report that parents are a primary source of information and encouragement to participate in youth programs, youth organizations should target publicity to families as well as directly to young people themselves. Many agencies consider it wise practice to obtain parental consent for youth participation in programs and to communicate regularly about what those programs entail.

Youth organizations typically involve parents and other family members as program volunteers, fund-raising assistants, program advisers, and board members. Many programs—including organized sports programs, religious youth organizations, and troop-based

For twenty-four years parents of children in a low-income South-Central Los Angeles neighborhood have helped shape, staff, and finance a remarkably successful youth service organization—Challengers Boys and Girls Club.

The club serves more than 2,200 young people aged six to seventeen each year. The club operates from 7:00 A.M. to 7:00 P.M. seven days a week and has served more than 25,000 youths since it was founded in 1968 by current Executive Director Lou Dantzler. Alumni have entered Cornell, UCLA, and Yale and include Los Angeles Dodger Eric Davis and *Boyz N the Hood* producer John Singleton.

As one measure of its standing in the community, the large club building was untouched in the April 1992 riots in South-Central Los Angeles, even though facilities surrounding it were extensively damaged.

Dantzler notes that parents are the key to Challengers' success. Parents in the Creative Services Program, which focuses on gang prevention and recruits first-time juvenile offenders aged ten to seventeen, teach photography, arts and crafts, wood shop, sports, and computer literacy.

Programs have evolved over the years as a result of parental involvement, according to Director of Community Programs John Kotick. "The program is all homegrown," he says, "the product of our existing relationship with the parents over twenty-four years. It worked out over a long period."

PARENTS AND THEIR CHILDREN SIGN A CONTRACT THAT SPELLS OUT MUTUAL RESPONSIBILITIES AND PROVIDES GUIDELINES OF DRESS AND CONDUCT. "ONCE WE HAD TO CALL PARENTS TO VOLUNTEER.... NOW, THE PARENTS CALL HERE AND ASK WHAT THEY CAN DO."

In Operation Safe Streets (OSS), parents provide after-school transportation and social support services for elementary school-age children. This team effort involves parents, the Los Angeles Police Department, eighteen elementary schools, and the club. OSS daily transports more than 1,600 youth to the club for supervised activities that include instruction in street safety, educational supports to deter dropping out, and health classes on basic physiology, sexually transmitted diseases, and drug and alcohol avoidance.

Parents help according to their talents and interests. They may assist in administration, staff the after-school snack bar, chaperone field trips, run fund-raising events, or help with homework. One knowledgeable parent teaches computer operation on IBM-donated equipment. Parents coach teams or travel to games, pass out refreshments, and wash uniforms.

More than 200 parents are involved in club activities every month, and from thirty-five to forty are at the club on any given day. They wear identification badges so young people know whom to seek out for help. Single parents, grandparents, foster parents, aunts and uncles, and other adult guardians are encouraged to participate.

Parents are required to volunteer for eight hours a month as long as they have a child enrolled in Challengers. When parents enroll their children, staff meets with the parents to explain rules, programs, and the importance of parental involvement. Parents pay an annual fee of $20 per child and agree to donate time to the club on a regular basis. Parents and their children sign a contract that spells out mutual responsibilities and provides guidelines of dress and conduct. "Once we had to call parents to volunteer," says Club Office Manager Bridget Iserhein. "Now, the parents call here and ask what they can do."

---

youth groups such as Camp Fire, 4-H, and scouting—rely heavily on parents and other family members as the adult leaders. Youth organizations should encourage but not require active family involvement in these efforts, because such a requirement might rule out the participation of young people who need the organizations' services. Similarly, youth organizations should use inclusive definitions of family, recognizing that families today come in many forms and constellations.

Program developers are increasingly seeing the value of building program components that encourage young people to view their families as resources during adolescence. Programs such as the Journey,[36] which focuses on the formation of a positive identity during adolescence, and the Choices and Challenges[37] series of life-options courses include homework assignments that involve young people in interviewing their parent(s) and other family members about such issues as family history and career choices.

Youth organizations may also have an unrecognized but critical role to play in assisting parents to become more skilled in their interactions with their children. Many parents recognize that their children's adolescence brings a need to renegotiate their relationships, but they are uncertain about how to proceed. Through parenting workshops, and in the company of other parents of teenagers, they can learn that effective, "authoritative" parenting consists of being warm toward one's children, engaging in a high degree of give-and-take, offering rational explanations of rules and limits, and affirming the young person's qualities coupled with setting clear standards for conduct.[38] Few youth organizations offer such support for parents, and programs currently available are directed largely toward middle- and upper-income parents.[39] Untapped potential would appear to exist both in the direct provision of parenting skills workshops through youth organizations and in the application of knowledge about authoritative parenting styles to staff-youth relationships within such organizations.

In addition to these four supportive ways that youth organizations can involve families in their work, some youth organizations choose to serve families directly. For example, the National Coalition of Hispanic Health and Human Services Organizations (COSSMHO) notes that all of its work with young people is done in the context of their lives within their families. COSSMHO offers family programs targeted toward contemporary youth issues such as teenage pregnancy and substance-abuse prevention. Several of these efforts, including the Strengthening Families model program, have incorporated experimental evaluations designed to determine their impact on low-income Hispanic families.

Still others view themselves as standing *in loco parentis* in serving young adolescents from families that are unable to provide adequate support for their children. These organizations offer intensive services for youth, perhaps for thirty to forty hours (or more) per week, and may include meals and transportation. Families become directly involved on an as-needed, individual basis. A key goal of most of the country's runaway shelters is to reunite young people with their families, and many of these organizations measure their effectiveness according to their ability to accomplish this end.[40]

Community-based youth organizations can stretch their dollars and staff to reach families of the young people they serve, but intensive family involvement may begin to dilute the strength of their service to youth. In these circumstances, the organizations may have to find ways to collaborate with other agencies in their communities to meet the totality of family needs.

Few would argue against the proposition that children would be better served by systems in which schools and other community institutions work together. Why does such cooperation not generally take place? Many barriers prevent school-community collaboration, including logistical, financial, legal, and bureaucratic barriers. Known solutions do exist, however.

At the simplest level, schools and community-based agencies should share information about individual students and effect appropriate referrals from one institution to another. Youth organizations should reach out to schools in publicizing their services and in eliciting suggestions from school personnel about the needs of their students. A second level of cooperation envisions community agencies delivering program services in school facilities, either during the school day or on a "wraparound" basis (that is, before and after school). A third level involves joint planning that focuses not just on individual students but also on the delivery of services for all students. A fourth level, one that has been realized in few communities, is a unified system of educational and human services; this system views its role as youth development and recognizes the common goals of the schools and community agencies while respecting their inherent differences and strengths.

This report's earlier analysis of adolescent time use pointed to the dual realities of America's relatively short school day and school year and of American adolescents' significant and often untapped resource—discretionary time. Effective school-community relationships would tackle this equation directly. In this effective system, schools would communicate high expectations for students' use of discretionary time and would assist them in making constructive choices. Community agencies would be flexible enough to respond to the needs of youth, families, and schools.

The current trend that sees youth organizations increasing their delivery of in-school, classroom-based programming should be viewed with some caution. These efforts may be doing more to meet the organizations' needs for increased membership and revenue than to address the most pressing needs of young people. Of particular concern are two lost opportunities: (1) students may be shortchanged in critical academic achievement areas if agency-sponsored programs are permitted to use academic time to teach nonacademic subjects; and (2) use of any agency's limited financial and human resources for the implementation of classroom-based programs may impede the expansion of efforts designed to promote constructive use of students' discretionary time. While community agencies can do much to support schools' basic academic program and to enrich the services offered to students,

When the country's largest school system joined forces with one of the nation's oldest and largest human service agencies to launch three new community schools in the Washington Heights–Inwood section of New York City, that event was significant enough to make the front page of *The New York Times*. But the news coverage about the partnership between the New York City schools and the Children's Aid Society (CAS) failed to report the most radical element of its design: the fact that these two New York institutions worked in full partnership on all aspects of the initiative, including planning of the facilities and services, fund raising, public relations, and day-to-day operations. Unlike many school-community partnerships, which see agencies' programs brought into existing schools on a piecemeal basis, the Washington Heights–Inwood experiment offers a new model for both process and outcome. The process is a fully collaborative approach, and the outcome is an innovative, comprehensive youth and family development center.

These new community schools focus on excellence in mathematics, reading, social studies, and science. This content is reinforced through community experiences such as service projects and internships. The core curriculum is organized around three themes— community service, business/ enterprise, and science/technology—and uses interdisciplinary teaching teams, peer tutoring, partnerships with older students and senior citizens, community residents as guest lecturers, parental involvement, and flexible grouping of students.

"IT IS APPROPRIATE THAT THE CHILDREN'S AID SOCIETY, WHICH CREATED THE FREE LUNCH PROGRAM AND OPERATED THE FIRST KINDERGARTENS IN NEW YORK CITY, SHOULD BE AT THE FOREFRONT IN HELPING US TO DEVELOP THE FIRST COMMUNITY SCHOOLS TO BE BUILT FROM THE GROUND UP."

These community schools will offer health services, preschool programs, day care, recreation, mental health counseling, food and nutrition programs, medical referrals, tutorial assistance, leadership development training, drug and teen pregnancy prevention counseling, sports and fitness programs, day camping programs, visual and performing arts, emergency assistance for homeless families, and adult education specifically tailored to residents' needs (English as a second language training, parent education, immigrant rights, and tenant rights). These services are offered twelve months a year, six days a week, from 7:00 A.M. until 9:00 P.M.

Funding is collaborative. The New York State legislature established the New York City School Construction Authority to oversee construction of the schools, which cost from $27 million to $52.8 million each. Operating funds come from a combination of city, state, and federal dollars. An additional $1 million per site underwrites the health and social services components, with government contracts supporting about a third of these costs, and private sources (local foundations and Special Initiatives grants from United Way of New York City) covering the rest.

New York City Schools Chancellor Joseph A. Fernandez added a historical perspective to the initiation of this partnership when he noted: "It is appropriate that the Children's Aid Society, which created the free lunch program and operated the first kindergartens in New York City, should be at the forefront in helping us to develop the first community schools to be built from the ground up." Founded in 1853, the society serves more than 100,000 children and families each year through neighborhood-based programs offered mainly in low-income areas throughout New York City. In the Washington Heights–Inwood initiative, the society has teamed up with local community groups, such as Alianza Dominicana, in sponsoring after-school programs for young adolescents. Such additional collaborations are critical in tailoring programs to the needs of area residents, most of whom are recent Dominican immigrants.

they should make decisions jointly with educators about how to achieve the most effective relationship. Schools need to consider the best ways to achieve educational goals, resolve competing priorities for students' classroom time, meet union regulations, and address a host of other complicated issues raised by community partnerships. Agencies must consider how to make best use of their limited resources, how to build on their strengths, and how to set priorities, given the many unmet needs of young people.

Another trend that the task force also views with some caution, again perceiving that there may be a lost opportunity, is the increasing number of schools that are operating their own after-school programs, using only their own personnel.[41] Although for many communities the decision to employ school facilities for after-school or "wraparound" care may well be the best choice, the task force questions the decision of some schools to employ only classroom teachers and traditional didactic teaching methods in after-school programs. This approach is likely to shortchange students, who need access to a wide range of adults and to a variety of avenues for learning. A more effective approach is to integrate community agencies into school-based extended-day programs—by asking these agencies actually to coordinate and run the overall program, by inviting them to conduct specific activities on a regularly scheduled basis, by hiring youth agency staff to train teachers in informal education techniques, or by teaming youth workers with teachers in conducting program activities. Another alternative is for schools to coordinate transportation to community programs for students who need and want such services.

Youth organizations should be proactive in reaching out to schools as youth development partners. They should work toward joint planning of youth development services and view these collaborative efforts as an ongoing way of working, not as a one-time event. They should build on the many excellent models of effective school-community partnerships that exist, and they should work with schools to develop creative financing packages, for example, by using federal Chapter 1 (remedial education) funds for collaborative after-school programs for low-income youth.

the organization to the media and policy makers.

Community programs should also ensure that youth have opportunities to provide meaningful service to the larger community in which they live. The program can act as a broker between youth and other community institutions, by developing and nurturing relationships with these groups and by working to publicize the good work that young people contribute. Youth should actively participate in determining what issues they wish to address through service activities and which strategies they will employ. Adult leaders may underestimate the creativity and concern for social justice that young adolescents bring to the design of such efforts. Current projects around the country find young people building neighborhood parks for younger children, planting trees and reclaiming trash-ridden streams, providing child-care services for mothers in battered women's shelters, and working to end the killing of dolphins in tuna fishing.[42]

In addition to encouraging young people to formulate the problems to be solved and work to be done, community programs should also encourage young people to reflect on the underlying causes of current social problems and to design appropriate action campaigns in response to these conditions. For example, staffing a soup kitchen might lead young people to examine the causes of hunger and homelessness in American society and subsequently to take responsive political or civic action, individually or as a group.

A related recommendation is that programs should assist young people in learning to use their communities *as* a resource. Programs can act as bridges to the larger community, helping young people identify and use the services they need, such as health clinics, legal aid, and employment.

YOUNG ADOLESCENTS CAN AND WANT TO CONTRIBUTE TO THEIR COMMUNITY, AND THEY LEARN MUCH FROM DOING SO. COMMUNITY PROGRAMS SHOULD ENHANCE THE ROLE OF YOUNG PEOPLE AS RESOURCES TO THEIR COMMUNITY.

YOUNG ADOLESCENTS CANNOT BE HEARD IN THE CLAMOR OF POLITICAL DEBATE AND NEED STRONG CHAMPIONS FOR THEIR INTERESTS. COMMUNITY PROGRAMS SHOULD SERVE AS VIGOROUS ADVOCATES FOR AND WITH YOUTH.

A good place to begin applying this principle is within youth organizations themselves. Community programs should involve young people in decision making at all levels, from choices about program activities to organizational governance. In addition to carrying out roles in organizational decision making, young people should have opportunities to participate in all other aspects of agency life, including teaching skills to other participants, caring for the physical facility, planning special events, and representing

Because children and youth do not vote, their best interests are often ignored or shunted to last place in the legislative process. Their need for strong and consistent advocates at the local, state, and national levels is clear.

A few strong advocates do exist at all levels. On the local level, a variety of adult service groups (including the Association of Junior Leagues and the National Council of Jewish Women) have been long-time supporters of more enlightened public policies for children and youth. These groups frequently join such state-wide coalitions as the Texas and California Collaborations for Youth and the New York State Advocates for Children. On the national level, such consistent voices for young people as the Children's Defense Fund, the Child Welfare League of America, and the National Collaboration for Youth frequently work together through multiagency vehicles, such as Generations United (a coalition of more than a hundred national organizations representing children, youth, families, and the aging that works to improve the quality of life for all generations) and the Coalition for America's Children (through which forty-five children's organizations joined forces to coordinate efforts and issues around the 1992 elections).

All types of organizations that sponsor community programs for youth—adult service clubs, senior citizens groups, sports organizations, national and local youth agencies, churches, museums—should become advocates for youth. Staff members and volunteers (board members, fund-raising associates, and program volunteers) should consider advocacy as part of their work with the agency. The organizations themselves should join local, state, and national advocacy coalitions in an effort to elevate youth issues in public policy debates.

Adults should work with young people as partners in the multiple advocacy processes of educating the public about youth needs and influencing youth-related public policy, including funding levels and mechanisms. Youth and other community organizations should educate funders that advocacy is a legitimate and ongoing part of youth work.

> GOOD INTENTIONS ARE NOT ENOUGH; GOOD RESULTS ARE THE GOAL, AND THEY FLOW FROM WELL-DESIGNED AND CAREFULLY EVALUATED PROGRAMS. TO THAT END, COMMUNITY PROGRAMS SHOULD SPECIFY AND EVALUATE THEIR OUTCOMES.

SPECIFYING OUTCOMES

Program developers should seek clarity and realism when defining outcomes of their efforts. As much as possible, these outcomes should focus on the end point of positive youth development rather than solely on preventing problem behaviors such as substance abuse, delinquency, and adolescent pregnancy. The outcomes should be stated in terms of behavioral functioning in the real world, and the indicators associated with each outcome should also be identified. Positive results are more likely to ensue if the frequency and duration of a program intervention matches well with its intended outcomes.

DESIGNING INTERVENTIONS

A critical need exists to anchor youth development programs in the best available knowledge, which can be drawn from the experience of similar programs as well as from research about adolescent development. Many current programs are based on outmoded theory and research or, worse yet, on no theory and research. It is not uncommon to find programs rooted solely in political or organizational philosophy.

Effective program development appears to combine art with science by calling on the designer's creativity, intuition, understanding, and experience as well as on research knowledge. Many good programs have been developed in a nonlinear fashion that one observer described as "ready, fire, aim." This observation connotes both the experimental quality and the immediacy that characterize much of youth work.

It is clearly easier to describe the science than the art of program development. The science involves a five-step process of conceptualization, design, implementation, evaluation, and maintenance and dissemination.[43]

The conceptualization phase draws on behavioral and social science theories and on research findings about proven or promising interventions in an effort to identify combinations of personal resources (skills, beliefs, knowledge) and environmental supports that will produce desired results. Program design involves creating potentially replicable program models, often including detailed program curricula and training mechanisms that flesh out the conceptual approach. The implementation phase often involves testing the model in a variety of settings to ensure its appropriateness with a wide variety of audiences; there are often several rounds of program adaptation during this third phase as program developers seek to refine and improve the model. The fourth phase, evaluation, usually occurs concurrently with the implementation component. Early evaluations may focus more on implementation or process aspects, in an effort to document whether the program is being carried out effectively and to provide information that will lead to program modifications and improvements. Once the model is refined, subsequent evaluations may focus more clearly on assessing the outcomes of the intervention on participants. In the fifth phase, maintenance and dissemination, efforts are made to support replication of the model in new sites and to ensure control over quality of implementation, using such vehicles as training and technical assistance.

Organizations that have implemented this process

have found it to be both practical and effective, revealing the wisdom of the notion—attributed to psychologist Kurt Lewin—that "there is nothing quite so practical as a good theory." On the national level, examples of theory-based interventions that have shown positive evaluation and replication results include the Salvation Army's Bridging the Gap Between Youth and Community Services program, the Boys and Girls Clubs' SMART Moves program, and Girls Incorporated's Friendly PEERsuasion and Preventing Adolescent Pregnancy programs.

On the local level, organizations that pay careful attention to program design are likely to engage in a modified version of this sequence, with less focus on model building and more on the planning, scheduling, and sequencing of activities. Nonetheless, there is a cyclic quality to the program planning, and clear steps that involve—either formally or informally—design, implementation, assessment, and redesign.

MEASURING PROGRESS TOWARD ACHIEVEMENT OF STATED OUTCOMES

Some type of assessment mechanism should be built into every community program for youth. The level of the assessment or evaluation should match the needs of the sponsoring organization and the state of the program's evolution. For example, a new program should be subject to process evaluation that is directed toward program improvement, while a more mature program that has shown promising initial results should undergo outcome evaluation to determine objectively whether the program is producing its intended effects.

Achieving more rigorous outcome evaluation of youth development programs raises a host of general and specific problems—none insurmountable but all nonetheless real. General problems include deciding what outcome variables (knowledge, attitudes, skills, behaviors) to measure; constructing valid and reliable assessment measures for determining change; building in sufficient controls to be able to argue that the intervention was responsible for causing these changes; and allowing enough time to elapse for the desired changes to occur. Specific problems include recruiting and retaining participants in the program and assessment (a challenge in any voluntary setting); and dealing with the issue of random assignment to treatment and control groups, which runs counter to the public-service orientation of most human service agencies. Youth organizations may find it useful to work with evaluation experts from other institutions, including universities and nonprofit technical assistance organizations.

In effective collaborations, outside evaluators should see themselves as equal partners with youth agency personnel in designing and implementing evaluations. Young people themselves should be

SOME TYPE OF ASSESSMENT MECHANISM SHOULD BE BUILT INTO EVERY COMMUNITY PROGRAM FOR YOUTH. THE LEVEL OF THE ASSESSMENT OR EVALUATION SHOULD MATCH THE NEEDS OF THE SPONSORING ORGANIZATION AND THE STATE OF THE PROGRAM'S EVOLUTION.

active participants in evaluations of all types. The methods used to evaluate youth development programs should be appropriate to the organizational setting and to the age of the participants as well as to the individual programs.

In a world of scarce resources, the best candidates for rigorous outcome evaluations are those programs that are carefully designed and implemented, that have shown promising results, and that seem amenable to replication.

In addition to their individual efforts, youth organizations should work in partnership with one another and with social science researchers to conduct longitudinal studies that can contribute to understanding the long-term effects of participation in youth development programs and to share information useful in evaluation.[44]

> THE YOUTH OF A COMMUNITY NEED THE STRONG COMMITMENT OF PEOPLE IN POWER, PEOPLE WHO SIT ON BOARDS OF NONPROFIT AGENCIES AND MAKE THINGS HAPPEN. THUS, COMMUNITY PROGRAMS SHOULD ESTABLISH SOLID ORGANIZATIONAL STRUCTURES, INCLUDING ENERGETIC AND COMMITTED BOARD LEADERSHIP.

Just as programs must be shaped to meet the changing needs of the youth population, so organizations that would present those programs effectively must be well structured and adequately supported. Effective programs are generally found in stable, well-governed, and well-managed organizations. Although there are exceptions to this rule—particularly small, locally developed programs that serve young people successfully at the neighborhood level—for the most part, the connection between programs and organizations is so close that it is difficult to know exactly where one ends and the other begins. Research and experience show that effective youth organizations make a serious commitment to both their programs and their staff.

In addition to providing direct program services, effective youth organizations frequently engage in one or more of these other mission-related functions:

▶ Public education: increasing community understanding of and support for the nonprofit agency's concerns, programs, and constituency;

▶ Advocacy: promoting public policies that respond to the needs of young adolescents; and

▶ Research: learning more about the needs of the young constituents and how to address them, as well as evaluating the results of programs.

To support their mission-related activities, effective youth organizations should also employ basic management techniques (such as day-to-day and annual planning, fiscal control, organization of staff and other resources),[45] plus more recent innovations that include strategic planning and marketing.[46] While day-to-day management is considered the responsibility of staff, particularly the executive director or chief executive officer, establishing policy, setting the organization's strategic direction, and ensuring financial stability are generally viewed as the responsibility of its board of directors or trustees.

The importance of board leadership cannot be overstated. Organizations with effective programs for young adolescents have generally made a board-level commitment to such work; this commitment may involve a decision to raise new funds for expanded program activity as well as the establishment of new organizational policies on such issues as adolescent sexuality, substance use, and youth employment. Board members also play a critical role in determining where to locate agency facilities and programs and whether to charge fees for program participation—decisions that determine, to a great extent, whether the organization will succeed in reaching out to young people living in low-income neighborhoods. Boards should also reflect the diversity of their communities so that decisions benefit from an understanding of the broader community.

Boards are generally considered responsible for conducting oversight of all organizational activities and for raising funds and overseeing their expenditure. A particular challenge for board members in carrying out their role as stewards of the organization is to determine how the agency will collaborate with other community institutions, especially other youth groups that may be viewed as their competition. To address this challenge, board members must analyze the strengths and limitations of their own organization and focus on the needs of youth rather than solely on the needs of their agency.

Board members should work with management staff to address issues of fund-raising and financial stability. Specifically, the board can diversify funding sources; make best use of existing resources; and continually work to develop innovative and stable sources of core support for the organization (comparable to sales campaigns for Girl Scout cookies, which provide an average of 60 percent of the core support for the work of local Girl Scout councils). The board and staff can also work collectively with other youth organizations to increase the stability and total level of support for the sector's work, through action directed toward both traditional sources and innovative new mechanisms. For example, a Children's Investment Trust[47] could earmark public funds for youth services or a semipostal stamp could allow individuals to make voluntary contributions to youth programs each time they purchase stamps through the U.S. Postal Service.[48]

Stability of programs is essential to maintaining continuity of relationships, especially for youth at critical junctures in their lives. Long-term commitment to their young constituents requires that community programs and organizational sponsors plan for lean funding years, by raising unrestricted operating and endowment funds to cover gaps in restricted funding.

Furthermore, youth organizations should view themselves as having an interdependent relationship with funders, which means educating funders about their real needs and responding to funders' requests for greater accountability and responsiveness to community needs.

CONCLUSION:

LINKING PROGRAMS TO POLICIES

Effective youth development programs come into the lives of young adolescents with the intention of helping them grow into healthy young adults. Effective programs and organizations stay with their young constituents, through thick and thin, to provide them with the levels and quality of adult guidance they need—for as long as they need it.

But nonprofit agencies rely on many individuals, businesses, foundations, government units, and other community institutions for sustenance. The next section offers recommendations for the kinds of policies that are needed to support effective youth development programs and organizations, and—more important—to promote positive youth development.

RESEARCH-COMMUNITY PARTNERSHIPS SHOW PROMISE

The research-community partnership is a key building block of strengthened youth development services—both in terms of designing specific programs and of determining community-wide needs. Current promising efforts include the following:

▶ The Los Angeles Roundtable for Children—a group of university-based researchers and community leaders, under the leadership of Jacquelyn McCroskey, a professor of social welfare at the University of Southern California, that conducted two studies that mapped the area's current youth programs and identified gaps in the service delivery system. Researchers from the University of North Florida have conducted similar activities in the Jacksonville area.

▶ The Policy, Research, and Interventions Designed for Early Adolescents (PRIDE) program— which was developed by Penn State's College of Health and Human Services' Dean Anne Petersen to bridge the gap between research and practice communities through workshops,

media conferences, adult education programs, and action research on existing youth programs. The goals of the program are to advance research on early adolescence, influence state policy for the benefit of young adolescents, and improve media and programs directed toward this age group.

▶ The Chapin Hall Center for Children of the University of Chicago—whose national and local studies have influenced youth work practice, contributing to such actions as the reorganization of public policies at the state level in Illinois and the development of a new youth services funding initiative by the Chicago Community Trust.

▶ The Teacher Context Center of Stanford University—where researchers Milbrey McLaughlin and Shirley Brice Heath are examining the resources and programs available to youth in diverse urban settings. Their work is directed toward strengthening the conceptual base of youth development programs and informing the education, research, and

policy communities about the actual and potential contributions of supportive services for adolescents.

▶ The Center for Youth Development and Policy Research, a division of the Academy for Educational Development—which was established in 1990 to link social science research with youth development practice through conceptual and action-oriented activities including public education, advocacy, and technical assistance activities.

Strengthening the ties between the research and practice communities will improve the quality of youth development services across the country. Improved outreach activities on the part of researchers and practitioners, increased incentives, especially on the part of universities, for participating in such community-based initiatives, additional funds for research-practice collaborations, and increased attention to nonschool issues in large-scale national surveys of youth will all be needed to improve these partnerships.

CONSTRUCTING SUPPORTIVE POLICIES FOR YOUNG ADOLESCENTS

YOUTH PROGRAMS AND ORGANIZATIONS ARE DYNAMIC STRUCTURES. THEY INTERACT WITH AND RESPOND TO YOUNG PEOPLE AND THEIR FAMILIES, AND TO BROADER SOCIAL INSTITUTIONS, INCLUDING PRIVATE FUNDING SOURCES, THE BUSINESS COMMUNITY, AND GOVERNMENT AGENCIES. SOCIAL AND PUBLIC POLICIES, THEREFORE, HAVE A STRONG INFLUENCE ON THE ABILITY OF YOUTH PROGRAMS AND ORGANIZATIONS TO CARRY OUT THEIR WORK. THIS SECTION OUTLINES RECOMMENDATIONS FOR IMPROVING THE POLICY CLIMATE THAT SURROUNDS YOUTH DEVELOPMENT PROGRAMS AND ORGANIZATIONS.

FUNDING INSTITUTIONS

Many types of funding are needed to ensure that the total amount of resources allocated to youth development is adequate to the task. Funders of all types—private and public, national and local—should work in partnership with youth development organizations and with one another to identify and address the pressing needs of youth in communities across the country.

Four major problems characterize the funding of America's youth programs and organizations: instability of overall funding, particularly of core support for programs and organizations; inadequacy of the total level of resources; an orientation toward fixing problems rather than promoting healthy development; and a piecemeal, categorical approach to youth issues rather than a comprehensive, holistic one.[49]

Youth organization funders should work individu-ally as well as collectively to help stabilize and expand the base of support for youth development. With these priorities in mind, the task force turns its attention to the various types of funders whose increased contributions are needed to strengthen the work of the youth development sector. It urges them to take the following actions:

▶ Local United Ways: Currently the largest single funder of youth development services on the community level, local United Ways should continue their emphasis on youth development programs; greatly expand their focus on services to children and youth in high-risk environments; play an active role in planning and coordination of services; not engage in direct service per se; place greater emphasis on program effectiveness and less emphasis on numbers served; and assist youth organizations in achieving visibility and recognition for their work. United Way of America should assist local United Way affiliates in implementing these community-oriented recommendations and in establishing training centers for youth service professionals.

▶ Community Foundations: According to the 1990 Community Foundations Survey, there are approximately 400 community foundations in the United States.[50] The assets of 123 of the largest U.S. community foundations now exceed $6.7 billion, and grants awarded by community foundations in 1990 reached a half billion dollars. In some areas, community foundations are key supporters of youth development programs, and promising new efforts in Chicago and Kansas City have seen community foundations playing an active role in the reorganization and strengthening of youth services. Community foundations should work in partnership with United Ways to coordinate, strengthen, and expand youth development programs in their areas; emphasize and advocate for improved services to children and youth in high-risk environments; support advocacy efforts of youth organizations themselves; and share their successes and challenges with other community foundations.

▶ National Foundations: Most national foundations place priority on national-level initiatives, such as national demonstration projects and generation of new knowledge with broad applicability. Relatively few currently place priority on youth development programs and services. The task force urges national foundations, large and small, to consider making youth development a higher priority for funding; supporting the efforts of youth development organizations to expand their services to youth living in high-risk environments, strengthen and evaluate their program services, replicate proven programs, train their staff members (both paid and unpaid), and advocate with and on behalf of youth; and making long-term commitments to these efforts.

▶ Businesses: Many corporations and other businesses contribute to the work of youth development organizations through their partnerships with United Ways and other federated campaigns. However, the role of the business community could be enhanced by supporting the work of national youth organizations that do not receive United Way dollars; providing additional support to local youth organizations, particularly in the areas near corporate plants and other facilities; lending executives to assist youth organizations in strategic planning and management; encouraging employees to volunteer their time and services in youth development organizations; and providing release time or other incentives for such volunteer work.

▶ Individuals: Many local youth organizations conduct annual fund-raising campaigns and special events fund-raisers that rely heavily on individual donations.

Many individual donors also contribute to the work of youth organizations through their annual gifts to United Ways. Individual donors should continue and expand both types of financial support; use the United Way "donor choice" option to direct at least some of their contributions to youth development services; learn more about the work of local youth development agencies; and become involved in that work through a variety of means in addition to providing financial support. Individuals can supplement their financial support by volunteering their time and energy to the work of youth organizations.

▶ Government: Governments at all levels—local, state, and federal—should expand their support of youth development services, particularly services directed toward adolescents living in low-income areas. Funding is, of course, only one aspect of the role of governments, but it is a critical role. Because government funding is related to larger policy questions, additional recommendations will be made in the following section on the role of local, state, and federal policies in supporting positive youth development.

GOVERNMENT POLICIES

Local, state, and federal policies all play a critical role in supporting or in failing to support healthy adolescent development. An ideal set of public policies would be integrated at all three levels; would be built on the best current knowledge; would be firmly rooted in the philosophical notion of youth as resources; would focus on increasing support for basic youth development services; would target services to areas of greatest need; and would give priority to locally generated solutions.

A community's ability to reconstruct itself as youth oriented depends in considerable measure on supportive public policy. One of the key findings of this report is that government at all levels in the United States tends to address youth issues on a fragmented, almost haphazard basis. With few exceptions, no coherent policy is noticeable at any level—local, state, or federal.

HOW LOCAL GOVERNMENTS CAN HELP

Although the 1990s have been a time of fiscal austerity for most municipal-level agencies, some local communities have taken a lead in improving the programs and services they offer to their children. Denver, Kansas City, New York, Seattle, and San Diego are among a small group of cities that have made serious efforts to provide leadership and funding for youth development services.

The initiatives of each of these cities have many common features:

▶ They are all designed to improve the delivery of youth services;

▶ Each has the leadership and blessing of top-level government officials;

▶ All build on existing services, while recognizing the need to plan, coordinate, and modify services;

▶ All seek to draw on the strengths of the voluntary sector in improving services for youth; and

▶ All have generated or allocated new financial resources as a part of their planning and implementation efforts.

In Denver the leadership of former mayor Federico Peña, followed by the support of current Mayor Wellington Webb, led to the development of two major efforts: the Mayor's Youth Initiative and the Denver Initiative for Children and Families. The Mayor's Youth Initiative allocated new funds for youth programs and convened local planning councils to determine the best use of those resources in their respective neighborhoods. The city also secured additional federal funds for the design of a program that provided Denver youth with alternatives to gang involvement. Following this effort, a number of public and private leaders formed the Denver Initiative for Children and Families. The program developed the *CAN DO* report, a blueprint for schools, neighborhood organizations, and government agencies to follow as they work to improve the quality of life for Denver's children and families.

In Kansas City a collaboration of service providers established YouthNet to improve the quality and increase the quantity of youth programs in low-income neighborhoods. This collaboration has resulted in significant improvements in local service delivery through the development and implementation of programs and joint fund-raising efforts. Young adolescents are a particular focus of YouthNet's activities.

In New York City a collaboration between the city's board of education and United Way of New York City, entitled CAPS (Community Achievement Projects in the Schools), has provided funding and oversight for a variety of community-based programs to prevent school failure and promote healthy adolescent development. CAPS matches young people who are likely to drop out of school with local agencies that provide counseling, tutoring, sports programs, and other relevant activities (such as a school newsletter for young Dominicans). When implemented in 1991, it involved 96 schools and 108 community-based organizations. The initiative is viewed by many as a model with important national implications.

In Seattle a number of youth-oriented initiatives have contributed to the city's reputation as a place that provides a positive environment for young people. Seattle's KidsPlace, a community-wide planning and public relations effort, has been adopted by a number of other cities. Seattle voters recently passed an education and human services levy that will provide public financial support for youth services. The city's government, school district, United Way, and corporate community are collaborating with Cities in Schools to coordinate the delivery of education, health, social, and other support services in twenty-five middle and senior high public schools.

San Diego has undertaken reform efforts designed to improve the delivery of education and social services to young people and their families. The city also crafted a statement of residents' beliefs about and visions for children:

We BELIEVE *that the society that we have tomorrow depends on how we nurture, educate and challenge our children today. The love, protection, wisdom and encouragement we invest in our children today will return to us in productive, useful citizens of the future.*

We PLEDGE *to promote the principles of self esteem, self discipline and respect for others, their diverse backgrounds, cultures and family structures. We will devote our energies to building harmonious environments in our homes, schools and city.*

We COMMIT *to reducing institutional barriers that prevent the joining of resources and providing the most effective services to our youth, families and city. A priority for prevention and a focus on the whole child and family will guide our activity.*

We ENCOURAGE *families, citizens, community organizations, schools and government to work together to create positive environments for all children that stimulate love of learning and inspire them to reach their full potential.*

Few cities have prepared such a statement, and yet the development process for this type of declaration can clarify areas of agreement and disagreement, serve as a consensus among diverse constituencies, and encourage ordinary citizens to take actions to serve their communities.

HOW STATES CAN HELP

No matter how diligent or well-meaning, most local communities lack the financial or other resources to plan and sustain comprehensive youth development programs. State and federal support is, therefore, essential to improving this nation's youth programs. In the context of the move toward block grants and federal revenue sharing with states over the past two decades, state policies toward youth development are of prime importance in building and modifying programs and services for adolescents.

For example, Social Services Block Grants, stemming from Title II of the Social Security Act amendments, serve as a funding stream for states to support programs for their low-income populations. These federal funds, supplemented by the states' own money, are in turn allocated to local services providers for their work with this segment of their community.

Recognizing the need to improve their youth programs, some states are now moving beyond their role as allocators of funds to the enactment of legislation that promotes community-based opportunities for youth. For instance:

▶ Some states have now passed community schools legislation that promotes the use of public school facilities during nonschool hours for youth-oriented programs and services;

▶ A handful of states—California, New Jersey, Oregon, Iowa, Kentucky, and Florida in particular—are attempting to foster coordination and collaboration among state agencies, cut down on program fragmentation and overlap, and provide support to low-income communities and school districts through grant programs that call for joint health, social services, and educational initiatives;[51]

▶ Several states have established Offices of Children and Youth in an effort to identify unmet needs of young people and to effect better coordination of youth services; and

▶ At least forty-seven states have taken steps to assist youth in low-income neighborhoods—unfortunately, many of these efforts focus on increasing public awareness of youth problems or address only small segments of the total youth population living in these environments.[52]

One of the most dramatic attempts to improve youth development services is taking place in Oregon. In 1989 Oregon passed legislation that mandated the establishment of state- and county-level youth services commissions to ensure that every child has the opportunity to graduate from high school healthy, literate, and skilled and receives the assistance needed to reach his or her full potential. The commission is responsible for coordinating all community efforts to provide programs and services for children from birth through age eighteen. County-level youth commissions are responsible for planning local services. Oregon's county youth services commissions are now involved in a community action planning process with public and private services providers, and they receive state support for some of those efforts.

The Oregon experiment is noteworthy on several fronts. First, it has quickly translated a state-level mandate into needed action on the local level. Second, communities are ensured some financial support to carry out the programs and services they believe are

needed in their area and, therefore, have an incentive to plan and implement youth-oriented programs. Third, the overall program has been built on the basis of experiences with earlier reform initiatives, such as the former governor's Children's Agenda. Finally, the state has continued to support the initiative, even after a change in state administration.[53]

A similar structure has been in place within New York State's Youth Bureau system for several decades. Comprehensive community-wide planning, combined with a shift in the allocation of resources from a largely rehabilitative to a more balanced approach that emphasizes youth development and primary prevention, has demonstrated many strengths. The Association of New York State Youth Bureaus is currently attempting to effect a national replication of its model, which involves locally administered planning and resource allocation structures that are supported by state policy and funds, through the enactment of federal legislation that would provide formula-based federal aid on an annual basis.[54]

According to the Council of Governors' Policy Advisors, the increase in state-level youth policy and program activity during the past decade has occurred because "the federal government turned to the states to shoulder the major public policy problems facing the nation."[55] At present, no two state initiatives are alike, and no state has realized the goal of a comprehensive, state-wide program—beyond the planning and demonstration project stage.[56] To achieve a comprehensive youth development program, states must first recognize that:

▶ Community initiatives must reach and encourage the participation of all youth—regardless of socioeconomic factors—within a community;

▶ Youth development problems—such as high school drop-out rates, teen pregnancy, substance abuse, lack of job skills, and mental heath problems—are often interrelated and must be addressed simultaneously;

▶ An existing state agency must be designated, or a new agency established, to lead and administer initiatives;

▶ A line item with funds for state staff and activities must be included in the state budget to ensure that stable support is provided for all initiatives—funds for services in low-income neighborhoods can be assembled by combining contributions for agencies that already receive allocations for such programs;

▶ Initiatives for youth in low-income neighborhoods must take local community processes into account;

▶ The legislatively established policies and funding for initiatives should extend beyond the term of any particular governor; and

▶ The capacity to implement programs must be established before programs are developed.[57]

RECOGNIZING THE NEED TO IMPROVE THEIR YOUTH PROGRAMS, SOME STATES ARE NOW MOVING BEYOND THEIR ROLE AS ALLOCATORS OF FUNDS TO THE ENACTMENT OF LEGISLATION THAT PROMOTES COMMUNITY-BASED OPPORTUNITIES FOR YOUTH.

A few communities around the United States are making strong efforts to marshal all available resources, coordinate policies and organizational missions, and aim for the most successful kind of community-wide youth services programs. This approach requires comprehensive planning and continuous coordination. The task force commissioned a study of how three American communities have committed themselves to this high level of effort.[58] (None of these programs focuses exclusively on young adolescents, but all include them.)

PINELLAS COUNTY, FLORIDA

The Juvenile Welfare Board of Pinellas County was established as a result of Juvenile Court Judge Lincoln Bogue's frustration at the lack of alternatives to incarcerating children with adult offenders. The judge persuaded the Florida legislature to create an independent special taxing district in the county that was dedicated to children's services. In November 1946, 80 percent of the county's voters approved formation of the Juvenile Welfare Board (JWB), with its taxing authority.

The voluntary sector was a major force behind the initiative. Led by the Junior League and a local community planning group, the voluntary sector ensured that the initiative was rooted in the community, provided legislative advocacy and public education, and offered a vehicle for channeling local concern about children. Close ties have continued: most JWB contracts are with the voluntary sector. In recent years, JWB's relations with the United Way have grown even stronger than before, which has led to increased emphasis on joint planning.

Today, JWB funds forty-nine community agencies that operate ninety-one programs. It is one of Florida's leading forces for children's services and child advocacy. Five other counties in Florida have created similar taxing districts, and several others are seeking voter approval. Moreover, in 1990 the residents of Pinellas County voted to increase their contributions to JWB from the 0.5 mill of the property assessment established in 1946 to a maximum of 1 mill.

IN 1989 AND 1990 JWB AGENCIES SERVED 75,866 CHILDREN, 94,679 ADULTS, AND 30,442 FAMILIES. THEY TRAIN BETWEEN 10,000 AND 11,000 LOCAL PROGRAM AND AGENCY STAFF MEMBERS EACH YEAR.

JWB'S FOUR BASIC GOALS ARE TO:

▶ Provide early intervention and prevention services—rather than rehabilitative services—to children and their families;

▶ Encourage creative solutions to human services problems, recognizing that risk taking and testing of unconventional strategies are legitimate functions in the search for new, more effective means for meeting human needs—that is, create a service delivery system based on the needs of families, not on institutional or previously established systems;

▶ Offer quality services for children and their families that are planned, implemented, and evaluated by a competent, well-trained staff and committed volunteers—JWB supports this standard even though achieving it may occasionally limit the kind or number of services provided; and

▶ Adopt policies for creating and funding programs that are based on the community's expected twenty-first-century demographics.

TO MEET THESE GOALS, JWB:

▶ Plans and coordinates services for Pinellas County's children and families (community organizations and resources are joined with JWB resources to help support these activities);

▶ Conducts research on topics that relate to children and families and provides social indicator data to the community;

▶ Provides training and enrichment opportunities for human service professionals and maintains a library of books and audiovisual materials;

▶ Contracts with and evaluates numerous social and human services within the county and provides technical support to human service organizations;

▶ Reviews and recommends legislative and public policies and engages in advocacy for children and families; and

▶ Promotes community awareness and understanding of the needs of children and their families.

In 1989 and 1990 JWB agencies served 75,866 children, 94,679 adults, and 30,442 families. They train between 10,000 and 11,000 local program and agency staff members each year. Some problems addressed are adolescent pregnancy, substance abuse, truancy and drop-out rates; family dysfunction, physical abuse and neglect, and adult domestic violence; chronic illness, developmental and physical disabilities, and emotional disorders; sexual offenses and other crimes by youth; employment and training; emergency housing; and runaway youth and youth without permanent homes.

Research and evaluation are essential components of all JWB activities, which sets JWB apart from many community youth initiatives. Research staff members analyze local, state, and national data on children's needs, outcomes, and services. Research information helps in funding decisions and is also made available to interested community members. Every agency that receives funding from JWB must develop a detailed set of outcome objectives and agree to measure its progress toward those objectives.

JWB activities are governed by a board of directors that includes judges of the circuit court, juvenile division, the vice chair of the county commission, the superintendent of public instruction, and five members who are appointed by the governor for four-year terms. The board is supported by a full-time staff.

EFFECTIVENESS OF JWB

Local program directors and service providers report that JWB has done more than merely provide funding; it has enabled new programs to get started and grow and helped existing programs improve and expand their services and lower the ratio of young people to adults.

Moreover, JWB has become the informational focal point and the major advocate for young people in the county, according to persons in the community. And, because of the stability of its funding, JWB has been able to make a long-term commitment to meet the needs of children and families in the county. (The county recently voted to double the tax contribution to JWB.)

Still, JWB has had difficulty obtaining and demonstrating success in, for example, reducing rates of some of the problems of youth that it set out to address. The board's latest funding priorities suggest a trend away from smaller, categorical efforts and toward more comprehensive approaches. The board will be putting more emphasis on local neighborhood development strategies. And additional funds generated by the millage increase will be concentrated on three areas that suggest long-term commit-

ment: providing appropriate, affordable child care; fighting crime and substance abuse; and supporting and strengthening families.

MINNEAPOLIS, MINNESOTA

The Minneapolis Youth Coordinating Board was established in 1986—at the initiative of Mayor Donald Fraser—through a state-authorized agreement among the city board of education, the park and recreation board, the public library, and the county board of commissioners. Founded as a part of the city's twenty-year commitment to children, this intergovernmental organization was promised a five-

> **...BY FOCUSING ON VALUES AND MISSION RATHER THAN EXCLUSIVELY ON PROGRAMS, YCB HAS RAISED AWARENESS OF YOUTH ISSUES, CREATED A COMMON VALUE BASE, AND LAID THE GROUNDWORK FOR A VARIETY OF EFFORTS TO IMPROVE THE LIVES OF CHILDREN AND FAMILIES.**

year tenure during which it was to enhance and promote healthy, comprehensive development of Minneapolis children and youth through collaborative actions with the city's public, private, and nonprofit organizations. The tenure of the Youth Coordinating Board (YCB) has since been extended for an additional five years.

Like JWB, YCB is a governmental entity; unlike JWB, YCB's role is formally limited to coordinating activities of organizations represented on its board. (The purpose of board composition is to amass governmental power, and the voluntary sector has no member on it.) YCB has worked, however, to strengthen relationships between some of its member agencies and the voluntary sector. It has, for example, helped plan and coordinate

its members' funding decisions in making grants or issuing contracts to such voluntary agency programs as prevention of gang involvement and early pregnancy.

AS DEFINED IN A 1990 REPORT TO THE MINNEAPOLIS BOARD OF EDUCATION, YCB'S GOALS ARE TO:

▶ Improve the ability of public agencies to promote the health, safety, education, and development of the community's children and youth;

▶ Create an organizational structure to improve coordination and cooperation among youth-serving agencies and local government bodies; and

▶ Identify and remedy conditions that hinder or prevent the community's youth from becoming healthy, productive members of society.

To achieve these goals, YCB:

▶ Provides a forum in which local elected officials can plan, strategize, and develop policies and programs—collaboratively—to improve the ways in which services are delivered to children and families;

▶ Provides elected officials with the information and resources needed to influence policy development;

▶ Is raising awareness about and advocates for youth issues through a long-term, community-wide planning process; and

▶ Is increasing funding for children and youth programs and services by requiring commitments from participating members and brokering additional funds from public and private sources.

YCB is composed of a twelve-member board of elected officials, including the mayor of Minneapolis; two city council members; two members of the school board; two county commissioners; the park board commissioner; a library board member; the chief judge of the county district court, juvenile division; and chairs of the Minneapolis delegation to the Minnesota house and senate. A four-member core staff, augmented as needed by temporary personnel, supports board activities.

Technically, YCB's function is to meet on a regular basis to discuss and make decisions about youth; however, because each member of YCB also holds a position of leadership with decision-making authority, board members have been highly successful in influencing the child- and youth-related policies, staffing, and funding decisions of the agencies and legislative bodies they represent.

Initially, much of the board's focus was on expanding services for and dealing with problems affecting adolescents in the community. Early on, it took a leadership role in addressing the gang issue, and in the summer of 1989, when a lack of constructive activities for youth threatened to create a crisis, it generated $1 million for fifty-three summer school, employment, and social/recreational programs that served 13,000 young people. For several years, YCB has also sponsored the Minneapolis Youth Organization—a project that attempts to involve young people in public policy, program formation and service activities, and that recognizes youth for their positive contributions to the community. The problems of adolescent pregnancy are also being addressed.

The primary vehicle YCB uses for creating a common value base for its programs is a twenty-year plan, City's Children: 2007, which was developed by the board in cooperation with the community over an eight-month period. Ninety people were selected from Minneapolis's public, private, and community sectors to help develop this plan. And, although youth involvement was minimal and the follow-up process has been limited, there is general agreement that City's Children: 2007 has elevated the importance of youth and has offered a common basis for the discussion of youth issues.

EFFECTIVENESS OF YCB

YCB is now considered one of Minneapolis's most important forces for positive child and youth development. It has successfully developed sound working relationships among high-level individuals concerned with youth development in Minneapolis, although it has been less successful in drawing youth and agency managers into its deliberations.

A willingness to tackle difficult issues has enhanced YCB's credibility. An example was its readiness to address the growing problem of gangs by opening up a broad dialogue on the subject. Indeed, by focusing on values and mission rather

> **BECAUSE EACH MEMBER OF YCB ALSO HOLDS A POSITION OF LEADERSHIP WITH DECISION-MAKING AUTHORITY, BOARD MEMBERS HAVE BEEN HIGHLY SUCCESSFUL IN INFLUENCING THE CHILD- AND YOUTH-RELATED POLICIES, STAFFING, AND FUNDING DECISIONS OF THE AGENCIES AND LEGISLATIVE BODIES THEY REPRESENT.**

than exclusively on programs, YCB has raised awareness of youth issues, created a common value base, and laid the groundwork for a variety of efforts to improve the lives of children and families.

CHICAGO, ILLINOIS

The Chicago Cluster Initiative emerged in 1989 from discussions among leaders from Chicago's public, private, and nonprofit sectors. This partnership among nine Chicago-based public and nonprofit agencies was established to reduce school drop-out rates and failure among disadvantaged inner-city children—two problems that have threatened to create a permanent underclass in the city.

The Cluster Initiative attempts to redeploy existing educational, youth development, and other public services in a more efficient, coordinated way and to engage principals and community leaders in an active process of school reform.

THE PROGRAM HAS SEVEN GOALS:

▶ Help both public and private agencies focus on education as a single, top priority;

▶ Revitalize neighborhoods that have been written off as hopeless;

▶ Encourage collaboration among city agencies;

▶ Coordinate city resources;

▶ Involve the community in change and renewal;

▶ Help students and parents develop a genuine stake in their schools; and

▶ Establish an environment where academic excellence is expected and can be achieved.

The Cluster Initiative will be implemented in four low-income neighborhoods over five years. Two sites serve youth from some of Chicago's largest public housing projects. Most program activities will be conducted at four high schools and their forty feeder schools in these neighborhoods. When fully implemented, the initiative will serve approximately 23,420 fifth- to twelfth-grade students. To date, it is operational at one site, the DuSable High School and elementary and middle schools that feed into it.

Because many of the Cluster Initiative's programs focus on education, efforts are being concentrated on curriculum reforms, faculty development, new teacher recruitment, and attendance rates. Auxiliary programs designed to meet the needs of children and families will include the establishment of study centers in empty apartments in Chicago Housing Authority buildings and the creation of after-school programs.

Local government agencies, school officials, community leaders, community-based organizations and local businesses, and foundation representatives are all participating. The decision-making body for the initiative is a board of trustees, which has the authority to allocate money. Some members serve as program implementers within their own agencies. Local cluster councils direct program development at each site, but most get approval of their plans for school-based programs from Chicago's local school councils (which function as local school boards).

Although the role of the voluntary sector in the Cluster Initiative is still being defined, United Neighborhood Organization and the Chicago Urban League are represented on the board of trustees, primarily as community organizers and not as service providers. The initiative is clearly focused on schools, and how community-based organizations will fit into the effort is not yet totally clear.

The Cluster Initiative received its initial funding from the John D. and Catherine T. MacArthur Foundation and the Chicago Community Trust, which is a community foundation. The agencies represented by board members are providing the other funds required to meet core operating costs. At the end of the initial five-year funding period it is hoped that the Cluster Initiative model will be replicated throughout the city.

As a final note, the Chicago Community Trust's Children, Youth, and Families Initiative is being implemented at two Cluster Initiative sites. Established in 1991, this program is attempting to make Chicago's service system for children more comprehensive, better integrated, more community-based, and more responsive to the needs of families—particularly those with special needs. The trust is prepared to invest $30 million in this program over nine years and expects to develop cooperative partnerships with

PLANNERS FACE THE FORMIDABLE PROBLEMS... THAT PLAGUE DELIVERY OF YOUTH PROGRAMMING IN MOST AMERICAN COMMUNITIES.

government agencies, as well as other foundations and corporations, to reach its goals. The emphasis on partnerships and collaborations is expected to enhance Cluster Initiative programs at the two sites.

LESSONS TO BE LEARNED FROM THE THREE EXAMPLES

Persuading various elements of a community to join in a coordinated plan for youth development is not easy, but the three examples cited suggest that it can be done. Planners face the formidable problems of fragmented services, inequity of availability and access, inadequacy of resources, and inappropriateness of services—problems that plague delivery of youth programming in most American communities.

The three examples reported on here suggest a prescription for overcoming these problems through comprehensive, community-wide planning. This prescription has five elements:

▶ Designated leadership: A permanent planning structure must be in place and it must have responsibility, accountability, visibility, relative stability, and financial and political clout;

▶ Needs assessment: This process identifies unmet needs of youth, preferably by involving youth themselves, as well as parents, service providers, and other community leaders;

▶ Assessment of current services: This process casts a wide net to ensure that a full array of services is examined, again preferably with youth involvement;

▶ Improvement of services: The mismatch between the assessments of needs and of current services must be rectified by action and change. This action may require reallocating existing resources, infusing new resources, strengthening existing services, expanding services to new areas or groups, or developing well-constructed mechanisms to make services more accessible to young people and their families; and

▶ Evaluation: This mechanism should be developed at an early stage in the total planning and implementation cycle, and it should address processes as well as outcomes.

HOW THE FEDERAL GOVERNMENT CAN HELP

The federal government has no coherent policy for youth, despite its many proclamations about the importance of children, youth, and families and its numerous units of government so named. The orientation of federal youth policy, to the extent that it has any orientation, and the majority of federal dollars and technical expertise are aimed at crisis intervention, reme-diation of problems, or control of antisocial and criminal behavior, which usually translates into incarceration or some other level of involvement with the juvenile justice system. Thus, federal programs for youth generally focus on helping or punishing young people who are already in trouble, not on helping them keep out of it.

But healthy youth development has a different focus. It strives to help young people develop the inner resources and skills they need to cope with pressures that might lead them into unhealthy and antisocial behaviors. It aims to promote and prevent, not to treat or remediate. Prevention of undesirable behaviors is one outcome of healthy youth development, but there are others: the production of self-reliant, self-confident adults who can take their place as responsible members of society.

A 1990 General Accounting Office (GAO) report to the U.S. House of Representatives Select Committee on Children, Youth, and Families indicated that, although GAO had produced more than 250 reports, had testified, and had undertaken a number of assignments and other activities related to children from birth through age eighteen in the preceding decade, not one of these efforts was concentrated on youth development. While the scope of the activities described in the report was broad, there was a decided emphasis on the treatment of problem behavior and on a categorical approach to addressing these problems.[59] Moreover, the U.S. Department of Agriculture is the only federal agency that uses the term "youth development" with any regularity; it frequently, although unofficially, cites the 4-H program (which is funded primarily by federal, state, and county government funds) as the "4-H Youth Development Program."

In recent years, programs provided through the Office for Substance Abuse Prevention (particularly its High-Risk Youth and Community Partnership Programs), the Centers for Disease Control's Division of Adolescent and School Health, and the Office of Juvenile Justice and Delinquency Prevention have begun to support efforts to prevent problem behaviors among youth and have therefore become reasonable sources of funding support for some youth development efforts. These few programs do not even begin, however, to meet the wide variety of needs of this nation's youth.

In short, the gap in federal support reflects three factors: an orientation toward pathology rather than health, a categorical approach to youth issues rather than a comprehensive one, and inadequate attention to and resources for youth programs.

In 1989 Congress began to address at least some of these problems when it passed the Young Americans Act. Designed to establish a national youth policy, this legislation declares that "children and youth are inherently our most valuable resource" and that "they deserve love, respect, and guidance as well as good health, shelter, food, education, productive work, and preparation for responsible community life."

To fulfill these goals, the act:

▶ Formally establishes the Administration for Children, Youth, and Families within the U.S. Department of Health and Human Services;

▶ Establishes the Federal Council on Children, Youth, and Families, which is charged with the responsibility of advising the president and Congress on matters related to the special needs of young Americans;

▶ Authorizes grants to states for state and community programs for children, youth, and families; and

▶ Authorizes grants to states for supportive services that demonstrate methods of filling service gaps identified during the planning and advocacy process.

The Young Americans Act is a solid basis for national youth policy. Unfortunately, Congress has not as yet appropriated any funds for its implementation. If funded at an adequate level, this legislation could accomplish what its authors originally intended: it could generate a national consensus on basic youth-related issues, and it could provide a floor of support for community-based services for children and youth, just as the 1965 Older Americans Act served to upgrade both policies and programs for older adults. When compared to the annual appropriation of more than $1 billion to support the activities of the Older Americans Act, the initial $30 million authorization for the Young Americans Act can hardly be considered extravagant. Action is needed to make this money available for implementation of the vital underpinning of American youth policy.

While the Young Americans Act provides a vital step forward in building the infrastructure needed to plan, coordinate, and implement effective youth development services at the national level and in all fifty states, unless substantially amended it will not allocate the level of new financial resources needed to support youth development services delivery at the local level. New proposals that illustrate ways to accomplish this step are under development in Washington and are worthy of serious consideration.

One such proposal calls for the initiation of a program of youth development block grants, which would channel federal resources to local communities; at least some of these resources would focus on young adolescents and on service to youth in low-income areas. Exemplary features of the youth development block grants include requirements that communities assess youth needs, examine current services, identify service gaps, and establish priorities for expanded services; targeting of some resources to underserved low-income areas; allowance for expenditures on staff and volunteer training; and realistic accountability requirements. As currently envisioned, this proposal calls for an expenditure level of $2 billion, with most of the money being reallocated from existing federal programs. The youth development block grant proposal would also underwrite the costs of operating the Youth Development Information Center. Established in 1988 but never fully funded, this center is intended to serve

CROSS-NATIONAL PERSPECTIVES ON THE PROMOTION OF YOUTH DEVELOPMENT

Cross-national perspectives can sharpen the focus on youth development in this country by providing alternative views of public and social policy, systems of services, and specific programs. The Task Force on Youth Development and Community Programs commissioned a study of cross-national perspectives in an effort to learn from the experience of selected countries, focusing on the most transferable lessons and models.[60]

The study examined youth policies and programs of the United Kingdom, Australia, Germany, Sweden, and Norway, with a view toward providing examples that could be informative for youth policy development in the United States. One major finding was that the content of youth policies and programs in the five countries studied tends to be *developmental, broadly based, inclusive, and participatory*. In contrast, U.S. youth policy is more oriented toward remediation of individual difficulties than broad development and socialization. A second major finding is that the national governments have identified youth development as a broad public responsibility, have established legal and organizational structures for carrying out that responsibility, and have appropriated significant funds on a stable basis to carry out youth policies and programs. In some countries, federal funding did not provide the majority support, but it was substantial enough to leverage local and voluntary resources and to create youth service partnerships guided by federal policy but adapted and implemented by local actors, both public and voluntary.

Although the voluntary sector in the United States is vibrant, it is largely independent of the public sector in terms of overall planning and coordination. This situation poses a sharp contrast to all of the countries examined—countries in which youth policies involve explicit public-voluntary cooperation and coordination to an extent that is unknown in the United States. This coordination occurs through both law and organizational structure. In each of the five countries studied, and in many other European nations, local youth boards are charged with implementing or overseeing public and voluntary youth services. Generally, these local bodies also provide significant financial support.

Another factor that differentiates the United States from other countries is the lack of a national perspective on, and system for, preparation of youth-work professionals. The United Kingdom, Germany, and Sweden in particular offer rich models for pre- and in-service education that address such issues as career ladders, adequate compensation, and other forms of professional recognition.

Research on youth issues represents another lesson that Americans might learn from their international colleagues. While research dollars in the United States are directed toward studies of youth problems, virtually no funding—public or private—is oriented toward youth development or community-based youth organizations. Researcher Michael Sherraden notes that:

"It would be difficult to overstate the problem. A researcher working in an urban area, for example, can more easily obtain a million dollars to study youth purse snatching than a thousand dollars to study youth theater and dance groups. This is a misallocation of research dollars. Unfortunately, it becomes a vicious circle—the more we study problems, the more we spend on problems; and the less we study solutions, the less we spend on solutions."[61]

With the Youth Education Studies Centre in Australia as a model, the United States should place far greater emphasis on studying ordinary youth development and successful youth services at the community level. Also noteworthy is the urgency of developing better information networks among youth work practitioners and researchers, including the need for the types of youth service magazines and journals that are available in several other countries.

Although discussion of youth development from a cross-national perspective provides many instructive lessons, perhaps the most elucidating aspect involves what is missing from current U.S. policy. And what is missing *is* a national policy on youth, particularly on positive youth development. One has only to read about the British Youth Service, an organized comprehensive system for implementing youth policy, built on a foundation of local youth clubs; or to learn of Australia's Office of Youth Affairs, which was established by the commonwealth government in 1977 in response to a federally sponsored study on youth issues; or to recognize that Germany's system of youth services, including its Federal Ministry of Youth, rests on national legislation (the Federal Youth Welfare Act) that was passed in 1922, to understand what national youth policy really looks like.

Sherraden concludes that, "Overall, U.S. youth services are less planned, less coordinated, less public, less funded, less egalitarian, less comprehensive, and less developmental"[62] than those in the other nations cited in his report.

A MATTER OF TIME

110

as a resource to the federally supported youth programs of the Cooperative Extension Service, including 4-H, as well as to other youth organizations. With additional funding from the youth development block grant legislation or through the Extension Service's annual appropriation, this center could collect and disseminate information about public- and private-sector program services, program curricula, professional contacts (consultants and experts on specific topics), funding, research, evaluation, and advocacy.

Two other current proposals also illustrate the more constructive approach to youth policy that the task force advocates. The Youth Development Act of 1992 calls for the allocation of new resources for developmentally oriented local programs for young adolescents. The legislation would authorize initial (1993) expenditures of $25 million for each of four program areas: educational performance, health and fitness, life skills, and family relationships. Although the $100 million of proposed first-year expenditures is not adequate to meet current demand, the legislation calls for "such sums as may be necessary for fiscal years 1994 and 1995."

The proposed Comprehensive Services for Youth Act of 1992 would make grants to community partnerships consisting of schools, health agencies, and community-based organizations for the purpose of expanding the delivery of "comprehensive education, health, and social services to improve school performance and future potential of at-risk youth." The legislation would also make grants to local and statewide consortia with a demonstrated commitment to the coordinated delivery of comprehensive services to in-school and out-of-school youth.

With the Young Americans Act, the federal government has taken its first steps toward improving support for youth development; however, the United States has much work to do before its youth policies are on a par with those of its international colleagues. Both short- and long-term strategies are needed to move American youth policy from piecemeal to comprehensive, from negative to positive, and from parsimonious to generous.

WITH THE YOUNG AMERICANS ACT, THE FEDERAL GOVERNMENT HAS TAKEN ITS FIRST STEPS TOWARD IMPROVING SUPPORT FOR YOUTH DEVELOPMENT; HOWEVER, THE UNITED STATES HAS MUCH WORK TO DO BEFORE ITS YOUTH POLICIES ARE ON A PAR WITH THOSE OF ITS INTERNATIONAL COLLEAGUES.

BUILDING A NETWORK
OF SUPPORTIVE SERVICES

Every level of government, every adult, and nearly every for-profit and nonprofit organization in this country has a role to play in the development of community-level support services for young adolescents. For some, their role involves research or program evaluation. For others it is program design, leadership, or participation—either on a paid or volunteer basis—or youth advocacy. For still others it is financial support.

WORKING TOGETHER TO PROMOTE YOUTH DEVELOPMENT

THE TASK FORCE PRESENTS IN THIS REPORT ITS VISION OF A COMMUNITY-WIDE NETWORK OF SUPPORTIVE SERVICES FOR YOUNG ADOLESCENTS. TO REALIZE THIS VISION, ALL SECTORS OF SOCIETY, INCLUDING THOSE THAT CURRENTLY APPEAR TO BE QUITE DISTANT FROM THE WORK OF PROMOTING HEALTHY ADOLESCENT DEVELOPMENT, HAVE IMPORTANT ROLES TO PLAY AND CONTRIBUTIONS TO MAKE.

The task force urges all concerned about young adolescents—national youth organizations, other community organizations, schools, parents and families, health organizations, higher education institutions, research and evaluation organizations, funders (including businesses and corporate philanthropies), media, government leadership, and young adolescents themselves—to join forces in developing sturdy mechanisms designed to achieve long-term and constructive social change that can benefit all Americans by serving the nation's twenty million young adolescents.

NATIONAL YOUTH ORGANIZATIONS

Because of their extensive resources and reach, national youth organizations are in a unique position to expand their work with young adolescents, particularly those living in poor neighborhoods. The task force calls on all of America's national youth organizations, and especially the twenty major groups in its study, to consider seriously at the national board and staff levels the recommendations outlined in Section One of Part III.

Separately, these groups should examine their current delivery systems and design strategic plans that will enable them to extend and deepen greatly their reach to the young people who most need their services. Together, these organizations should strengthen current efforts by engaging in joint planning, sharing training resources, conducting joint evaluations, and collaborating in advocacy activities.

Other priorities for national youth organizations include improving data about the populations they are currently serving and perhaps creating a uniform data system; investing in staff development, with a particular focus on increasing the skills of paid and volunteer staff in working with diverse populations; and increasing active youth participation in organizational governance and decision making at both local and national levels.

OTHER COMMUNITY ORGANIZATIONS

Many other types of community organizations—including grassroots independent youth agencies, religious institutions, adult service clubs, senior citizens groups, sports organizations, museums, libraries, and parks and recreation departments—currently sponsor some programs for youth. A key task force finding is that many of these institutions are failing to reach young adolescents in poverty areas.

These groups represent many strengths, including considerable potential to expand their current efforts. Such expansion should not occur in a vacuum; rather, community programs for youth—regardless of sponsorship—should view themselves as part of a services network and engage in joint planning and coordination at the local and national levels. Whether they are new or expanding efforts, such networks should take an inclusive approach, enlisting the participation of both established and emerging organizations. They should also take a systematic approach, gathering and using reliable information, including the views of youth, in their planning processes.

As a first step, these networks should examine ways to realign and reconfigure existing resources; a subsequent step may well involve generating new resources to meet identified needs. Community-wide planning efforts should address issues of staff development, drawing on one another's demonstrated strengths and abilities in expanding available training efforts; access to services for *all* adolescents, examining relevant factors such as program location, transportation, and fees; and active youth involvement at all levels of the planning process.

As part of these collective efforts, boards of directors of individual agencies should make policy decisions about strategic directions (especially about program content and target populations), resource allocation, and long-term commitments. Board members should work with staff to elicit the best available information on which to base these decisions.

SCHOOLS

Youth programs and organizations can reach out to schools as partners in youth development. Schools and educators can activate and solidify such partnerships.

Schools should work with community agencies to construct a unified system of youth development, a joint enterprise that recognizes the common goals of schools and community agencies while respecting their inherent differences and strengths. Such a system should involve joint planning and decision making; build on existing institutional and organizational resources; and devote financial and human resources to assess needs, identify service gaps, improve access to and coordination of current resources, and provide new services as required. In this effective system, schools should communicate high expectations for students' use of out-of-school time and should assist them in making constructive choices.

PARENTS AND FAMILIES

Like schools, parents and families can help young adolescents make wise choices about constructive use of nonschool time. Parents and families can encourage participation in youth development activities by seeking information about community programs; volunteering in youth organizations as leaders, board members, or fund-raisers; providing feedback to the organizations on the quality of their services; acting as advocates for youth needs (of their own children and others) in community forums; and participating in parent-family components of youth organizations, including parent education workshops and recognition events.

HEALTH ORGANIZATIONS

Public and private health and mental health agencies should work as partners with youth organizations to increase adolescents' access to health information and services. Health and mental health organizations can help youth organizations enrich their current health and fitness programs. Working together, health and youth organizations can sponsor joint programs, develop and implement mutual referral systems, team up as advocates for youth, and cooperate on staff development activities. In addition, health and mental health organizations—including health clinics and community mental health agencies—can themselves provide community-based programs for youth, such as group activities, individual support and counseling, and parent education workshops.

HIGHER EDUCATION INSTITUTIONS

Community colleges, four-year colleges, and universities have much to contribute to, and gain from, partnerships with community programs for youth. Higher education institutions should collaborate with community programs to enhance the knowledge base from which these programs operate; increase their accountability, especially through more systematic and rigorous evaluation; strengthen pre- and in-service training efforts for youth workers and volunteers; and conduct joint programs that directly serve youth.

From a research perspective, faculty at higher education institutions can conduct relevant research that can be applied to youth development programs; assist community programs in designing theory-based interventions; convene forums for researchers and practitioners to join forces in developing data-based plans for service delivery improvement; and inform new publics (particularly the education, research, and policy communities) about the actual and potential contributions of supportive services for adolescents.

Institutions of higher education can also strengthen youth-work practice by helping design and conduct program evaluations within youth organizations. In the most effective models, university-based researchers see themselves as teammates in this process and take the time to familiarize themselves with the strengths, needs, and constraints of the setting before recommending any particular evaluation approach.

Faculty members at colleges and universities can contribute new information and approaches to youth organizations' staff development efforts at both the national and local levels. Training workshops can offer an interactive vehicle that allows youth-work practitioners to stay abreast of current research and theories about adolescent development, while enabling university staff to learn more about the contemporary experiences of youth from those who work with them on a regular basis. In addition, colleges and universities have an important role to play in preparing youth workers for jobs and careers in youth development. Schools of social work, academic departments of human development and leisure and recreation, and schools of theology and public health can actively promote youth work as a viable career option and incorporate academic content that focuses on normal adolescent development and group facilitation skills. Schools of education can prepare teachers and school administrators to work collaboratively with community-based organizations to promote positive youth development.

Colleges and universities can also conduct joint programs with youth organizations that encourage mentoring and other forms of community service among college students, that provide academic enrichment programs for young adolescents, and that offer young people opportunities to explore future college attendance by visiting campuses, meeting slightly older peers, and learning about admissions processes and financial aid.

RESEARCH AND EVALUATION ORGANIZATIONS

Research organizations that specialize in social science research can help youth organizations improve and expand their current services. Such nonprofit groups as the Manpower Development Research Corporation, High/Scope Educational Research Foundation, and Public/Private Ventures, which conduct systematic evaluations of national demonstration programs, should expand their current efforts by forming partnerships with national youth organizations around program development and evaluation. Similarly, such intermediary organizations as the Education Development

COLLEGES AND UNIVERSITIES CAN ALSO CONDUCT JOINT PROGRAMS WITH YOUTH ORGANIZATIONS THAT ENCOURAGE MENTORING AND OTHER FORMS OF COMMUNITY SERVICE AMONG COLLEGE STUDENTS, THAT PROVIDE ACADEMIC ENRICHMENT PROGRAMS FOR YOUNG ADOLESCENTS, AND THAT OFFER YOUNG PEOPLE OPPORTUNITIES TO EXPLORE FUTURE COLLEGE ATTENDANCE BY VISITING CAMPUSES, MEETING SLIGHTLY OLDER PEERS, AND LEARNING ABOUT ADMISSIONS PROCESSES AND FINANCIAL AID.

Center, Milton S. Eisenhower Foundation, and Center for Youth Development and Policy Research of the Academy for Educational Development have key roles to play in helping community organizations strengthen the conceptual base of their youth programming and in providing training and technical support for these efforts.

FUNDERS

Funders have a critical function in addressing many of the challenges facing the youth development sector, including those of strengthening and stabilizing the funding base for youth development programs and services; moving from categorical (problem-specific) funding to core support for youth development; adding public dollars to private funds that currently support youth development services; targeting new resources to low-income neighborhoods; and establishing funding priorities that focus on professional development of youth workers, outcome evaluations of youth development programs, replication of proven programs, and advocacy with and on behalf of youth.

The task force urges local United Ways and other federated campaigns, community foundations, national foundations, corporations and other businesses, and government to work not only individually but also collectively—with one another and with service providers—to expand their roles and make long-term commitments to the work of youth development.

MEDIA

The task force urges all media to join with other sectors of society in expanding opportunities for young people to serve as resources for their communities by developing creative ways to integrate the voices of youth into their publications and programs. The media—television, radio, magazines, newspapers, and films—can and should be one of this nation's strongest forces for improving and expanding public understanding of youth services. Public opinion is often shaped by what Americans see, read, or hear through the media. Equally important, public opinion is also affected by the willingness of elected officials and community leaders to make youth a priority.

The media can further youth development in four ways: through expanded coverage of youth activities and legislative and programmatic efforts designed to support adolescents; through increased publication or broadcasts of editorial opinions, news stories, and videos written or produced by young people; through programs that feature young adults in new anchor

THE TASK FORCE URGES ALL MEDIA TO JOIN WITH OTHER SECTORS OF SOCIETY IN EXPANDING OPPORTUNITIES FOR YOUNG PEOPLE TO SERVE AS RESOURCES FOR THEIR COMMUNITIES BY DEVELOPING CREATIVE WAYS TO INTEGRATE THE VOICES OF YOUTH INTO THEIR PUBLICATIONS AND PROGRAMS.

roles—such as the show "In the Mix," which is produced by WNYC-TV, New York City's public television station; and by expanding the use of media to publicize youth services directly to young audiences and their families.

GOVERNMENT LEADERSHIP

Local, state, and federal policies play a critical role in supporting or failing to support healthy adolescent development. Although young people grow and develop in the immediate context of their families and communities, the ability of these direct influences to fulfill their nurturing and guiding responsibilities rests in no small measure on indirect, often hidden, policy decisions.

Ideal public policies would be integrated at the local, state, and federal levels; focus on increasing support for basic youth development services; target services to areas of greatest need; give priority to locally generated solutions; and energetically support and nurture local association and involvement, avoiding centralized control. All elements of such a system would be built on the best current knowledge—knowledge of principles of youth development, intervention techniques, social change, and community problem solving.

Local governments should develop public policy that articulates citizens' beliefs about, and vision for, the children and youth in their communities. This basic public policy, which should spell out the rights and responsibilities of adults and children, can then serve as a blueprint for future community action directed toward improving conditions for children and youth. Local governments should also take the lead in convening community-wide planning bodies that work to improve direct service delivery for children and youth and should generate or allocate needed financial resources to support youth development. The role of local governments is enhanced by the designation of strong staff leadership, such as a commission for children and youth, whose role and responsibilities would involve coordination and facilitation of services for all of the community's young people, including its young adolescents.

State governments should contribute to positive youth development efforts at the local level by monitoring and using existing federal vehicles that provide local youth development funding; establishing their own initiatives to coordinate education, health, and social services; allocating or generating new resources to support community youth development programs; and targeting new and reallocated resources to low-income areas. Although strengthening school-based services is one important effort that states can undertake, it is

AMERICANS HAVE LET THEIR COMMUNITY SUPPORTS FOR YOUTH FALL INTO DISREPAIR. IT IS TIME TO START THE TASK OF REBUILDING. THE EMPHASIS SHOULD BE ON THE HUMANIZING QUALITIES OF COMMUNITY, AND NOTABLY, THEIR EFFECTS ON THE NEXT GENERATION. THAT UNDERTAKING IS THE FOCUS OF THIS REPORT.

important for them to pay concerted attention to other community-based approaches as well. States should foster the development of local community planning processes that include both public and private service providers and should offer technical and some financial assistance for planning and coordination efforts as well as for direct services.

On the federal level, both macro-level public policies (dealing with such issues as employment, poverty, housing, health, education, and civil rights) and specific youth development policies contribute to the climate of improvement or deterioration of adolescent well-being. The federal government currently shows little commitment to the promotion of positive youth development, either from a policy and leadership perspective or from a legislative and funding point of view. Over the short term, the federal government should formulate an explicit policy that defines the nation's commitment to children and youth and that spells out the federal role in honoring that commitment. As a second step, the federal government should allocate public resources to supplement the already considerable but clearly inadequate private support for youth development services nationwide, with a focus on expansion of services in poverty areas. Furthermore, federal policy should encourage and enable communities to take a more comprehensive approach to the provision of health and social services for adolescents by modifying eligibility requirements within existing federal programs to allow for the use of categorical funds for comprehensive services.

Finally, the strong traditional federal role of providing equal access to impartial information should be extended to the field of youth development. Although the federal government sponsors clearinghouses on alcohol and other drug abuse, on child abuse, and on a host of other problem behaviors, it has only recently—and in a very limited fashion—established a Youth Development Information Center. Expansion of that effort could address an important, documented national need for a permanent information source that is available to all.

These short-term solutions, if fully funded and conscientiously implemented, could pave the road toward more solid long-term change that would recognize young adolescents as a true national resource, ripe for development and with the potential to enrich the entire country with each succeeding generation.

YOUNG ADOLESCENTS

Young adolescents will leap at the opportunity to design their own activities for nonschool hours, and their ideas for programs will contribute much to their own healthy development.

Young people should also be called on to serve their communities. The task force believes that they will answer that call. With appropriate adult supervision, young people can develop their own expressions of community service and action such as tutoring their peers and younger children, implementing substance abuse prevention campaigns, conducting surveys of teen needs, and registering voters. Neighborhood and municipal leaders should look on young adolescents as a valuable asset. And young people should be encouraged to seize these and other opportunities to contribute to their own healthy development as well as to community betterment.

A TIME FOR ACTION

Americans have let their community supports for youth fall into disrepair. It is time to start the task of rebuilding. The emphasis should be on the humanizing qualities of community and, notably, their effects on the next generation. That undertaking is the focus of this report.

All sectors of society will be needed to bring about the new understanding and appreciation of young adolescents that the task force advocates. Understanding and appreciation must lead to action. Previous reports of the Carnegie Council on Adolescent Development have focused attention on the urgent need to transform middle-grade schools to improve education for all young adolescents and to step up efforts to promote their physical and mental health. In this report, the task force extends this youth-centered agenda by advocating a new national effort to make use of nonschool hours for the vast and important job of promoting development among American youth, thus preparing them for their own and the country's future.

It is time to end the costly and senseless cycle of despair for so many young people that begins with an early life in neighborhoods with substandard schools, little or no medical care, and few supportive and healthy activities during the nonschool hours. As a result, young people will not be able to cope with the demands of the contemporary American workplace, the demands of citizenship, family, and parenthood—the demands of life itself. All young adolescents deserve a full and fair chance to pursue a better destiny. It is time for action.

N O T E S

EXECUTIVE SUMMARY

1. Dryfoos, J. (1990). *Adolescents at risk: Prevalence and prevention*. New York: Oxford University Press.

2. Ianni, F. A. J. (1990). *The search for structure*. New York: The Free Press.

3. Csikszentmihalyi, M., & Larson, R. (1984). *Being adolescent: Conflict and growth in the teenage years* (p. 63). New York: Basic Books.
   Medrich, E. A., & Marzke, C. (1991). *Young adolescents and discretionary time use: The nature of life outside school* (p. 14). Unpublished manuscript prepared for the Carnegie Council on Adolescent Development, Washington, DC.
   Timmer, S. G., Eccles, J., & O'Brien, I. (1985). How children use time. In F. T. Juster and F. B. Stafford (Eds.), *Time, goods and well-being*. Ann Arbor: University of Michigan, Institute for Social Research.

4. U.S. Department of Education, Office of Educational Research and Improvement, National Center for Education Statistics. (1990). *National education longitudinal study of 1988: A profile of the American eighth grader* (pp. 50–54). Washington, DC: U.S. Government Printing Office.

5. Ibid., p. 55.

6. Ibid.

PART I

1. U.S. Bureau of the Census. (1990). Washington, DC: U.S. Government Printing Office.

2. U.S. Bureau of the Census. (1990). *Age, sex, race and Hispanic origin information from the 1990 Census: A comparison of Census results with results where age and race have been modified* (CPH-L-74). Washington, DC: U.S. Government Printing Office. The reader should note that the categories of race and ethnicity currently used by the U.S. Bureau of the Census may not reflect how individuals choose to identify themselves. Rounding errors account for the fact that these figures do not total 100 percent.

3. Children's Defense Fund. (1991). *The state of America's children, 1991* (p. 143). Washington, DC: Author.

4. Adolescents surveyed about health issues. (Spring 1989). *Family Life Educator, 7*(3), 16.

5. Carnegie Council on Adolescent Development. (1989). *Turning points: Preparing American youth for the 21st century*. Report of the Task Force on Education of Young Adolescents. Washington, DC: Author.

6. National Center for Health Statistics. (1991). *Data from the National Survey of Family Growth* (Series 23). Washington, DC: U.S. Department of Health and Human Services, Public Health Service, Centers for Disease Control.

7. Planned Parenthood Federation of America. (1986). *American teens speak: Sex, myths, TV, and birth control* (The Planned Parenthood Poll by Louis Harris and Associates). New York: Author.

8. National Institutes on Allergies and Infectious Disease Study Group. (1980). *Sexually transmitted diseases—Summary and recommendations*. Washington, DC: U.S. Department of Health, Education, and Welfare, National Institutes of Health.

9. Dryfoos, J. (1990). *Adolescents at risk: Prevalence and prevention*. New York: Oxford University Press.

National Commission on Children. (1991). *Beyond rhetoric: A new American agenda for children and families*. Washington, DC: Author.

Children's Defense Fund. (1991). *The state of America's children, 1991*. Washington, DC: Author.

10. Johnston, L. D., O'Malley, P. M., & Bachman, J. G. (1991). *Drug use among American high school seniors, college students, and young adults 1975–1991: Vol. I: High school seniors* (pp. 40–45). Washington, DC: U.S. Department of Health and Human Services, National Institute on Drug Abuse.

11. Timmer, S. G., Eccles, J., & O'Brien, I. (1985). How children use time. In F. T. Juster and F. B. Stafford (Eds.), *Time, goods and well-being*. Ann Arbor: University of Michigan, Institute for Social Research.

Medrich, E. A., & Marzke, C. (1991). *Young adolescents and discretionary time use: The nature of life outside school* (p. 14). Unpublished manuscript prepared for the Carnegie Council on Adolescent Development, Washington, DC.

Csikszentmihalyi, M., & Larson, R. (1984). *Being adolescent: Conflict and growth in the teenage years* (p. 63). New York: Basic Books.

12. Dryfoos, J. (1990). *Adolescents at risk: Prevalence and prevention*. New York: Oxford University Press.

13. U.S. Department of Education, Office of Educational Research and Improvement, National Center for Education Statistics. (1990). *National education longitudinal study of 1988: A profile of the American eighth grader*. Washington, DC: U.S. Government Printing Office.

14. These vignettes are based on composites of focus group interviews conducted for the Carnegie Council by staff of S. W. Morris & Company, a social marketing research firm based in Bethesda, MD. Vignettes were written by Janice Lynch.

15. Children's hours. (1991, March 24). *The New York Times*.

16. The following sections on adolescent time use draw heavily on Medrich, E. A., & Marzke, C. (1991). *Young adolescents and discretionary time use: The nature of life outside school*. Unpublished manuscript prepared for the Carnegie Council on Adolescent Development, Washington, DC.

17. Csikszentmihalyi, M., & Larson, R. (1984). *Being adolescent: Conflict and growth in the teenage years* (p. 73). New York: Basic Books.

18. Greenberger, E., & Steinberg, L. (1986). *When teenagers work: The psychological and social costs of adolescent employment*. New York: Basic Books.

19. Medrich, E. A., & Marzke, C. (1991). *Young adolescents and discretionary time use: The nature of life outside school*. Unpublished manuscript prepared for the Carnegie Council on Adolescent Development, Washington, DC.

20. U.S. Department of Education, Office of Educational Research and Improvement, National Center for Education Statistics. (1990). *National education longitudinal study of 1988: A profile of the American eighth grader*. Washington, DC: U.S. Government Printing Office.

21. Timmer, S. G., Eccles, J., & O'Brien, I. (1985). How children use time. In F. T. Juster and F. B. Stafford (Eds.), *Time, goods and well-being*. Ann Arbor: University of Michigan, Institute for Social Research.

22. U.S. Department of Education, Office of Educational Research and Improvement, National Center for Education Statistics. (1990). *National education longitudinal study of 1988: A profile of the American eighth grader*. Washington, DC: U.S. Government Printing Office.

23. Zelnik, M., & Kantner, J. F. (1977). Sexual and contraceptive experience of young unmarried women in the United States, 1976 and 1971. *Family Planning Perspectives, 9*, 55–71.

24. Richardson, J. L., Dwyer, K., Hansen, W. B., Dent, C., Johnson, C. A., Sussman, S. Y., Brannon, B., & Flag, B. (1989). Substance use among eighth-grade students who take care of themselves after school. *Pediatrics, 84*(3), 556–566.

25. Marx, F. (1989). *After school programs for young adolescents: Overview and program profiles*. Wellesley, MA: Wellesley College Center for Research on Women.

Steinberg, L. (1986). Latchkey children and susceptibility to peer pressure: An ecological analysis. *Developmental Psychology, 22*(4), 433–439.

26. Clark, R. M. (1988). *Critical factors in why disadvantaged students succeed or fail in school*. New York: Academy for Educational Development.

27. Bergstrom, J. M. (1990). *School's out: Resources for your child's time*. Berkeley, CA: Ten Speed Press.

28. Independent Sector. (1990). *Volunteering and giving among American teenagers 14 to 17 years of age: Findings from a national survey*. Washington, DC: Author.

29. National Crime Prevention Council. (1990). *Changing perspectives: Youth as resources*. Washington, DC: Author.

30. This section of the report draws heavily on a 1991 paper by Karen Pittman and Marlene Wright, entitled *A rationale for enhancing the role of the non-school voluntary sector in youth development*. Unpublished manuscript prepared for the Carnegie Council on Adolescent Development, Washington, DC.

31. Bronfenbrenner, U. (1979). *The ecology of human development: Experiments by nature and design*. Boston: Harvard University Press.

32. Benson, P. L. (1990). *The troubled journey: A portrait of 6th–12th grade youth*. Minneapolis: Lutheran Brotherhood.

33. Bogenschneider, K., Small, S., & Riley, D. (1990, September). *An ecological risk-focused approach for addressing youth-at-risk issues*. Paper presented at the Youth-at-Risk Summit of the National Extension Service, Washington, DC.

34. Benard, B. (1991). *Fostering resiliency in kids: Protective factors in the family, school and community* (pp. 18–19). Portland, OR: Northwest Regional Educational Laboratories, Western Regional Center for Drug-Free Schools and Communities.

35. Wynn, J., Richman, H., Rubenstein, R. A., & Littell, J. (1987). *Communities and adolescents: An exploration of reciprocal supports*. Chicago: University of Chicago, Chapin Hall Center for Children. Paper prepared for the William T. Grant Foundation Commission on Work, Family and Citizenship.

36. Clark, R. M. (1988). *Critical factors in why disadvantaged students succeed or fail in school*. New York: Academy for Educational Development.

37. Lipsitz, J. S. (1986). *After school: Young adolescents on their own*. Carrboro, NC: University of North Carolina at Chapel Hill, Center for Early Adolescence.

Sarason, S. S. (1982). *The culture of the school: The problems of change* (2nd ed.). Boston: Allyn and Bacon.

Raizen, S. (1989). *Reforming education for work: A cognitive science perspective*. Berkeley, CA: National Center for Research in Vocational Education.

38. Pittman, K., & Wright, M. (1991). *A rationale for enhancing the role of the non-school voluntary sector in youth development*. Unpublished manuscript prepared for the Carnegie Council on Adolescent Development, Washington, DC.

39. National Association of Elementary School Principals. (1988). *NAESP principals' opinion survey: Before- and after-school child care*. Alexandria, VA: Author.

40. Hedin, D., et al. (1986). *Summary of the family's view of after-school time* (p. 7). Minneapolis: University of Minnesota.

41. Ladewig, H., & Thomas, J. K. (1987). *Assessing the impact of 4-H on former members*. College Station, TX: Texas A&M University System.

42. Allen, J. P., & Philliber, S. (1991). *Process evaluation of the Teen Outreach Program: Characteristics related to program success in preventing school dropout and teen pregnancy in year 5 (1988–89 school year)*. New York: Association of Junior Leagues International.

43. Girls Incorporated. (1991). *Truth, trust and technology: New research on preventing adolescent pregnancy*. New York: Author.

44. WAVE, Inc. (1991). *Summary of the first year of WAVE*. Washington, DC: Author.

45. Boys and Girls Clubs of America. (1991, March). *The effects of Boys and Girls Clubs on alcohol and other drug use and related problems in public housing projects*. A demonstration study sponsored by the Office for Substance Abuse Prevention. New York: Author.

1. This summary of views of youth draws heavily on focus group discussions with young adolescents conducted for the Carnegie Council by S. W. Morris & Company, a social marketing research firm based in Bethesda, MD. Its full report to the task force, entitled *What young adolescents want and need from out-of-school programs*, is available from the Carnegie Council on Adolescent Development.

2. National Collaboration for Youth. (1990). *Making the grade: A report card on American youth—report on the nationwide project* (p. 1). Washington, DC: Author.

3. This study builds on a small but important body of professional literature over the past two decades that has sought to document and analyze particular aspects of the work of youth organizations. At least two earlier studies sought to document the work of some youth organizations: (1) Hanson, R. F., & Carlson, R. E. (1972). *Organizations for children and youth.* Englewood Cliffs, NJ: Prentice-Hall; and (2) James, D. (1979). *Description study of selected national youth serving organizations.* Washington, DC: U.S. Department of Agriculture, Science and Education Administration/Extension.

The research of sociologist Judith Erickson over the past twenty-five years has contributed greatly to our appreciation of the rich history and traditions of the country's mainline agencies as well as to our understanding of their basic organization, structure, and functioning. See, for example, (1) Erickson, J. B. (1986). Non-formal education in organizations for American youth. *Children Today, 15*(1), 17–25; and (2) Erickson, J. B. (1991). *1992–1993 Directory of American youth organizations* (4th ed.). Minneapolis: Free Spirit Publishing.

Three reports—two published in the early 1980s that examined the educational role of youth organizations, and one in 1986 that analyzed public policy issues related to school-age child care—have also made valuable contributions to the literature on youth organizations: (1) Kleinfeld, J., & Shinkwin, A. (1982). *Youth organizations as a third educational environment particularly for minority group youth* (Final Report to the National Institute of Education). Washington, DC: U.S. Government Printing Office; (2) LaBelle, T. J., & Carroll, J. (1981, October). An introduction to the nonformal education of children and youth. *Comparative Education Review, 25*, 313–329; and (3) Lipsitz, J. S. (1986). *After school: Young adolescents on their own.* Carrboro, NC: University of North Carolina at Chapel Hill, Center for Early Adolescence.

4. Erickson, J. B. (1991). *1992–1993 Directory of American youth organizations* (4th ed.). Minneapolis: Free Spirit Publishing.

5. Size was one criterion used by the task force in selecting which national organizations to examine closely. Age was another factor: groups that served primarily younger children or older teens were considered outside the parameters of the present inquiry. The twenty national youth organizations that were interviewed and examined as part of the task force research included the fifteen member agencies of the National Collaboration for Youth and five others that emphasize intensive summer programming (American Camping Association) or service to low-income and minority youth (ASPIRA, COSSMHO, NAACP Youth and College Division, National Urban League). Although settlement houses represent an important network of community-based organizations for children, youth, and families, the national organization to which many settlements belong—United Neighborhood Centers of America—disbanded during the period of research for this study, and, therefore, its leadership was not interviewed.

6. Readers should be alerted to the fact that figures indicating the numbers of youth served may reflect some duplication among organizations. For example, some of the camps that belong to the American Camping Association are operated by local Boy Scout, Girl Scout, and Camp Fire councils and by affiliates of other national youth organizations. Furthermore, the factors that constitute membership in national youth organizations vary. Technically speaking, the memberships of several of these groups (American Camping Association, National Network of Runaway and Youth Services) are their local affiliates. Young people join or are served by these local units and have no direct connection to the national structure. Other agencies (Boy Scouts of America, Girl Scouts of the U.S.A.) follow a different model, enrolling individual youth as members of the national organization. In addition, some agencies make a distinction between "members" and "numbers of youth served," indicating that there may be different levels of involvement of young people in their programs.

7. Salamon, L. M., & Abramson, A. J. (1992). *The federal budget and the nonprofit sector: FY 1992.* Baltimore: The Johns Hopkins University.

8. This section draws heavily on Stern, L. (1992). *Funding patterns of nonprofit organizations that provide youth development services: An exploratory study.* Unpublished manuscript prepared for the Carnegie Council on Adolescent Development, Washington, DC.

9. The finding from the Stern paper is corroborated in Weber, N. (1991). *Independent youth development organizations: An exploratory study.* Unpublished manuscript prepared for the Carnegie Council on Adolescent Development, Washington, DC.

10. The survey and interviews were conducted by consultant Nathan Weber, whose full report to the task Force, entitled *Independent youth development organizations: An exploratory study,* is available from the Carnegie Council on Adolescent Development. This survey is considered exploratory because of the limitations in its methodology and response rate of organizations. Methodology: Recipients of the questionnaire used for this study were selected from the nation's most comprehensive and best classified database of nonprofit organizations. The database is part of the National Center for Charitable Statistics, a unit of Independent Sector, and organizations are classified in accordance with the National Taxonomy of Exempt Entities (NTEE). From this database, questionnaire recipients included (a) all groups classified under the category of Youth Development, with annual revenues of at least $25,000, and which were unaffiliated with national organizations and were not primarily religious, fund-raising, or advocacy groups; (b) all groups classified as Multipurpose Youth Services (a subset of Human Service organizations) with incomes of at least $25,000; and (c) random samples of Youth Development and Multipurpose Youth Services groups with revenues under $25,000. Response rate: Virtually none of the organizations from (c) above—those that do not file income statements—responded to the questionnaire. Therefore, they are not represented in this study, and the mailing to those groups is discounted in computing the respondent rate. Of the approximately 700 independent youth development organizations with annual budgets of at least $25,000 in (a) and (b) above that were identified through the Independent Sector database, 252 (or approximately 35 percent) responded.

11. Weber, N. (1991). *Independent youth development organizations: An exploratory study* (p. 42). Unpublished manuscript prepared for the Carnegie Council on Adolescent Development, Washington, DC.

12. This pattern was confirmed in Stern, L. (1992). *Funding patterns of nonprofit organizations that provide youth development services: An exploratory study.* Unpublished manuscript prepared for the Carnegie Council on Adolescent Development, Washington, DC.

13. This section draws heavily on Dean, K. C. (1991). *A synthesis of research on, and a descriptive overview of Protestant, Catholic, and Jewish religious youth programs in the United States.* Unpublished manuscript prepared for the Carnegie Council on Adolescent Development, Washington, DC.

14. With few exceptions, religious youth programs share an uncertainty about the numbers of youth they serve. A handful of national studies have offered estimates on the percentage of youth who participate in religious youth organizations. For example, the well-regarded National Education Longitudinal Study found that 34 percent of eighth graders reported such participation, with girls participating at a higher rate than boys. U.S. Department of Education, Office of Educational Research and Improvement, National Center for Education Statistics. (1990). *National education longitudinal study of 1988: A profile of the American eighth grader.* Washington, DC: U.S. Government Printing Office.

The 1980 High School and Beyond survey reported that 36.5 percent of sophomores participated in church activities, including youth groups. The Boys Town Center for the Study of Youth Development. (no date). *A profile of participants in religious youth activities—1980: From the High School and Beyond Study of the National Center for Education Statistics.* Boys Town, NE.

The Search Institute's 1990 study of more than 46,000 Midwest teenagers found that 57 percent of respondents claimed involvement in a church or synagogue (which does not necessarily imply participation in a religious youth organization). Benson, P. L. (1990). *The troubled journey: A portrait of 6th–12th grade youth.* Minneapolis: Lutheran Brotherhood.

15. Erickson, J. B. (1991). *1992–1993 Directory of American youth organizations* (4th ed.). Minneapolis: Free Spirit Publishing.

16. This trend was cited in several denominational interviews conducted by Dean in the preparation of her paper, *A synthesis of research on, and a descriptive overview of Protestant, Catholic, and Jewish religious youth programs in the United States* (February 1991), prepared for the Carnegie Council on Adolescent Development, Washington, DC.

Osmer, R. (1989). Challenges to youth ministry in the mainline churches: Thought provokers. *Affirmation, 2*, 1–25.

17. Kilstein, S., Board of Jewish Education of Greater New York. (1991, January). [Personal interview with the Reverend Kenda Creasy Dean, January 16, 1991.]

Plutzer, A., Associate Director, Department of Religious Affairs, UJA/Federation (1991, January). [Personal interview with the Reverend Kenda Creasy Dean, January 16, 1991.]

18. Amoateng, A. Y., & Bahr, S. J. (1986). Religion, family, and adolescent drug use. *Sociological Perspectives, 29*, 256–263.

Cochran, J. K. (1988). The effect of religiosity on secular and ascetic deviance. *Sociological Focus, 21*, 293–306.

Forliti, J., & Benson, P. L. (1986). Young adolescents: A national survey. *Religious Education, 81*, 199–224.

Hadaway, C. K., Elifson, K.W., & Petersen, D. M. (1984). Religious involvement and drug use among urban adolescents. *Journal for the Scientific Study of Religion, 23*, 109–128.

Jessor, R., Costa, F., Jessor, L., & Donovan, J. E. (1983). Time of first intercourse: A prospective study. *Journal of Personality and Social Psychology, 44*, 600–626.

19. This section draws heavily on Fitzgerald, A. K., & Collins, A. M. (1991). *Adult service clubs and their youth programs*. Unpublished manuscript prepared for the Carnegie Council on Adolescent Development, Washington, DC

20. Association of Junior Leagues International, Inc. (1991). Teen outreach program: A three-year proposal for replication/institutionalization. New York: Author.

21. This section draws heavily on Seefeldt, V., Ewing, M., & Walk, S. (1992). *An overview of youth sports programs in the United States*. Unpublished manuscript prepared for the Carnegie Council on Adolescent Development, Washington, DC.

22. Martens, R. (1986). Youth sport in the USA. In M. Weiss & D. Gould (Eds.), *Sport for children and youth: Vol.10*. Champaign, IL: Human Kinetics Press.

23. Data in this chart were drawn primarily from telephone interviews conducted by Vern Seefeldt, Martha Ewing, and Stephan Walk in the preparation of their paper, *An overview of youth sports programs in the United States* (November 1992), prepared for the Carnegie Council on Adolescent Development, Washington, DC.

24. Ewing, M. E., & Seefeldt, V. (1989). *Participation and attrition patterns in American agency-sponsored and interscholastic sports: An executive summary*. Final report to the Athletic Footwear Council of the Sporting Goods Manufacturers Association.

25. National Association for Sport and Physical Education, Youth Sports Coalition. (1986). *Guidelines for coaching education: Youth sports*. Reston, VA: Author.

26. This section draws heavily on Freedman, M., Harvey, A. C., and Ventura-Merkel, C. (1992). *The quiet revolution: Elder service and youth development in an aging society*. Unpublished manuscript prepared for the Carnegie Council on Adolescent Development, Washington, DC.

27. The Freedman, Harvey, and Ventura-Merkel paper lists twenty-four evaluation studies that have been conducted of the Foster Grandparent program from 1966 through 1988.

28. National Endowment for the Arts. (1974). *Museums USA: Art, history, science, and other museums* (pp. 8–9). Research conducted by the National Research Center of the Arts, Inc., an affiliate of Louis Harris and Associates, Inc., under contract to the National Endowment for the Arts. Washington, DC.

29. Association of Science-Technology Centers. (1991, October). *Report to DeWitt Wallace–Reader's Digest Fund on the development of a national initiative to seed and support programs for adolescents at science-technology centers and children's museums nationwide* (planning grant). Washington, DC.

30. Matyas, M. L. (1990). *Report on analysis of data: Association of Science-Technology Centers survey of programs for adolescents at science centers and youth museums*. Washington, DC: American Association for the Advancement of Science.

31. Ibid.

32. Ibid.

33. National Center for Education Statistics. (1988). *Services and resources for young adults in public libraries* (Survey report on a Fall 1987 national survey conducted by Westat, Inc.). Washington, DC: U.S. Department of Education, Office of Educational Research and Improvement.

National Center for Education Statistics. (1990). *Services and resources for children in public libraries, 1988–89* (Survey report on a March 1989 national survey conducted by Westat, Inc.). Washington, DC: U.S. Department of Education, Office of Educational Research and Improvement.

The 1989 survey, which focused on services and resources for children in public libraries, indicated that children (defined as young people fourteen years of age or under) represent 37 percent of library users nationally. The 1987 survey, on services and resources for young adults (aged twelve to eighteen) in public libraries, found that this age group represents 25 percent of library users. Recognizing the overlap in age groups between these two studies, it appears that approximately one-half of current library users are children and youth.

34. National Center for Education Statistics. (1988). *Services and resources for young adults in public libraries* (Survey report on a Fall 1987 national survey conducted by Westat, Inc.). Washington, DC: U.S. Department of Education, Office of Educational Research and Improvement.

35. National Center for Education Statistics. (1990). *Services and resources for children in public libraries, 1988–89* (Survey report on a March 1989 national survey conducted by Westat, Inc.). Washington, DC: U.S. Department of Education, Office of Educational Research and Improvement.

36. National Center for Education Statistics. (1988). *Services and resources for young adults in public libraries* (Survey report on a Fall 1987 national survey conducted by Westat, Inc.). Washington, DC: U.S. Department of Education, Office of Educational Research and Improvement.

37. Ibid.

38. Public Library Association, Service to Children Committee. (1988). *Latchkey children in the public library: A position paper.* Chicago: American Library Association.

39. Ibid.

40. A book on the project, entitled *Information in Empowering: Developing Public Library Services for At-Risk Youth* (BALIS, 1992), was published describing the lessons learned in the project.

41. This section draws heavily on Smith, C. (1991). *Overview of youth recreation programs in the United States.* Unpublished manuscript prepared for the Carnegie Council on Adolescent Development, Washington, D.C.

42. Ibid., pp. 32–38.

43. U.S. Department of the Interior, President's Commission on Outdoors. (1989). *National urban recreation study: An executive report.* Washington, DC: Author. See also Littell, J., & Wynn, J. (1989). *The availability and use of community resources for young adolescents in an inner-city and suburban community.* Chicago: University of Chicago, Chapin Hall Center for Children.

44. Office of Technology Assessment. (1991). *Adolescent health: Vol. I. Summary and policy options* (OTA-H-468) (p. I–81). Washington, DC: U.S. Government Printing Office.

45. U.S. Department of Education, Office of Educational Research and Improvement, National Center for Education Statistics. (1990). *National education longitudinal study of 1988: A profile of the American eighth grader.* Washington, DC: U.S. Government Printing Office.

46. Ibid.

47. Hofferth, S. L., Brayfield, A., Deich, S., & Holcomb, P. (1991). *National childcare survey, 1990: A National Association for the Education of Young Children (NAEYC) Study* (p. 116). Washington, DC: Urban Institute Press.

48. McLaughlin, M. W., & Smrekar, C. (1988). *School-linked comprehensive service delivery systems for adolescents.* Unpublished manuscript prepared for the Carnegie Council on Adolescent Development, Washington, DC.
Policy Analysis for California Education. (1989). *Coalition of children in California.* Berkeley, CA: Author.
Kulla, R. J., & Richards, P. (1991). *Children's social services in metropolitan Chicago: Vol. 3. Children's services in metropolitan Chicago: The current system and alternative approaches.* Chicago: University of Chicago, Chapin Hall Center for Children.

49. Ianni, F. A. J. *The search for structure.* (1990). New York: The Free Press.

50. These themes are echoed in Bruner, C. (1991, April). *Thinking collaboratively: Ten questions and answers to help policy makers improve children's services* (p. 6). Washington, DC: Education and Human Services Consortium. This report indicates that current social services for children are not organized to support coherent responses to the needs of youth. The

Education and Human Services Consortium found that most services are crisis-oriented; the social welfare system divides problems of families and children into rigid and distinct categories that fail to reflect interrelated causes and solutions; communication among public and private service providers is lacking; specialized agencies cannot easily craft comprehensive solutions to complex problems; and existing services are insufficiently funded. Clearly, greater coordination and collaboration are needed across welfare, health, and other service systems.

51. Littell, J., & Wynn, J. (1989). *The availability and use of community resources for young adolescents in an inner-city and suburban community*, (p. ix). Chicago: University of Chicago, Chapin Hall Center for Children.

PART III

1. National Commission on Children. (1991). *Beyond rhetoric: A new American agenda for children and families*. Washington, DC: Author.

2. Committee for Economic Development. (1987). *Children in need: Investment strategies for the educationally disadvantaged*. New York: Author.

3. This series of focus groups was conducted by S. W. Morris & Company, a social marketing research firm based in Bethesda, MD. Its full report to the task force, entitled *What young adolescents want and need from out-of-school programs: A focus group report*, is available from the Carnegie Council on Adolescent Development, Washington, DC.

4. This section draws on the work of Dryfoos, J. (1990). *Adolescents at risk: Prevalence and prevention*. New York: Oxford University Press.
    Hamburg, D. A. (1986). *Preparing for life: The critical transition of adolescence*. Reprinted from the Annual Report of Carnegie Corporation of New York.
    Heath, S. B., & McLaughlin, M. W. (1991, April). Community organizations as family: Endeavors that engage and support adolescents. *Phi Delta Kappan*, pp. 623–627.
    Honnet, E. P. and Poulsen, S. J. (1989). *Principles of good practice for combining service and learning* (Wingspread Special Report). Racine, WI: Johnson Foundation.
    Lipsitz, J. S. (1986). *After school: Young adolescents on their own*. Carrboro, NC: University of North Carolina at Chapel Hill, Center for Early Adolescence.
    Pittman, K., & Wright, M. (1991). *A rationale for enhancing the role of the non-school voluntary sector in youth development*. Unpublished manuscript prepared for the Carnegie Council on Adolescent Development, Washington, DC.

Schorr, L., & Schorr, D. (1988). *Within our reach: Breaking the cycle of disadvantage*. New York: Doubleday.
    Snider, B. A., & Miller, J. P. (1991, July). *Land-grant university system and 4-H: A mutually beneficial relationship of scholars and practitioners in youth development (Draft paper)*. State College, PA: Pennsylvania State University, Department of Agricultural and Extension Education.
    United Way of America. (1991). *Investing in children: A strategy to change at-risk lives* (A report of the Task Force on Children at Risk). Alexandria, VA: Author.
    United Way of America. (1991). *Promising prevention programs for children* (A report prepared by Sonenstein, F. L., Ku, L., Juffras, J., & Cohen, B., of the Urban Institute). Alexandria, VA: Author.
    Amherst H. Wilder Foundation. (1988). *Funders' guide manual: A guide to prevention programs in human services—focus on children and adolescents*. St. Paul, MN: Author.

5. Pittman, K. & Wright, M. (1991). *A rationale for enhancing the role of the non-school voluntary sector in youth development*. Unpublished manuscript prepared for the Carnegie Council on Adolescent Development, Washington, DC.

6. Walker, G., & Vilella-Velez, F. (1992). *Anatomy of a demonstration*. Philadelphia: Public/Private Ventures.
    Girls Incorporated. (1991). *Truth, trust and technology: New research on preventing adolescent pregnancy*. New York: Author.

7. Heath, S. B. & McLaughlin, M. W. (1991, April). Community organizations as family: Endeavors that engage and support adolescents. *Phi Delta Kappan*, pp. 623–627.

8. The following section on gender issues draws heavily on Nicholson, H. J. (1992). *Gender issues in youth development programs*. Unpublished manuscript prepared for the Carnegie Council on Adolescent Development, Washington, DC.

9. The following section on race, ethnicity, and culture draws heavily on Camino, L. A. (1992). *Racial, ethnic, and cultural differences in youth development programs*. Unpublished manuscript prepared for the Carnegie Council on Adolescent Development, Washington, DC.

10. Benson, P. L. (1990). *The troubled journey: A portrait of 6th–12th grade youth.* Minneapolis: Search Institute.

Girl Scouts of the United States of America. (1990). *Girl Scouts survey on the beliefs and moral values of America's children.* New York: Author.

Peng, S. S., Fetters, W. B., & Kolstad, A. J. (1981). *High school and beyond: A national longitudinal study for the 1980's.* A capsule description of high school students. Washington, DC: Statistical Information Office, National Center for Education Statistics, U.S. Department of Education.

11. Independent Sector. (1990). *Volunteering and giving among American teenagers 14 to 17 years of age: Findings from a national survey.* Washington, DC: Author.

Medrich, E. A., Roizen, J. A., Rubin, V., & Buckley, S. (1982). *The serious business of growing up: A study of children's lives outside school.* Berkeley, CA: University of California Press.

U.S. Department of Education, Office of Educational Research and Improvement, National Center for Education Statistics. (1990). *National education longitudinal study of 1988: A profile of the American eighth grader.* Washington, DC: U.S. Government Printing Office.

12. "Race," "ethnicity," and "culture" are sometimes used synonymously, yet they have distinct meanings that may be useful for program planners. "Race" generally refers to physical and genetic distinctions. The notion that race holds significant explanatory power to account for genetic and physiological differences among broadly defined racial groups has been discredited, because more variation has been found to exist *within* races than between them. However, race remains a powerful social and political category in this country. (See Camino, L. A., note 9.)

"Ethnicity' is conventionally used to denote the social or cultural heritage of a group of people, passed on from one generation to the next. References to ethnicity commonly include customs, language, religion, rituals, and ceremonies that mark distinctions between groups.

"Culture" represents the means by which ethnicity is maintained and expressed. Most references to culture emphasize its manifestations—knowledge, language, belief, art, morals, laws, and conventions—yet culture also operates at deeper levels. Learning a culture takes place through conscious, purposeful techniques as well as through observation and experience.

13. Dryfoos, J. (1990). *Adolescents at risk: Prevalence and prevention* (p. 21). New York: Oxford University Press. Current information from the Centers for Disease Control confirms this observation. In 1991 (provisional data), among young people aged five to fourteen, the death rate for African American males was 43.5 per 100,000; for white males, it was 26.2; for African American females, it was 27.9; and for white females it was 17.1. National Center for Health Statistics. *Monthly Vital Statistics Report, September 30, 1992.* Washington, DC: U.S. Department of Health and Human Services, Public Health Service, Centers for Disease Control.

14. U.S. Department of Education, Office of Educational Research and Improvement, National Center for Education Statistics. (1990). *National education longitudinal study of 1988: A profile of the American eighth grader* (p. 45). Washington, DC: U.S. Government Printing Office.

15. Dryfoos, J. (1990). *Adolescents at risk: Prevalence and prevention* (p. 22). New York: Oxford University Press.

16. Ibid.

17. Brumberg, J. J. (1989). *Fasting girls: The surprising history of anorexia nervosa.* New York: Plume.

18. Petersen, A. C., Sarigiani, P. A., & Kennedy, R. E. (1991). Adolescent depression: Why more girls? *Journal of Youth and Adolescence, 20,* 247–271.

19. Benson, P. L. (1990). *The troubled journey: A portrait of 6th–12th grade youth.* Minneapolis: Search Institute.

20. Girls Clubs of America. (1988). *Facts and reflections on girls and substance use.* New York: Author.

Johnston, L. D., O'Malley, P. M., & Bachman, J. G. (1991). *Drug use among American high school students, college students and young adults, 1975–1990: Vol. I. High school seniors* (DHHS Publication No. [ADM] 91–1813). Washington, DC: U.S. Department of Health and Human Services, Public Health Service, Alcohol, Drug Abuse, and Mental Health Administration.

21. National Center for Health Statistics. (1991). *Data from the National Survey of Family Growth* (Series 23). Washington, DC: U.S. Department of Health and Human Services, Public Health Service, Centers for Disease Control.

Hayes, C. C. (Ed.) (1987). *Risking the future: Adolescent sexuality, pregnancy and childbearing* (Vol. 1). Washington, DC: National Academy Press.

22. Billingsley, A. (1968). *Black families in white America.* New York: Simon & Schuster.

Bowman, P. J. & Howard, C. (1985). Race-related socialization, motivation, and academic achievement: A study of black youth in three generation families. *Journal of the American Academy for Child Psychiatry, 24:* 134–141.

23. Jeff, M. F. X. (in press). Afrocentrism and the African American Male. In R. Mincy (Ed.) *Nurturing young black males: Challenges to agencies, programs, and social policy.* Washington, DC: Urban Institute Press.

24. Montero-Sieburth, M. (1988). Conceptualizing multicultural education: From theoretical approaches to classroom practices. *Equity and Choice, 4*(3), 3–12.

25. Bernal, M. E., & Padilla, A. M. (1982). Status of minority curricula and training in clinical psychology. *American Psychologist, 37,* 780–787.

Irving, J., Perl, H., Trickett, E., & Watts, R. (1984, March). Minority curricula or a curriculum of cultural diversity? Differences that make a difference. *American Psychologist,* 320–324.

26. Batchold, L. (1982). Children's social interactions and parental attitudes among Hupa Indians and Anglo-Americans. *Journal of Social Psychology, 116,* 9–17.

Spencer, M. B., & Dornbusch, S. M. (1990). Challenges in studying minority youth. In S. S. Feldman & G. R. Elliott (Eds.), *At the threshold: The developing adolescent* (pp. 123–146). Cambridge, MA: Harvard University Press.

27. Schapiro, A. (1988, June). Adjustment and identity formation of Lao refugee adolescents. *Smith College Studies in Social Work,* 157–171.

Tobin, J. J., & Friedman, J. (1984). Intercultural developmental stresses confronting Southeast Asian refugee adolescents. *Journal of Operational Psychiatry, 15,* 39–45.

28. See, for example, Jankowski, M. S. (1991). *Islands in the street: Gangs and American urban society.* Berkeley and Los Angeles, CA: University of California Press.

29. Hagedorn, J., & Macon, P. (1988). *People and folks: Gangs, crime and the underclass in a rustbelt city* (p. 106). Chicago: Lake View Press.

30. Vigil, J. D. (in press). Gangs, social control, and ethnicity: Ways to redirect. In S. B. Heath & M. W. McLaughlin (Eds.), *Building identities with inner-city youth: Beyond ethnicity and gender* (p. 6). New York: Teachers College Press.

31. Tobler, N. (1989). *Drug prevention programs can work: Research findings* (p. 14). Paper presented at the conference What Works: An International Perspective on Drug Abuse Treatment and Prevention Research.

32. S. W. Morris & Company. (1992). *What young adolescents want and need from out-of-school programs: A focus group report.* Unpublished manuscript prepared for the Carnegie Council on Adolescent Development, Washington, DC.

33. This statement is made with the knowledge that many youth workers belong to professional membership organizations within their own disciplines, e.g., National Association of Social Workers, American Association for Leisure and Recreation. However, youth workers have no opportunity to join an interdisciplinary organization that focuses its attention on youth development issues.

34. This statement is made with the knowledge that, although many youth development professionals subscribe to such journals as *Youth Policy* (published by the Youth Policy Institute) and *New Designs for Youth Development* (published by Associates for Youth Development), the actual circulation of these publications is small. Other journals, such as *Children Today* (published by the federal government), occasionally deal with youth development topics, although their scope is intentionally broader. A new publication of the American Youth Work Center, *Youth Today,* is designed to fill this current void.

35. Ianni, F. A. J. (1990). *The search for structure.* New York: The Free Press.

36. Oldfield, D. (1987). *The journey: A creative approach to the necessary crises of adolescence.* Washington, DC: Author.

37. Bingham, M., Edmondson, J., & Stryker, S. (1984). *Choices: A teen woman's journal for self-awareness and personal planning.* Santa Barbara: Advocacy Press.

Bingham, M., Edmondson, J., and Stryker, S. (1984). *Challenges: A young man's journal for self-awareness and personal planning.* Santa Barbara: Advocacy Press.

38. Baumrind, D. (1978). Parental disciplinary patterns and social competence in youth. *Youth and Society, 9,* 239–276.

39. For a useful, although not exhaustive, review of preventive family support programs, see Small, S. A. (1990). *Preventive programs that support families with adolescents*. Working paper of the Carnegie Council on Adolescent Development, Washington, DC.

40. National Network of Runaway and Youth Services. (1991). *To whom do they belong?* Washington, DC: Author.

41. Seligson, M., & Fink, D. B. (1989). *No time to waste: An action agenda for school-age child care* (p. 20). Wellesley, MA: Wellesley College Center for Research on Women.

42. For additional program examples and a description of program experiences, see National Crime Prevention Council. (1990). *Changing perspectives: Youth as resources*. Washington, DC: Author. See also Rolzinski, C. A. (1990). *The adventure of adolescence: Middle school students and community service*. Washington, DC: Youth Service America. See also Schine, J. (1989). *Community service for young adolescents*. Working paper of the Carnegie Council on Adolescent Development, Washington, DC.

43. Weissberg, R. P., Caplan, M. Z., & Sivo, P. J. (1989). A conceptual framework for establishing school-based social competence promotion programs. In L. A. Bond & B. E. Compas (Eds.), *Primary prevention and promotion in the schools* (pp. 255–296). Newbury Park, CA: Sage.

44. Carnegie Council on Adolescent Development. (1992, January). *Report on the consultation on evaluation of youth development programs*. Washington, DC: Author.

45. Newman, W. H., Warren, E. K., & Schnee, J. E. (1991). *The process of management: Strategy, action, results* (pp. 14–16). Englewood Cliffs, NJ: Prentice-Hall.

46. Sumariwalla, R. D. (1988). Modern management and the nonprofit sector. In P. R. Keys & L. H. Ginsberg (Eds.), *New management in human services* (pp. 202–203). Silver Spring, MD: National Association of Social Workers.

47. Sugarman, J. (no date). *About the children's investment trust*. Washington, DC: Center for Effective Services for Children.

48. Stern, L. W. (1992). *Funding patterns of nonprofit organizations that provide youth development services: An exploratory study*. Unpublished manuscript prepared for the Carnegie Council on Adolescent Development, Washington, DC.

49. Ibid.

50. The Columbus Foundation. (1991). *Highlights: 1990 community foundation survey*. Columbus, OH: Author.

51. Levy, J., & Copple, C. (1989). *Joining forces: A report from the first state year*. Alexandria, VA: National Association of State Boards of Education.

52. Dryfoos, J. G. (1991, January 18). *States' response to youth-at-risk issues: Preliminary report to the Carnegie Corporation on work in progress in 1990*. Unpublished manuscript.

53. Ibid.

54. Association of New York State Youth Bureaus. (1990, October 10). *Concept paper: Federal funding for youth development*. New City, NY: Author.

55. *Council of Governors' Policy Advisors 1991 Annual Report* (p. 2). Washington, DC: Council of Governors' Policy Advisors.

56. Dryfoos, J. G. (1991, January 18). *States' response to youth-at-risk issues: Preliminary report to the Carnegie Corporation on work in progress in 1990*. Unpublished manuscript.

57. Ibid.

58. O'Brien, R., Pittman, K., & Cahill, M. (1992). *Building supportive communities for youth: Local approaches to enhancing youth development*. Unpublished manuscript prepared for the Carnegie Council on Adolescent Development, Washington, DC.

59. General Accounting Office. (1990, September). *Children's issues: A decade of GAO reports and recent activities* (GAO/HRD-90–162). Report to the Select Committee on Children, Youth and Families, House of Representatives. Washington, DC: Author.

60. The following section is based on a paper written by Michael Sherraden in 1991, entitled *Community-based youth services in international perspective*. Unpublished manuscript prepared for the Carnegie Council on Adolescent Development, Washington, DC.

61. Ibid., p. iv.

62. Ibid., p. 51.

ACKNOWLEDGMENTS

The healthy development of young adolescents represents a long-standing concern and commitment for Carnegie Corporation of New York President David A. Hamburg. Working with the Carnegie board of trustees, Dr. Hamburg in 1986 established the Carnegie Council on Adolescent Development, and as one of its major efforts the council in 1990 convened the Task Force on Youth Development and Community Programs. Dr. Hamburg actively participated in all of the task force deliberations and provided valuable guidance throughout the research and writing phases of the preparation of this report. His passion, vision, and caring spirit are integrated into the fabric of its content.

One of the early translations of this vision involved the selection of James Comer and Wilma Tisch to serve as cochairs of the task force. Their skilled leadership fostered lively discussions, and ultimately consensus, among members of the task force. Working in partnership with Project Director Jane Quinn, the cochairs identified emerging issues that required task force involvement and made themselves available to render substantive decisions. As the primary author of the report, Jane Quinn designed the approach of the study, synthesized a wide range of knowledge from research and practice, and facilitated solid working relationships among all members of the task force.

Several members of the Carnegie Corporation staff contributed substantial time, energy, and wisdom to the work of the task force. Barbara D. Finberg, Elena O. Nightingale, Fred M. Hechinger, Avery Russell, Vivien Stewart, Gloria Primm Brown, Anthony W. Jackson, and Allyn Mortimer participated in task force meetings, reviewed drafts of the report, and made constructive suggestions throughout these endeavors. Julia Chill offered practical assistance with computer technology.

Similarly, staff members of the Carnegie Council on Adolescent Development deserve special recognition. Executive Director Ruby Takanishi provided essential support that strengthened the work of the task force and made important substantive and editorial contributions to the report. Project Assistant Winifred Bayard maintained close relations with all members of the task force throughout the duration of the project, ensuring the effective execution of all details of meetings and the production of the report. Her quiet, cheerful competence is especially appreciated. Office Administrator Katharine Beckman brought fiscal and other management oversight to the project, while Tasha Campos, Greg Curran, Darnice Curtis, Leigh Frazier, Caitlin Schneider, and Linda Schoff assisted in proofreading, fact-checking, and other behind-the-scenes support.

Professional colleagues who reviewed early drafts of the report and offered invaluable advice on ways to improve its structure and substance include Marvin Cohen, Dennis Fleming, Marc Freedman, Eric Goplerud, Lorraine Klerman, Robert Long, Neal Mazer, Richard Munger, Gordon Raley, Michael Sherraden, Leonard Stern, and Joan Wynn. Countless other colleagues contributed in ways large and small—by agreeing to be interviewed formally, by providing informal suggestions, by sharing information about their programs and organizations, or by responding to requests for information or materials. Staff of the National Collaboration for Youth assisted in a variety of ways, as did the collaboration's member agencies and its Program Support Group.

The task force acknowledges with deep gratitude the substantive contributions of the authors of commissioned papers, the participants in the consultations on professional development and program evaluation, and the consultants—especially Pamela Wilson, Nathan

Weber, Susan Morris, and Sue Korenbaum—who produced original research and summary reports that are integrated into the final report. A listing of these papers and reports is contained in the appendices. Other consultants, including Lisle Carter, Francis Ianni, and Karabelle Pizzigati, made presentations to the task force and engaged in thoughtful dialogues about youth development trends and issues. Another consultant, Janice Lynch, used focus group interviews to craft the "voices of youth" vignettes that appear in Part I of the report.

The task force also thanks the scores of teenagers who participated in focus group discussions, telling about their lives and their dreams, as well as members of the Teen Council of the Center for Population Options, who jointly facilitated the focus groups with staff from S.W. Morris & Company.

Joseph Foote brought editorial artistry to the final report and helped in devising the most effective strategies for communicating the report's content to its multiple audiences. Sara Blackburn assisted in editing the report's executive summary, and EEI, Inc., proofread the final draft. Marc Meadows and Robert Wiser lent their creativity and imaginations to the design of the report.

There is no question that *A Matter of Time* is a matter of teamwork. The task force thanks all of the individuals, both named and unnamed, who contributed to this report, which it offers to readers as a resource to enrich the lives of America's twenty million young adolescents, now and in the future.

APPENDIX A

COMMISSIONED PAPERS AND OTHER PROJECT REPORTS

COMMISSIONED PAPERS

1. *Adult Service Clubs and Their Programs for Youth.* Ann K. Fitzgerald and Ann M. Collins. August 1991.

2. *Building Supportive Communities for Youth: Local Approaches to Enhancing Youth Development.* Raymond O'Brien, Karen Pittman, and Michele Cahill. November 1992.

3. *Community-based Youth Services in International Perspective.* Michael Sherraden. January 1992.

4. *Funding Patterns of Nonprofit Organizations that Provide Youth Development Services: An Exploratory Study.* Leonard W. Stern. February 1992.

5. *Gender Issues in Youth Development Programs.* Heather Johnston Nicholson. February 1992.

6. *Overview of Youth Recreation Programs in the United States.* Christen Smith. September 1991.

7. *An Overview of Youth Sports Programs in the United States.* Vern Seefeldt, Martha Ewing, and Stephan Walk. November 1992.

8. *The Quiet Revolution: Elder Service and Youth Development in an Aging Society.* Marc Freedman, C. Anne Harvey, and Catherine Ventura-Merkel. September 1992.

9. *Racial, Ethnic, and Cultural Differences in Youth Development Programs.* Linda A. Camino. August 1992.

10. *A Rationale for Enhancing the Role of the Non-School Voluntary Sector in Youth Development.* Karen Pittman and Marlene Wright. August 1991.

11. *A Synthesis of the Research on, and a Descriptive Overview of, Protestant, Catholic, and Jewish Religious Youth Programs in the United States.* Kenda Creasy Dean. February 1991.

12. *Young Adolescents and Discretionary Time Use: The Nature of Life Outside School.* Elliott Medrich. June 1991.

SPECIAL REPORTS

13. *Evaluation of Youth Development Programs.* Summary report of the January 1992 consultation.

14. *Independent Youth Development Organizations: An Exploratory Study.* Nathan Weber. May 1992.

15. *Professional Development of Youthworkers.* Summary report of the May 1991 consultation.

16. *What Young Adolescents Want and Need From Out-of-School Programs: A Focus Group Report.* S. W. Morris & Company. January 1992.

CONSULTATION PARTICIPANTS

CONSULTATIONS OF THE
TASK FORCE ON YOUTH
DEVELOPMENT AND
COMMUNITY PROGRAMS

**PROFESSIONAL
DEVELOPMENT OF YOUTH
WORKERS**

MAY 13, 1991
NEW YORK, NEW YORK

COCHAIRS

PHILIP COLTOFF
Executive Director
The Children's Aid Society
New York, New York

WILMA S. TISCH
Chairman of the Board
WNYC Foundation
Member of the Executive
   Committee
United Way of New York City
New York, New York

PARTICIPANTS

CAROL BEHRER
Associate Commissioner
Family and Youth Services
   Bureau
Human Development Services
Washington, D.C.

JUDITH J. CARTER
Director of Career Development
Boys and Girls Clubs of America
New York, New York

JOAN COSTELLO
Faculty Associate
Chapin Hall Center for Children
University of Chicago
Chicago, Illinois

KENDA CREASY DEAN
Director
Wesley Foundation
Associate Pastor
University United Methodist
   Church
University of Maryland
College Park, Maryland

JUDITH B. ERICKSON
Director of Research Services
Indiana Youth Institute
Indianapolis, Indiana

LUIS GARDEN-ACOSTA
Executive Director
El Puente
Brooklyn, New York

LEAH COX HOOPFER
Deputy Administrator
4-H Extension Service
U.S. Department of Agriculture
Washington, D.C.

ANNA HOPKINS
Executive Director
Grand Street Settlement
New York, New York

SHARON LYNN KAGAN
Associate Director
Bush Center in Child
   Development and Social Policy
New Haven, Connecticut

MICHAEL J. LENAGHAN
President
American Humanics, Inc.
Kansas City, Missouri

ROBERT LONG
McElroy Professor
Youth Leadership Studies
   Program
University of Northern Iowa
Cedar Falls, Iowa

JANET OBEID
Vice President and Director
National Academy for
   Volunteerism
United Way of America
Alexandria, Virginia

KAREN JOHNSON PITTMAN
Director
Center for Youth Development
   and Policy Research
Academy for Educational
   Development
Washington, D.C.

JOHN RAMEY
Membership Secretary and
    Coeditor
*Social Work with Groups
    Newsletter*
Association for the Advancement
    of Social Work with Groups, Inc.
University of Akron
Akron, Ohio

PETER SCALES
Deputy Director
Center for Early Adolescence
University of North Carolina
Carrboro, North Carolina

MICHELLE SELIGSON
Director
School Age Child Care Project
Center for Research on Women
Wellesley College
Wellesley, Massachusetts

JOHN TURNER
Dean
School of Social Work
University of North Carolina
Chapel Hill, North Carolina

WENDY WHEELER
Director
Certification of Instructors and
    Training
Girl Scouts of the U.S.A.
New York, New York

PAMELA WILSON
Consultant
Carnegie Council on Adolescent
    Development
Washington, D.C.

DOLORES WISDOM
Program Associate
Lilly Endowment, Inc.
Indianapolis, Indiana

OBSERVER

GARY L. HEUSEL
Director
Community Cares
National 4-H Council
Chevy Chase, Maryland

**EVALUATION OF YOUTH
DEVELOPMENT PROGRAMS**

JANUARY 15, 1992
NEW YORK, NEW YORK

CHAIR

JUDITH TORNEY-PURTA
Professor of Human
    Development
University of Maryland
College Park, Maryland

PARTICIPANTS

ALVIA BRANCH
Vice President and Director of
    Qualitative Research
Public/Private Ventures
Philadelphia, Pennsylvania

SYLVIA BROWN
Director of Research
Girl Scouts of the U.S.A.
New York, New York

MARCIA CHAIKEN
Director of Research
LINC
Lincoln, Massachusetts

THOMAS D. COOK
Professor
Center for Urban Affairs
Northwestern University
Evanston, Illinois

DONNA V. DUNLOP
Program Director
DeWitt Wallace–Reader's Digest
    Fund
New York, New York

LARRY EISENBERG
Director of Research and
    Strategic Planning
Boy Scouts of America
Irving, Texas

S. SHIRLEY FELDMAN
Professor
Stanford Center for the Study of
    Families, Children, and Youth
Stanford University
Stanford, California

KAREN FULBRIGHT
Program Officer
The Ford Foundation
New York, New York

DAGMAR E. MCGILL
Deputy National Executive
    Director
Big Brothers/Big Sisters of
    America
Philadelphia, Pennsylvania

MATTHEW MILES
Senior Research Associate
Center for Policy Research
New York, New York

MIRKA NEGRONI
National Director for Youth
    Services
ASPIRA Association, Inc.
Washington, D.C.

HEATHER JOHNSTON
    NICHOLSON
Director
National Resource Center
Girls Incorporated
Indianapolis, Indiana

KAREN JOHNSON PITTMAN
Director
Center for Youth Development
    and Policy Research
Academy for Educational
    Development
Washington, D.C.

HECTOR SANCHEZ
Public Health Adviser
Office for Substance Abuse
    Prevention
Rockville, Maryland

STEVEN SCHINKE
Professor
Columbia University School of
    Social Work
New York, New York

ROXANNE SPILLETT
Assistant National Director of
    Program Services
Boys and Girls Clubs of America
New York, New York

RUSSY SUMARIWALLA
Senior Consultant
United Way Strategic Institute
United Way of America
Alexandria, Virginia

WILMA S. TISCH
Chairman of the Board
WNYC Foundation
Member of the Executive
    Committee
United Way of New York City
New York, New York

PAMELA WILSON
Consultant
Carnegie Council on Adolescent
    Development
Washington, D.C.

RENÉE WILSON-BREWER
Associate Director
Center for Health Promotion and
    Education
Education Development Center,
    Inc.
Newton, Massachusetts

JOAN R. WYNN
Research Fellow
Chapin Hall Center for Children
University of Chicago
Chicago, Illinois

OBSERVERS

LINETTA GILBERT
Program Officer
Greater New Orleans
    Foundation
New Orleans, Louisiana

IMRE KOHN
Director of Evaluation
Milton S. Eisenhower
    Foundation
New York, New York

MARTHA TAYLOR
Director
Market Research and Program
    Evaluation
United Way of America
Alexandria, Virginia

BIOGRAPHIES OF MEMBERS OF THE TASK FORCE

JAMES P. COMER

James P. Comer is Maurice Falk Professor of Child Psychiatry at the Yale University Child Study Center and director of the center's School Development Program. His interest in changing conditions surrounding child rearing in this country, particularly of black children, led to his work on preventive strategies for low-income children in elementary schools. A successful intervention program initially developed in the New Haven, Connecticut, schools is now being implemented in several other states and was the subject of one of Dr. Comer's books, *School Power: Implications of an Intervention Project*. Dr. Comer is a columnist for *Parents Magazine*, as well as a consultant for the Children's Television Workshop and associate dean of the Yale University School of Medicine. He describes his own family and educational experiences in his 1988 book, *Maggie's American Dream*.

WILMA S. TISCH

Wilma S. (Billie) Tisch, a civic leader, has served as chairman of the board of WNYC Foundation (New York Public Broadcasting) since 1988. She is vice president of the Jewish Communal Fund; trustee of the Federation of Jewish Philanthropies of New York (now UJA Federation); member of the Council of Advisors, Hunter College School of Social Work; member of the American Jewish Joint Distribution Committee; and member of the executive committee of United Way of New York City. From 1980 to 1983, Ms. Tisch was president of the Federation of Jewish Philanthropies of New York. Ms. Tisch received the Louis D. Marshall Medal from the Jewish Theological Seminary and the Doctor of Humane Letters from Skidmore College and from the Mount Sinai School of Medicine of the City University of New York.

RAYMOND G. CHAMBERS

Raymond G. Chambers is chairman of the Amelior Foundation, the READY Foundation, and the New Jersey Performing Arts Center. He is founding chairman of the Points of Light Foundation and co-chairman of the One-to-One Partnership. Mr. Chambers is also a member of the board of the Enterprise Foundation, the Center for Educational Innovation, the Newark Museum, the Governor's Committee on Scholastic Achievement, Cities in Schools, Junior Achievement, Drew University, Community Foundation of New Jersey, United Way of New York City, Committee for Economic Development, and New Community Foundation.

PHILIP COLTOFF

Philip Coltoff is executive director of the Children's Aid Society and adjunct professor at Adelphi University School of Social Work. He has written one book as well as many articles on child welfare issues. Mr. Coltoff is a frequent speaker and lecturer on issues affecting adolescents and families. He recently led a delegation of American youth development specialists who consulted with Soviet colleagues on strengthening their social welfare services for children and youth.

JANE L. DELGADO

Jane L. Delgado has served as president and chief executive officer of COSSMHO, the National Coalition of Hispanic Health and Human Services Organizations, since 1985. She came to her position at COSSMHO after serving in the office of the secretary of the U.S. Department of Health and Human Services, which she joined in 1979. Before working for HHS she held a variety of positions, including children's talent coordinator for "Sesame Street" from 1973 to 1975. Dr. Delgado is chairperson-elect of the National Health Council and a trustee of the Foundation for Child Development.

JOY G. DRYFOOS

Joy G. Dryfoos is an unaffiliated researcher, writer, and lecturer from Hastings-on-Hudson, New York. Her volume *Adolescents at Risk: Prevalence and Prevention* summarizes youth program successes and prevention strategies. Ms. Dryfoos's current efforts focus on school-based health and social services. She serves on the National Research Council's Panel on High-Risk Youth and as a trustee of the Milton S. Eisenhower Foundation. Ms. Dryfoos also serves on many advisory panels concerned with youth and was recently appointed by Governor Cuomo to the Alcohol, Drug and Mental Health Block Grant Advisory Council of New York.

JUDITH B. ERICKSON

Judith B. Erickson joined the staff of the Indiana Youth Institute as Director of Research Services in July 1989. She is responsible for the *Indiana Youth Polls* and *The State of the Child in Indiana* reports. Previously, she was an associate professor at the University of Minnesota's Center for Youth Development and Research and a visiting fellow at the Boys Town Center for the Study of Youth Development in Boys Town, Nebraska. She was on the sociology faculty at Macalester College for several years and also spent two years with the Science Education Directorate of the National Science Foundation in Washington, D.C. Dr. Erickson has written extensively about the history of youth agencies and is author of the *Directory of American Youth Organizations* (currently in its fourth edition).

JOHN W. GARDNER

John W. Gardner holds the Miriam and Peter Haas Centennial Professorship of Public Service at Stanford University. He was secretary of Health, Education, and Welfare from 1965 to 1968 and was founder of Common Cause. A former president of Carnegie Corporation of New York, Dr. Gardner is the author of *Excellence* (rev. 1984), *Self-Renewal* (rev. 1981), and *On Leadership* (1990), among many other works.

WILLIAM H. GRAY III

William H. Gray III became president and chief executive officer of the United Negro College Fund in Sep-

tember 1991. During his tenure in the U.S. House of Representatives, from 1978 to 1991, Mr. Gray became the first black member of Congress to hold a position in the House leadership, as chairman of the Democratic Caucus and as majority whip. Mr. Gray served as Chairman of the House Budget Committee and was a leading advocate for strengthening America's education system. He has been pastor of the 5,000-member Bright Hope Baptist Church in Philadelphia for more than twenty years.

C. ANNE HARVEY

C. Anne Harvey, as director of the Programs Division of the American Association of Retired Persons (AARP), is responsible for the association's education, advocacy, employment, legal services, and community service programs. Before joining AARP in 1976, Ms. Harvey was assistant director of the National Student Nurses Association, a consultant on legislative affairs with the American Nurses Association, and a health claims adviser with the Guardian Life Insurance Company. She is currently a member of the American Fund for Dental Health's Oral Health 2000 Steering Committee, the National Rehabilitation Hospital's Board of Advisors, and the American Society of Association Executives (ASAE) Planning Committee.

THOMAS J. HARVEY

The Reverend Thomas J. Harvey is president of Catholic Charities U.S.A., a federation of organizations and individuals who carry out the Catholic Church's social mission in the United States. A priest of the Diocese of Pittsburgh, Father Harvey completed his theological studies at the Gregorian University in Rome and earned an M.S. degree in community organization and planning at the Columbia University Graduate School of Social Work in New York. Father Harvey serves as an officer, member, and contributor to a wide variety of national commissions and boards that concern themselves with social issues.

LEAH COX HOOPFER

Leah Cox Hoopfer is currently the program director, Extension Youth and Family Programs, and associate director, Institute for Children, Youth, and Families at Michigan State University. She gives leadership to Michigan State University Extension youth and family programs and works conjointly with the research institute on children, youth, and families. Dr. Hoopfer is an educational psychologist and human ecologist. During most of her tenure with the task force, she was the deputy administrator for 4-H Youth Development

Education at the U.S. Department of Agriculture, where she provided national leadership for the 4-H youth development program.

DAVID S. LIEDERMAN

David S. Liederman has served as executive director of the Child Welfare League of America (CWLA) since 1984. He is national cochair of Generations United and chairman of the National Collaboration for Youth. Mr. Liederman began his professional career in the early 1960s as a street worker for a settlement house in the Boston area. He served two terms in the Massachusetts House of Representatives and in 1973 became the first commissioner of the Massachusetts State Office for Children. Mr. Liederman served as chief of staff to Governor Michael Dukakis of Massachusetts from 1975 to 1979. He was executive director for public affairs of the Federation of Jewish Philanthropies of New York from 1979 to 1984.

DAGMAR E. MCGILL

Dagmar Edith McGill, deputy national executive director, Big Brothers/Big Sisters of America, has dedicated her career to children and youth through her leadership in two national youth development organizations—Girl Scouts of the U.S.A. and, for the past seventeen years, the Big Brothers/Big Sisters movement—having served at the local and national levels of both organizations. She advises a number of Philadelphia and national organizations related to youth services and is president of the Girls' Coalition of Southeastern Pennsylvania and vice president of development for the Educational Foundation of the American Association of University Women.

MILBREY W. MCLAUGHLIN

Milbrey W. McLaughlin is professor of education and public policy at Stanford University. Before joining the Stanford faculty, Professor McLaughlin was a policy analyst with the RAND Corporation. Her research interests focus on issues of policy implementation, contexts of schooling, and productive settings for youth development. She is director of the Center for Research on the Context of Secondary School Teaching at Stanford and coprincipal investigator, with Shirley Brice Heath, of a multiyear study of neighborhood-based organizations for inner-city youth.

THOMAS W. PAYZANT

Thomas W. Payzant has served as superintendent of San Diego city schools, the nation's eighth largest urban school district, since November 1982. His previous superintendencies were in Oklahoma City; Eugene, Oregon; and suburban Philadelphia. A native of Boston, Dr. Payzant earned his doctorate in educational administration at Harvard. He serves on several local, state, and national boards, including the Trustees of the College Board, the National Board for Professional Teaching Standards, and the Council for Basic Education. He regularly writes for professional journals and magazines on issues related to urban education.

FEDERICO PEÑA

Federico Peña is president and chief executive officer of Peña Investment Advisors. From 1983 to 1991 he served as mayor of Denver. During this period, the city of Denver launched several youth development initiatives. A former civil rights lawyer, Mr. Peña served two terms in the Colorado House of Representatives where, in 1981, he was elected Democratic leader.

KAREN JOHNSON PITTMAN

Karen Johnson Pittman is vice president of the Academy for Educational Development (AED) and director of its Center for Youth Development and Policy Research. She came to AED in 1990 after serving six years as director of the Adolescent Pregnancy Prevention Policy Division at the Children's Defense Fund. Ms. Pittman has written numerous articles on youth development and is widely respected as a speaker on youth issues. She has written two books: *Black and White Children in America: Key Facts* and *Testing the Social Safety Net: The Impact of Changes in Support Programs During the Reagan Administration.* Ms. Pittman is a member of various advisory boards.

HUGH B. PRICE

Hugh B. Price is a vice president at the Rockefeller Foundation. He is responsible for managing initiatives in education for at-risk youth and for overseeing the foundation's program to increase minority opportunities in the United States. Mr. Price is a former senior vice president of WNET/Thirteen, the public television station in New York City. A former member of the editorial board of *The New York Times*, he wrote editorials on a broad range of public policy issues including public education, urban affairs, welfare, criminal justice, and telecommunications. As a member of the City of New Haven mayor's cabinet, he supervised the Head Start program and services for youth and senior citizens.

STEPHANIE G. ROBINSON

Stephanie G. Robinson joined the office of the superintendent of the Kansas City, Missouri, school district in 1991. She is assistant to the superintendent for funding/development and special initiatives. Before this Dr. Robinson was director of education and career development at the National Urban League. She serves on the board of Learning Initiatives, Inc., an IBM Education Software User Group, and the Benjamin E. Mayes Foundation. In 1982, Dr. Robinson received an award for outstanding achievement in education from the National Council of Negro Women.

TIMOTHY M. SANDOS

Timothy M. Sandos was elected in 1991 to a four-year term on the Denver City Council as an at-large representative. Immediately before his election, Mr. Sandos served as Mayor Federico Peña's assistant for education and family issues. His extensive volunteer history includes service on the board of directors for University Hospital, Girl Scouts Mile High Council, Boys and Girls Clubs of Metro Denver, the Latin American Research and Service Agency, the cabinet for Mile High United Way, and the steering committee for the Denver Cooperative for Educational Excellence.

CHRISTEN G. SMITH

Christen G. Smith is the executive director of the American Association for Leisure and Recreation. She holds a doctorate in park and recreation administration and business administration from Texas Woman's University. Dr. Smith has had eight years of experience with municipal park and recreation departments in Colorado and Texas. She has also served as a consultant with numerous municipal park and recreation departments.

KENNETH B. SMITH

The Reverend Dr. Kenneth B. Smith is an ordained minister of the United Church of Christ. He has served as president of the Chicago Theological Seminary since October 1984. During his tenure as senior minister of the Church of the Good Shepherd in Chicago, the church congregation initiated programs in preschool education, after-school care and recreation, nutritional and recreation programs for retired persons, and a special program for teenagers with unique needs. Dr. Smith currently serves on a number of local and national voluntary boards and committees. His publications include the *Lenten Book of Meditation*, published by Eden Publishing Company, and *The United Church of Christ—Issues in Its Quest for Denominational Identity*, edited with Dr. Dorothy C. Bass and published by Exploration Press.

JUDITH TORNEY-PURTA

Judith Torney-Purta is professor of human development and affiliate professor of psychology at the University of Maryland at College Park. She is a developmental and educational psychologist with special interests in social development, cross-cultural education, and community psychology. Since the 1960s she has conducted research to study young people's views of social and political institutions as well as their motivation in educational settings (both formal and informal). She is a fellow of the American Psychological Association and the American Psychological Society.

JO UEHARA

Jo Uehara is assistant executive director for member association services, YWCA of the U.S.A., a national organization serving women, girls, and their families. Her experience includes serving as chair of the Washington Support Group of the National Collaboration for Youth and organizer and cofounder of a state coalition of youth-serving organizations established to deinstitutionalize dependent youth from state institutions for juvenile offenders, a youth service bureau that served first-time juvenile offenders, and a medical-dental clinic for children and their families living in a public housing project. She has an extensive background in providing training and consultation to multicultural constituencies of the United States.

ROBERTA VAN DER VOORT

Roberta van der Voort has been executive director of United Way of King County, Washington, since 1989. She was formerly the senior vice president, Marketing Group, at United Way of America. Dr. van der Voort began her professional career for the Crook County public schools in Prineville, Oregon, where she received the outstanding educator award. She worked for fifteen years with the Seattle–King County Council for Camp Fire. From 1977 to 1982 she served as the national director of Camp Fire, Inc. She currently serves on numerous national, regional, and local civic and voluntary boards and committees.

PROFILES OF TWENTY NATIONAL ORGANIZATIONS

The following twenty national organizations were active participants in the task force study:

AMERICAN CAMPING ASSOCIATION

ORGANIZATION DESCRIPTION

American Camping Association was founded in 1910 to advance the popularity of organized camping. In 1986 the organization underwent a restructuring to become an individual membership organization. It now serves as a professional society for camp staff and volunteers. American Camping Association establishes and monitors professional standards for camps and provides accreditation and site approval. Approved camps are listed in the ACA directory, which is published annually. In addition to its national office, the organization has thirty-two section offices and accredits 2,100 camps.

PROGRAM DESCRIPTION

American Camping Association does not offer programs as such, but promotes and recommends programs and activities through its publications. Publication topics include nature, games and activities, arts and crafts, music and stories, outside adventures, special activities, understanding human needs, philosophy, standards for accreditation, management and administration, and counselor training. American Camping Association also sponsors conferences and workshops for camp personnel and runs a certified camp director program.

MEMBERSHIP

American Camping Association has 5,063 members: camp owners and administrators, staff and volunteers from agencies serving youth, private independent entrepreneurs, church organizations, and public and municipal agencies. Five million young people go to camp each summer, some for a week or two, some for all summer, some to sleepaway camps, others to day camps. According to ACA, fees for camp generally range from $15 to $55 a day for camps run by nonprofit groups and $35 to $80 a day for private camps.

OUTREACH STRATEGIES

American Camping Association has a camper scholarship program through which it encourages its members to provide scholarships to low-income youth. Individual camps can make tax-deductible contributions to this scholarship fund, which is administered by ACA.

BUDGET

In 1991 the national organization spent $2,958,574 and received $3,041,972 in support and revenue. Assets were $1,549,418.

National Contact Information: John A. Miller, Executive Vice President, American Camping Association, Bradford Woods, 5000 State Road 67 North, Martinsville, IN 46151-7902, 317-342-8456.

AMERICAN RED CROSS

ORGANIZATION DESCRIPTION

The American Association of Red Cross was formed in 1881 by Clara Barton. Its mission is to provide disaster relief services and also to help people prevent, prepare for, and respond to emergencies. The Junior Red Cross was founded in 1917 to provide opportunities for young people to be involved in Red Cross activities through education, training, and volunteer activities. The extent of youth involvement and activities varies among chapters and is determined by local chapter leadership. The organization has a national headquarters office, three operation headquarters, and 2,675 chapters.

Red Cross's programs for young people cover four areas: health promotion, leadership development, community service, and international understanding. The organization offers its programs and volunteer opportunities through local Red Cross chapters, local schools, and other youth organizations. For the most part activity fees are required for participation in programs, and there are age restrictions on classes. Activities for young people between ten and fifteen years of age include first aid, money management, babysitting training, preparation for parenthood, nutrition and health (including courses on sexuality and HIV/AIDS education), volunteer opportunities, and swimming and lifeguarding.

MEMBERSHIP

In 1988, the most recent year for which data are available, more than 90 percent of Red Cross's 2,817 chapters had activities for youth.

OUTREACH STRATEGIES

One goal of the American Red Cross is to have its paid and volunteer staff reflect the diversity of the community served. Another goal is to make greater use of volunteer resources, particularly of young people.

BUDGET

In 1991 the national and local offices of the American Red Cross combined spent $1,402,000,018 and received $1,410,000,019 in support and revenue. Combined assets were $1,802,939,000.

National Contact Information: Elizabeth Dole, President, American Red Cross, 17th and D Streets, N.W., Washington, DC 20006, 202-737-8300.

ASPIRA ASSOCIATION, INC.

ORGANIZATION DESCRIPTION

ASPIRA Association, Inc., is a national organization dedicated to promoting education and leadership development among Hispanic youth. Its name is derived from the Spanish verb *aspirar*, meaning to aspire to something greater. Founded in New York City in 1961, ASPIRA now has several community-based affiliates in six states—Florida, Illinois, New Jersey, New York, Connecticut, and Pennsylvania—and Puerto Rico, with its national office in the District of Columbia. The national office coordinates programs that develop out of local needs, including school drop-out prevention, leadership development, and career exploration. In addition, it provides its associates with monitoring of federal policies, conducts and disseminates research on the needs of Hispanic youth through its Institute on

Policy Research, advocates on behalf of Hispanic youth, and provides network building.

PROGRAM DESCRIPTION

Young people participate in ASPIRA's programs through ASPIRA Clubs, where they develop leadership and academic skills, explore careers, and provide service to their communities. They also testify before political and education committees on issues of concern to Hispanic youth and attend career conferences and cultural awareness events. Parental involvement is integral to program success.

MEMBERSHIP

In 1991 ASPIRA's membership included 17,000 young people from preschool to college age and 5,000 parents. Participants were 99 percent Hispanic, and almost exclusively of lower socioeconomic backgrounds. Breakdown by age and gender is currently available only in the Florida sites.

OUTREACH STRATEGIES

Organization growth is an important goal for ASPIRA. It wants to address the requests for services from more communities and increase its visibility and sphere of influence by expanding its research and advocacy efforts.

BUDGET

In 1991, ASPIRA's national office spent $1,187,408 and received $1,290,716 in support and revenue. National office assets were $677,132.

National Contact Information: Janice Petrovich, National Executive Director, ASPIRA Association, Inc., 1112 16th Street, N.W., Suite 340, Washington, DC 20036, 202-835-3600.

BIG BROTHERS/BIG SISTERS OF AMERICA

ORGANIZATION DESCRIPTION

Big Brothers/Big Sisters, founded as Big Brothers in 1904, is an organization that matches one child, usually from a single-parent, low-income family, with one adult volunteer, who serves as a mentor, friend, and role model. The organization consists of a national office and 500 independent, locally run agencies. Agencies also provide counseling, referral, and family support services.

PROGRAM DESCRIPTION

The core Big Brothers/Big Sisters program is based on a one-to-one match between an adult volunteer and a young person. The theory behind the program is that personal attention can unlock potential in ways that cannot be addressed by schools or group programs alone. Adult volunteers commit three to six hours per week, for a minimum of one year, to spend with their Little Brothers or Sisters. These relationships are created and supervised throughout the duration of the match by professional staff. Topic-specific national programs include EMPOWER, a child sexual abuse education and prevention program; ALTERNATIVES, a substance abuse education and prevention program; and the Volunteer Education and Development program.

MEMBERSHIP

In 1991, 90,000 young people were matched in a one-to-one relationship with a volunteer. Approximately 67 percent of young people matched are between the ages of ten and fifteen. Thirty-one percent of young people who participate are minority, most live in single-parent homes, and at least 42 percent live in families below the poverty line. Counseling and family support services were provided to 110,000 families in 1991.

OUTREACH STRATEGIES

Big Brothers/Big Sisters' priority is to reach more at-risk youth. It has four national initiatives to accomplish that goal: recruiting minority volunteers, involving older adults as mentors, developing school-linked programs, and training mentors.

BUDGET

In 1991 Big Brothers/Big Sisters' national office had expenses of $3,995,088 and support and revenue of $3,789,159. National organization assets were $1,946,030.

National Contact Information: Thomas M. McKenna, National Executive Director, 230 North 13th Street, Philadelphia, PA 19107, 215-567-7000.

BOY SCOUTS OF AMERICA

ORGANIZATION DESCRIPTION

Boy Scouts of America is a national organization, founded in 1910, that strives to build character; foster citizenship; and develop mental, moral, and physical fitness in young people, while also endeavoring to meet the needs for fun, adventure, and meaningful learning. Members of Boy Scout programs must take an oath to do their duty to God and country. Local administrative units are called councils, and local delivery units—called packs, troops, teams, or posts, according to age levels of participants—are sponsored by local chartered partners. These partners are churches, schools, and civic groups.

PROGRAM DESCRIPTION

The basic program for Cub Scouts and Boy Scouts (boys aged six to fourteen) involves participating in ac-

tivities and learning skills in order to earn merit badges. Activities include outdoor skills, citizenship, first aid, family and community living, communications, and physical fitness. Boy Scout troops and Cub Scout dens meet weekly. Explorer Scouts, a program for high school-aged youth, is devoted to exploring career opportunities. Varsity Scouts is a program for high adventure. Boy Scouts has also instituted a new in-school program designed to reach inner-city and rural youth called Learning for Life.

MEMBERSHIP

In 1991, 4,292,992 boys and girls were enrolled in Boy Scouts programs. One-fourth of participants are aged eleven to fourteen. Boy Scout units allow only male participation, except for the Explorer Program, which is 40 percent female, and the new Learning for Life initiative. Boy Scouts does not keep records on members' race, ethnicity, family composition, or family income. A recent survey, however, indicated that 18 percent of Boy Scout participants were minorities.

OUTREACH STRATEGIES

Boy Scouts of America has taken some steps to diversify its membership. The organization has translated some of its publications into Spanish. Several local councils have established programs to reach boys living in welfare hotels. One program, Varsity Scouts, was initiated to attract boys who would not normally be interested in scouting. The Boy Scouts' in-school program, Learning for Life, is also designed to reach inner-city and rural youth.

BUDGET

In 1991 the national organization spent $75,491,000 and received $85,214,000 in support and revenue. Its assets were $255,639,000.

National Contact Information: Ben H. Love, Chief Scout Executive, Boy Scouts of America, 1325 West Walnut Hill Lane, P.O. Box 152079, Irving, TX 75015-2079, 214-580-2000.

BOYS AND GIRLS CLUBS OF AMERICA

ORGANIZATION DESCRIPTION

Boys and Girls Clubs of America is a nationwide federation of local autonomous Boys and Girls Clubs. The organization was founded in 1906 as Boys Clubs of America, but changed its name in 1990 to reflect its change to coeducational participation. Boys and Girls Clubs programs are building-centered, have an open-door policy, and offer diverse activities designed to teach good work habits, teamwork, perseverance, self-reliance, and consideration of others.

Boys and Girls Clubs programs are facility-based. Activities are offered in six core areas: health and physical education, citizenship-leadership development, cultural enrichment, social recreation, personal-educational development, and outdoor environmental education. Programs are designed to meet the developmental needs of competence, usefulness, belonging, and influence. The organization's national programs include drug and alcohol abuse prevention, discouragement of early sexual involvement, and delinquency and gang prevention as well as programs in career exploration and job search skills, educational support, outdoor and environmental education, fine arts and photography, leadership development, and sports tournaments.

MEMBERSHIP

In 1991, 1,700,000 young people between the ages of six and eighteen participated in Boys and Girls Clubs of America's programs. Thirty percent of these participants were female. Forty-four percent were aged eleven to sixteen. Fifty-one percent of participants were minority, and 66 percent came from families with incomes under $15,000. Seventy-one percent live in urban areas.

OUTREACH STRATEGIES

A primary goal of Boys and Girls Clubs of America is to reach more young people, including those living in public housing projects. The organization has made significant strides in this area and now serves 33 percent more young people than in 1986. It has exceeded its goal of establishing 100 new clubs in public housing units, bringing the total number of public housing clubs to 175.

BUDGET

In 1991 the national organization spent $16,097,026 and received $15,564,619 in support and revenue. Its assets were $31,819,100.

National Contact Information: Thomas G. Garth, National Director, Boys and Girls Clubs of America, 771 First Avenue, New York, NY 10017, 212-351-5900.

CAMP FIRE BOYS AND GIRLS

ORGANIZATION DESCRIPTION

Camp Fire Boys and Girls, founded in 1910 as Camp Fire Girls, is a national youth development organization that strives to provide self-development, skills development, and social development to young people. The organization has undergone significant changes in the past twenty years. Not only has it moved from being a single gender to a coeducational organization, but it has also expanded its delivery systems to include more than the club program and has given greater autonomy to its local councils. Every year the organization recognizes local programs of excellence through its PRIDE Acknowledgment Awards. These awards make it possible to expand and replicate innovative programs and provide incentives for creative programming.

PROGRAM DESCRIPTION

Camp Fire delivers its programs in five ways: the club program provides a group experience over a long period of time that focuses on developing planning and decision-making skills of youth; camp and environmental education programs offer children from diverse backgrounds an appreciation and commitment to the natural environment; child-care programs provide an enriching alternative to latchkey care for school-age children whose parents are at work; self-reliance courses teach youth personal life skills; and youth leadership programs empower teens to implement projects they choose.

MEMBERSHIP

In 1991 a total of 600,000 young people between the ages of five and eighteen were enrolled in Camp Fire programs. Approximately 50 percent of those were between the ages of ten and fifteen. Twenty-six percent of participants are minority. Around 62 percent are female and 38 percent male.

OUTREACH STRATEGIES

Expansion of services to at-risk youth, in inner cities and rural areas, is a national priority for this organization. At least fourteen councils deliver programs in housing projects. Camp Fire strives to increase adolescent participation by developing new ways to involve teens and adults in partnerships.

BUDGET

In 1991 the national organization spent $4,116,579 and received $3,818,429 in support and revenue. Its assets were $3,111,430.

National Contact Information: K. Russell Weathers, National Executive Director and CEO, Camp Fire Boys and Girls, 4601 Madison Avenue, Kansas City, MO 64112, 816-756-0258.

CHILD WELFARE LEAGUE OF AMERICA

ORGANIZATION DESCRIPTION

The Child Welfare League of America is a seventy-two-year-old association of 660 public and private child welfare agencies devoted to improving life for at-risk children and youth. At the local level agencies provide casework, group work, and family counseling. At the national level, CWLA develops standards, conducts and publishes research, provides training, advocates for legislative reform, and administers special projects.

PROGRAM DESCRIPTION

Local agencies provide a wide array of child welfare services including services for children in their homes, family foster care, and group care. There are ten basic child welfare services; some agencies offer only one, others offer several, and a few offer all ten. CWLA is currently encouraging its member agencies to involve adolescents actively in organizational leadership through peer programs, community service, and advocacy on their own behalf. The Child Welfare League of America has special national departments for purposes of developing standards, disseminating research findings, advocating for children's needs at the state and federal policy levels, providing consultation services, and developing training curricula.

MEMBERSHIP

A disproportionate number of CWLA's 660 member agencies are located in urban areas. CWLA's member agencies serve more than two million children and their families annually. A large percentage of children served are of preschool age. Approximately 51 percent of clients are white, 34 percent black, 10 percent Hispanic, 2 percent Asian, and 3 percent other. A high percentage of those served are from single-parent and low-income families.

OUTREACH STRATEGIES

The Child Welfare League of America is coordinating a Children's Campaign to build a stronger national voice for children and seeks to recruit thousands of new members to write letters and make phone calls to legislators. The organization's Florence Crittenton Division, which focuses on adolescent pregnancy and parenting issues, has begun to work with young men to focus on male responsibility.

BUDGET

In 1991 the national office spent $6,269,838 and received $6,423,994 in support and revenue. Its assets were $10,635,220.

National Contact Information: David S. Liederman, Executive Director, Child Welfare League of America, 440 First Street, N.W., Suite 310, Washington, DC 20001, 202-638-2952.

GIRL SCOUTS OF THE U.S.A.

ORGANIZATION DESCRIPTION

Girl Scouts of the U.S.A. is an informal education program for girls aged five to seventeen, founded in 1912. Experiential learning is a fundamental tenet of the Girl Scouts. The organization's guiding principle is that girls can learn and grow through experiences that involve making decisions and discoveries for themselves. A local Girl Scout council applies for and receives a charter from the national organization giving it authority to supervise the Girl Scout program in a particular jurisdiction. Programs for five age levels are delivered to girls who often meet in troops in a variety of settings, including leaders' homes, schools, and churches. Participants earn badges in different areas of activity. All members must accept the Girl Scout Promise and Law, which includes honoring God and country.

PROGRAM DESCRIPTION

Girl Scouts' skill-building activities are developed at the national level and are divided into five areas: personal well-being and fitness (including interpersonal relationships); awareness of other cultures; exploring new technologies; the arts; and the out-of-doors.

MEMBERSHIP

In 1991 approximately 2.5 million girls were members of Girl Scouts. Of those girls about 6 percent were eleven to fourteen years old. Another 30 percent were aged eight to eleven (ages overlap because statistics are kept by grade). The youth membership is 100 percent female. In 1991, 14.1 percent of girl and adult members were minority.

OUTREACH STRATEGIES

Girl Scouts recognizes current issues that put girls at risk and addresses them through its Contemporary Issues booklet series. These booklets are resources for adult leaders. The Girl Scouts' National Center for Innovation is experimenting with new delivery systems. The organization is making active efforts to diversify the composition of membership and leadership from racial, ethnic, and economic standpoints.

BUDGET

In 1991 the national organization spent $32,631,000 and received $33,853,000 in support and revenue. National organization assets were $90,492,000.

National Contact Information: Mary Rose Main, National Executive Director, Girl Scouts of the U.S.A., 420 Fifth Avenue, New York, NY 10018-2202, 212-852-8000.

GIRLS INCORPORATED

ORGANIZATION DESCRIPTION

Founded in 1945 as Girls Clubs of America, Girls Incorporated is a national organization devoted to meeting girls' needs and helping them overcome the effects of gender discrimination and patterns of passivity. The organization's programs are designed to help girls develop skills and realize their capabilities and potential. The organization is composed of a national headquarters, a research and training center, four regional offices, and 300 local centers. Local centers provide a weekly average of thirty hours of activities after school, on weekends, and during the summer.

PROGRAM DESCRIPTION

Girls Incorporated's programming encompasses activities pertinent to all areas of a girl's life. Activities are designed to build self-esteem and foster independence. National programs are based on research done at the organization's National Resource Center. Specific programs offer girls hands-on experience in math and science, encourage girls to postpone early sexual activity and avoid drug and alcohol abuse, teach them about AIDS, increase interest and participation in sports activities, and teach girls to recognize and avoid sexual abuse.

MEMBERSHIP

In 1991, 250,000 young people between the ages of six and eighteen participated in Girls Incorporated's programs; 37 percent of these young people were nine to eleven. Another 26 percent were twelve to eighteen years old. Some clubs serve boys, although the primary focus of most local affiliates and all national programs is girls. Ethnic and racial breakdown was 49 percent white, 40 percent black, 8 percent Hispanic, 2 percent Asian, and 1 percent Native American. Fifty-four percent of participants were from single-parent families, and 55 percent live in families whose income is $15,000 or less.

OUTREACH STRATEGIES

Girls Incorporated has implemented several new programs addressing at-risk behavior. The organization is working to reach more girls by establishing program partnerships with other organizations, including the Salvation Army and YWCA.

BUDGET

In 1991 the national organization's expenses were $3,670,248, and support and revenue was $3,598,412. National office assets were $5,953,420.

National Contact Information: Margaret Gates, National Executive Director, Girls Incorporated, 30 East 33rd Street, New York, 10016, 212-689-3700.

JUNIOR ACHIEVEMENT

ORGANIZATION DESCRIPTION

Junior Achievement is a national organization that teaches economic and business concepts to young people in grades K–12. Its original program, JA Company Program, was founded in 1919 and its in-school curriculum introduced in 1975. The in-school programs now account for most of Junior Achievement's activity. The organization structure consists of a national headquarters and local franchises governed by local boards.

PROGRAM DESCRIPTION

Junior Achievement has several programs geared to specific grades. Each program involves volunteers from the business community who lead hands-on activities that are age-appropriate and relevant.

Students in grades K–3 learn about the economic roles they play in their families and communities. In grades four to six the emphasis shifts to business operation in state, national, and world economies. In its middle-school program, Project Business, students explore basic theoretical and personal economic concepts and business principles. At the high school level students may take a semester-length economics course, Applied Economics, or participate in the JA Company program.

MEMBERSHIP

In 1992 nearly 1.4 million students in grades K–12 participated in Junior Achievement. Of those roughly 68 percent were young adolescents in grades seven to nine (twelve to fourteen years old). Fifty-five percent of participants were male and 45 percent female. Student ethnicity was approximately 21 percent black, 10 percent Hispanic, 3 percent Asian, 1 percent Native American and other and 65 percent non-Hispanic white.

OUTREACH STRATEGIES

Programs designed for at-risk youth include Success Now (still in the pilot stage), an experience-based program that helps students make the transition between school and work, and Economics of Staying in School, a program that helps students explore the personal and societal impact of dropping out of school. A partnership program, with the National Urban League, provides mentors to minority students in danger of dropping out.

BUDGET

In 1991 the national organization spent $8,739,487 and received $9,370,216 in support and revenue. National organization assets were $10,863,687.

National Contact Information: Karl Flemke, President and CEO, Junior Achievement Inc., One Education Way, Colorado Springs, CO 80906-4477, 719-540-8000.

NATIONAL ASSOCIATION FOR THE ADVANCEMENT OF COLORED PEOPLE (NAACP)

ORGANIZATION DESCRIPTION

The NAACP was founded in 1909 to ensure the political, educational, social, and economic equality of rights and eliminate racial prejudice through nonviolent means. Its Youth and College Division, created in 1935, is its oldest initiative and is devoted to developing youth leadership and citizenship skills. The NAACP is organized into seven regions and has more than 1,700 adult branches and 400 local youth councils and college chapters.

PROGRAM DESCRIPTION

Youth involvement in NAACP activities include membership drives, voter registration and work in political campaigns, tutoring other Afro-American students and implementing diversity courses in secondary and post-secondary schools, fund raising, community service, and attending conferences and rallies. National programs for young people include antidrug and teenage pregnancy workshops, tutorials, stay-in-school and back-to-school programs, scholarships and counseling services.

MEMBERSHIP

In 1989 the NAACP had more than 400,000 members, 40,000 of whom were young people under the age of twenty-one. Very few members were young adolescents. Some youth members were fourteen and fifteen, but most were older. Although members are primarily black, they may be from any racial or ethnic background.

OUTREACH STRATEGIES

In the 1980s the NAACP made a strategic decision to expand its mission beyond its traditional legal and legislative advocacy and develop programmatic initiatives to reach less advantaged and underserved black populations. The NAACP reaches out to at-risk youth through tutoring and stay-in-school programs, as well as counseling, often conducted in community centers or churches.

BUDGET

In 1991 the national organization spent $7,697,320 and received $7,063,392 in public support and revenue. Its assets were $7,306,528.

National Contact Information: James Williams, Director of Public Relations, NAACP, 4805 Mt. Hope Drive, Baltimore, MD 21215, 410-358-8900.

NATIONAL COALITION OF HISPANIC HEALTH AND HUMAN SERVICES ORGANIZATIONS (COSSMHO)

ORGANIZATION DESCRIPTION

COSSMHO is a membership organization of individuals, community organizations, national organizations, and educational institutions devoted to improving community-based health and human services for Hispanics. The organization was founded in 1973 to represent Mexican Americans, Puerto Ricans, Cubans, and Central and South Americans. It conducts national model programs, coordinates research, disseminates information, provides technical assistance, develops and analyzes policies, and sponsors community-based programs and interventions.

PROGRAM DESCRIPTION

To serve a population with limited access to health and human services, COSSMHO pursues programs in health research, health promotion and disease prevention, and education and training. Programs for adolescents use peer counseling, teen theater, and family intervention. Model programs for youth are located in ten cities around the country. Demonstration projects for young people include AIDS education for out-of-school Hispanic youth, health education, alcohol and drug abuse prevention, gang prevention, and inhalant abuse prevention. COSSMHO publishes books and videos pertinent to adolescent concerns.

MEMBERSHIP

COSSMHO's membership consists of approximately ten national organizations, 240 community-based organizations, and 800 individuals, including researchers; community-based providers of health, mental health, and social services; and practitioners and officials in the fields of public health, nursing, social work, psychology, and youth services.

COSSMHO sponsors demonstration projects in several cities to reach at-risk youth. COSSMHO works with community organizations (its own members and others) in targeting local problems and reaching young people and their families where they live. COSSMHO maintains Hispanic Health Link, a computer bulletin board, to disseminate information to 350 agencies throughout the United States.

BUDGET

In 1991 the organization spent $2,512,157 and received $2,765,618 in revenue. Its assets were $1,534,233.

National Contact Information: Jane L. Delgado, President and CEO, COSSMHO, 1501 16th Street, N.W., Washington, DC 20036, 202-387-5000.

NATIONAL 4-H CLUBS

ORGANIZATION DESCRIPTION

The National 4-H Program is part of the U.S. Department of Agriculture's Cooperative Extension Service, which was established by Congress in 1914. The purpose of the 4-H Program is to provide practical education through hands-on projects. The goal is to create a learning environment that is stimulating to the development of life skills. Originally 4-H targeted rural youth, but it now has programs for suburban and urban areas as well. 4-H programs, which operate out of land grant universities and colleges, are conducted in 3,150 counties of the United States. Programs vary from county to county and state to state.

PROGRAM DESCRIPTION

In 4-H programs, young people work on individual projects to gain hands-on knowledge. Young people can participate in programs through clubs, special-interest units, school enrichment units, individual study units, and instructional television series. Project areas include agriculture and natural sciences, science and technology, nutrition and diet, drug abuse prevention, family and economic well-being, career education and leadership development, community service and communications. Individuals enroll in one or several organized activities a year.

MEMBERSHIP

In 1991, 5,657,657 boys and girls between the ages of five and nineteen were enrolled in 4-H programs. Of those, 68 percent were aged nine to fourteen. Fifty-two percent were female, and 25 percent were minority. Ten percent lived in suburbs of cities of more than 50,000 people, and 22 percent lived in cities of more than 50,000.

The organization has been moving toward more centralized planning in order to focus more on particular initiatives, including a Youth-at-Risk Initiative, which is designed to extend the organization's reach to underserved groups. Other programs in effect in some states are designed to teach urban children good nutrition habits, teach survival skills to latchkey children, prevent teen suicide, and serve young people in public housing.

BUDGET

Information on revenue and expenses is not available; however, the federal appropriation for the Cooperative Extension Service, of which 4-H is a part, is approximately $300 million annually. 4-H is supposed to receive 20 to 22 percent of this appropriation, but 4-H officials estimate they actually receive less. State, county, and private dollars supplement these federal resources and collectively are estimated to exceed them.

National Contact Information: Richard Sauer, President and CEO, National 4-H Council, 7100 Connecticut Avenue, Chevy Chase, MD 20815, 301-962-2820, and Alma Hobbs, Assistant Deputy Administrator, 4-H Youth Development, Cooperative Extension Service, U.S. Department of Agriculture, Washington, DC 20250, 202-720-6527.

NATIONAL NETWORK OF RUNAWAY AND YOUTH SERVICES

ORGANIZATION DESCRIPTION

The National Network of Runaway and Youth Services is a national not-for-profit organization representing approximately 900 agencies that serve runaway, homeless, and other youth in high-risk situations. The mission of the organization, which was founded in 1971, is to emphasize the importance of youth, empower youth, strengthen families, and promote healthy alternatives for youth, through its programs and networking activities. The national office holds an annual symposium, publishes two newsletters, and serves as a resource for information on shelters and agencies and on effective intervention strategies and service delivery. It also promotes its members' programs.

PROGRAM DESCRIPTION

On the local level the principal program processes are individual counseling and group work. The average network agency provides fourteen services including individual and family counseling, crisis intervention, a hotline, recreation, shelter, educational training, and drug abuse and pregnancy prevention. National programs include an AIDS/HIV education program and a peer counseling program to prevent drug abuse.

Although the Network represents 900 agencies, only 300 of these are dues-paying members. Based on a 1990 survey of 178 representative membership agencies serving 404,279 youth, 38 percent of youth served were under fifteen years old and another 54 percent were fifteen to eighteen years old. Fifty-three percent were female and 47 percent were male. Sixty-four percent were white, 20 percent black, 10 percent Hispanic, and 6 percent other. Thirty-nine percent were from families living below the poverty line.

OUTREACH STRATEGIES

The National Network of Runaway and Youth Services is strengthening its membership base by developing a more formal and unified linkage with state and regional networks and by reaching those in allied professions. They plan to expand the development and dissemination of model programs, materials, and standards.

BUDGET

In 1991 the national organization spent $783,748 and received $782,247 in support and revenue. Its assets were $124,172.

National Contact Information: Della Hughes, Executive Director, National Network of Runaway and Youth Services, Inc., 1319 F Street, N.W., Suite 401, Washington, DC 20004, 202-783-7949.

NATIONAL URBAN LEAGUE

ORGANIZATION DESCRIPTION

The National Urban League was founded in 1910 in New York City for the purpose of helping black people from the rural South find jobs and housing in the city. The organization's newly revised mission is to assist all African Americans to achieve social and economic equality and to promote equal opportunity for African Americans, other minorities, and the poor. In 1991 the National Urban League had 112 affiliates in thirty-four states. These local affiliates conduct programs of direct service in their communities in the areas of employment, education, and economic development. The Urban League's national programs include advocacy and public education, race relations, research, program services in employment, job training, education, and career development, and technical assistance to affiliates.

PROGRAM DESCRIPTION

All local affiliates have education initiative programs or support activities for academic achievement. National programs for young people, adopted by some affiliates, address the areas of academic improvement and motivation, leadership development, community service, business and career education, pregnancy and parenting-related programs, adolescent male responsibility, and drug abuse prevention.

MEMBERSHIP

The National Urban League provides programs of direct service to approximately one to 1.2 million people each year. Approximately 100,000 to 150,000 of these are youth (aged twelve to twenty-four). Eighty-five percent are African American and 15 percent are Hispanic, Asian, or working-class white. Generally, they are from low-income families (earning under $15,000 a year).

OUTREACH STRATEGIES

In 1985 the National Urban League called on all affiliates to establish programs to improve academic achievement of African American students. In 1988 youth services were added as a national priority. A new club-based program called NULITES (National Urban League Incentives to Excel and Succeed) was launched in 1991 for youth aged twelve to eighteen.

BUDGET

In 1991 the national organization spent $26,208,003 and received $26,801,452 in support and revenue. Its assets were $18,211,175.

National Contact Information: John E. Jacob, President and CEO, National Urban League, 500 East 62nd Street, New York, NY 10021, 212-310-9000.

THE SALVATION ARMY

ORGANIZATION DESCRIPTION

The Salvation Army is an international religious and charitable organization that is organized and operated in a quasimilitary manner. Its mission is twofold: spiritual redemption and social service. The basic unit of delivery for programs and services is the corps community center, which combines a ministry of religious programs, social service work, education, training, fellowship, and recreation. In 1990 there were 1,133 of these centers. Although basic Salvation Army program guidelines are followed, programming at the local level is determined by community needs. Through the four U.S. regional offices, national headquarters coordinates programs and activities.

PROGRAM DESCRIPTION

The Salvation Army's various youth programs fit generally into two categories: youth development and social services. Youth development activities include Christian Education, Boy Scouts, Girl Guards and Adventure Corps, Boys/Girls Clubs/Community Centers, and camping. These programs offer activities and projects to young people that teach skills, develop good health habits, develop leadership and citizenship, and provide opportunities for community service. Social service programs for young people include day care, family emergency assistance, residential care, and programs for pregnant and parenting teens.

MEMBERS

In 1990, 83,952 young people from the ages of six to nineteen participated in Salvation Army group activities such as Boy Scouts and Girl Guards/Adventure Corps, 20,780 young people were involved in the youth band, 96,774 attended Salvation Army camps, and 108,873 were members of Boys/Girls Clubs/Community Centers (a total of 310,379). On the social services side, 1,711 children were served through residential care and 34,983 through day care. Children helped through shelter, emergency, and seasonal service totaled approximately 4.1 million.

OUTREACH STRATEGIES

Most of the community centers are located in economically disadvantaged areas, and their services are designed to reach individuals and families in these areas. Strengthening services for youth is one of this organization's continuing priorities.

BUDGET

In 1991 the national office spent $7,012,958 and received $9,299,241 in support and revenue. Its assets were $24,105,147.

National Contact Information: James Osborne, National Commander, The Salvation Army, P.O. Box 269, 615 Slaters Lane, Alexandria, VA 22313, 703-684-5500.

WAVE, INC.

ORGANIZATION DESCRIPTION

WAVE, Inc., originally named 70001, was founded in 1969 to provide young people who had dropped out of high school with training and employment services. It has since expanded its programs to include young people still in school but in danger of dropping out. In addition to providing direct employment assistance, the organization helps young people develop self-sufficiency and the desire to achieve. WAVE programs operate in twenty-three states. The national office provides training, educational materials, support, and monitoring to schools and community organizations that implement its programs.

PROGRAM DESCRIPTION

Two programs are operated by WAVE: WAVE In Communities and WAVE In Schools. The ultimate goal of WAVE In Schools is to encourage students to complete high school. Its curriculum, designed for grades nine to twelve, emphasizes life skills, employability, personal development, and career awareness. The program's approach is experiential, allowing students to work at their own pace and to receive immediate feedback. The In School curriculum can be adapted to use in drop-out prevention efforts, school-to-work transition programs, and enhancement of alternative education initiatives. Students attend WAVE classes one period each day for the entire school year. Much emphasis is placed on the importance of the teacher, and teachers are provided with substantial training and ongoing support. WAVE In Communities, for young people who have dropped out of high school, provides education in basic skills, employment training, motivational development, and placement services.

MEMBERSHIP

In 1991, 10,068 young people aged fourteen to twenty-one were enrolled in WAVE's programs. Of these, approximately 7 percent were aged fourteen. Membership was 49 percent female and 51 percent male, 47 percent white, 40 percent black, 11 percent Hispanic, 1 percent Asian, and 1 percent other. Students enrolled in WAVE In Schools are often behind grade levels, receive low test scores, and have behavioral difficulties and problems with absenteeism. Approximately 32 percent of WAVE In Schools participants and 83 percent of WAVE In-Communities participants are economically disadvantaged.

OUTREACH STRATEGIES

One of WAVE's current goals is to expand its services to middle schools.

BUDGET

In 1991 the national organization spent $5,880,445 and received $5,929,328 in support and revenue. Assets were $1,623,075.

National Contact Information: Lawrence C. Brown, President, WAVE, Inc., 501 School Street, S.W., Suite 600, Washington, DC 20024-2754, 202-484-0103.

YMCA OF THE USA

ORGANIZATION DESCRIPTION

The first U.S. YMCA opened in Boston in 1851 to meet the spiritual and social needs of rural young men moving to the city. Local YMCAs now offer programs that meet health and social service needs in the communities they serve. In 1991, 958 member YMCAs operated 1,120 branches for a total of 2,078 service delivery units that offer different programs depending on local decisions and local needs.

PROGRAM DESCRIPTION

YMCA programs for youth are designed to build self-esteem, improve personal health, develop employment skills and career goals, provide education and training, and develop leadership. Local YMCAs run summer camps, operate school-age child-care programs, and offer various sports activities for young people as well as their traditional Trail program, in which a young person participates with a parent. Programs typically consist of classes that last eight weeks. The national YMCA has a Teen Leadership Program, various aspects of which may be offered by local YMCAs. In addition, many local YMCAs offer specific programs for at-risk youth.

MEMBERSHIP

The YMCA reports it had 12,781,793 registered constituents in 1991. This number includes 5,964,787 registered members and 6,817,006 program members. Of the total constituents, 5,800,000 were six to eighteen years old.

OUTREACH STRATEGIES

In 1989 the YMCA recommitted itself to youth programming with its ten-year plan: Youth Work 2000. Its goal is to become a significant leader in work with teens and have all local branches serve at least 10 percent of the youth in their areas. Particular emphasis is placed on targeting hard-to-reach youth who have not traditionally participated in YMCA programs. Local YMCAs have programs targeted to at-risk youth (534 YMCAs), low-income youth (657 YMCAs), and teen parents (125 YMCAs).

BUDGET

In 1990 the national organization spent $32,958,892 and received $32,790,053 in support and revenue. In 1991, 884 YMCAs reported expenses of $1,513,399,965 and revenue of $1,538,054,038.

National Contact Information: David Mercer, National Executive Director, YMCA of the USA, 101 North Wacker Drive, Chicago, IL 60606-7386, 312-997-0031.

YWCA OF THE U.S.A.

ORGANIZATION DESCRIPTION

The YWCA of the U.S.A. was founded in 1858 to help women and girls who were moving to the city during the Industrial Revolution find housing and jobs. Today its mission is twofold: to empower women and eliminate racism. The YWCA consists of a national headquarters, three other national offices, and 445 community and student YWCAs operating in 4,000 locations. Local YWCAs are autonomous, designing their own programs to meet the needs of their own communities. Of the YWCA's 445 member associations, about forty are student associations at the college level and approximately 140 have Y-teen programs.

PROGRAM DESCRIPTION

Local YWCAs offer classes, workshops, and seminars designed to promote health, well-being, and personal development. Programs for young people include health instruction, teen pregnancy prevention, family life education, self-esteem enhancement, informed decision making, parenting, nutrition, delinquency prevention and career exploration. The YWCA also offers sports and fitness activities.

MEMBERSHIP

In 1990 YWCAs served approximately 2,000,000 women, girls, and their families. No breakdown is available on age, gender, or ethnicity, but "membership focuses on women and girls (from age twelve on), reflecting diversity in age, ethnicity, religion, race, lifestyles, and interests."

OUTREACH STRATEGIES

The YWCA has recently reaffirmed its focus on women and girls, a single-gender membership structure, and youth programming. The YWCA is working in collaboration with Girls Incorporated to pilot a project called Partnership for Tomorrow's Women, designed to expand services to girls and young women.

BUDGET

In 1991 the national organization spent $12,108,987 and received $8,843,208 in support and revenue. Its assets were $41,989,411.

National Contact Information: Gwendolyn Calvert Baker, National Executive Director, YWCA of the U.S.A., 726 Broadway, New York, NY 10003, 212-614-2821.